ANDREY AVIN

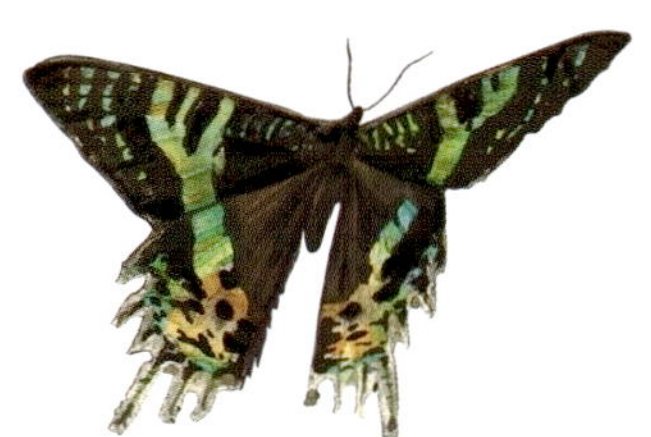

NOFF IN PURSU

LOUISE LIPPINCOTT   CARNEGIE MUSEUM OF ART, PITTSBURGH, PENNSYLVANIA

T OF BEAUTY

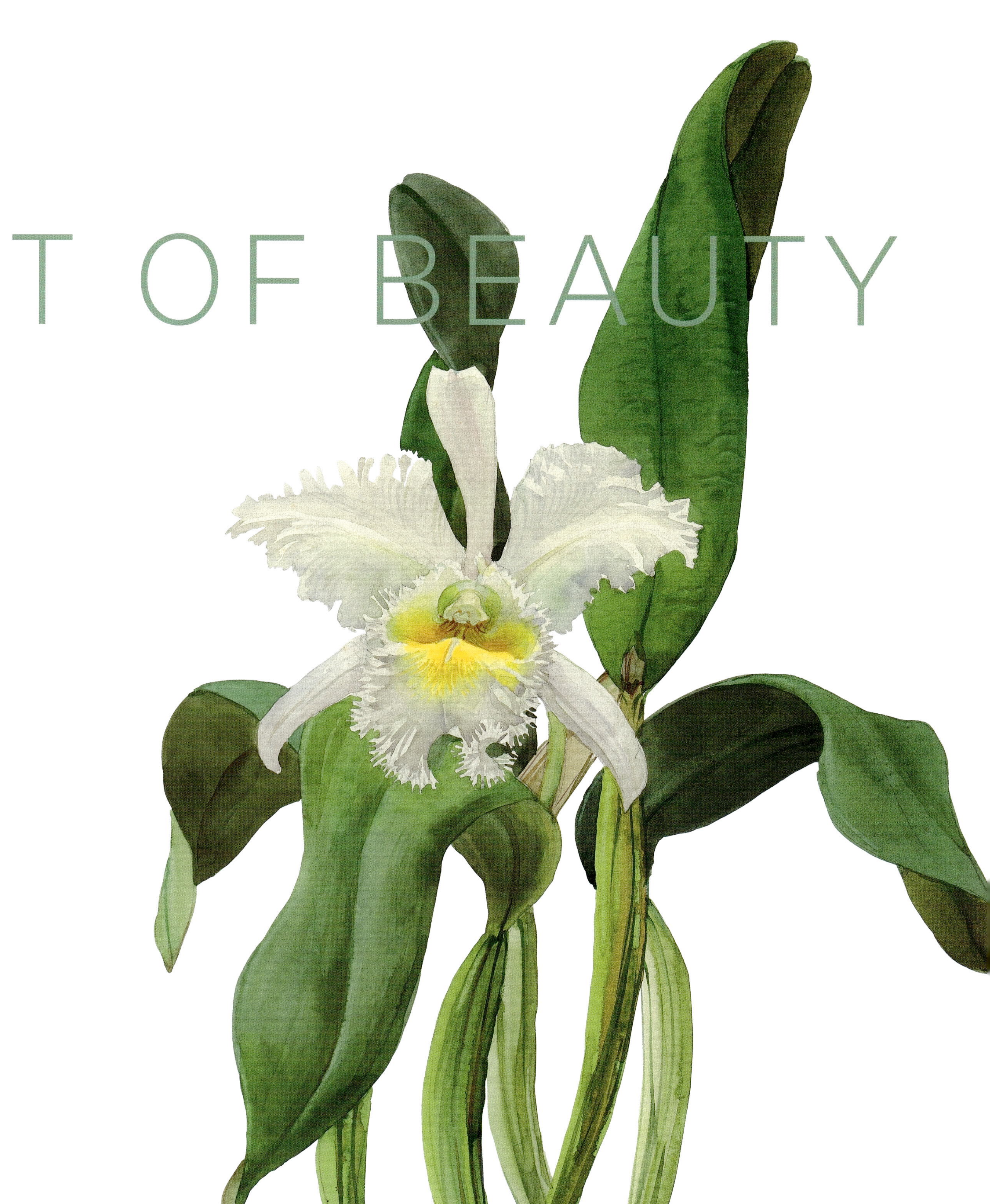

This book is published to coincide with the exhibition *Andrey Avinoff: In Pursuit of Beauty* at Carnegie Museum of Art, February 26–June 5, 2011.

Published by
Carnegie Museum of Art
4400 Forbes Avenue
Pittsburgh, Pennsylvania 15213-4080
www.cmoa.org

Available through D.A.P. / Distributed Art Publishers
155 Sixth Avenue, 2nd Floor, New York, New York 10013
Tel.: 212.627.1999 Fax: 212.627.9484
www.artbook.com/dap.html

Major support for *Andrey Avinoff: In Pursuit of Beauty* is provided by Dr. Richard and Priscilla Hunt, the Virginia Kaufman Fund, and the Beal Publication Fund. General operating support for Carnegie Museum of Art is provided by The Heinz Endowments and Allegheny Regional Asset District. Carnegie Museum of Art receives state arts funding support through a grant from the Pennsylvania Council on the Arts, a state agency funded by the Commonwealth of Pennsylvania.

ISBN 978-0-88039-053-8

Katherine E. Reilly, Head of Publications
Melinda Harkiewicz, Publications Associate
Laurel Mitchell, Coordinator of Rights and Reproductions
Norene Walworth, Production Coordinator

Designed and produced by Glue + Paper Workshop LLC, Chicago
Edited by Jane Friedman
Color separations by Professional Graphics, Rockford
Printed in Hong Kong by Asia Pacific Offset

Half title page: Detail of *Frustration*, 1948 (figure 62)
Title page: Detail of *White Orchid*, 1948–1949 (figure 43)
Page 6: Detail of *Cup Plant*, 1941–1943 (figure 35)
Page 11: Detail of *Dutch Bouquet*, 1948 (figure 38)

Library of Congress Cataloging-in-Publication Data

Lippincott, Louise, 1953–
Andrey Avinoff : in pursuit of beauty / Louise Lippincott.
p. cm.
Published to coincide with an exhibition held at Carnegie Museum of Art, Pittsburgh, Penn., Feb. 26–June 5, 2011.
Includes bibliographical references.
1. Avinoff, Andrey, 1884–1949 —Exhibitions. I. Avinoff, Andrey, 1884–1949. II. Carnegie Museum of Art. III. Title.

N6537.A945A4 2010
709.2—dc22 2010040735

CONTENTS

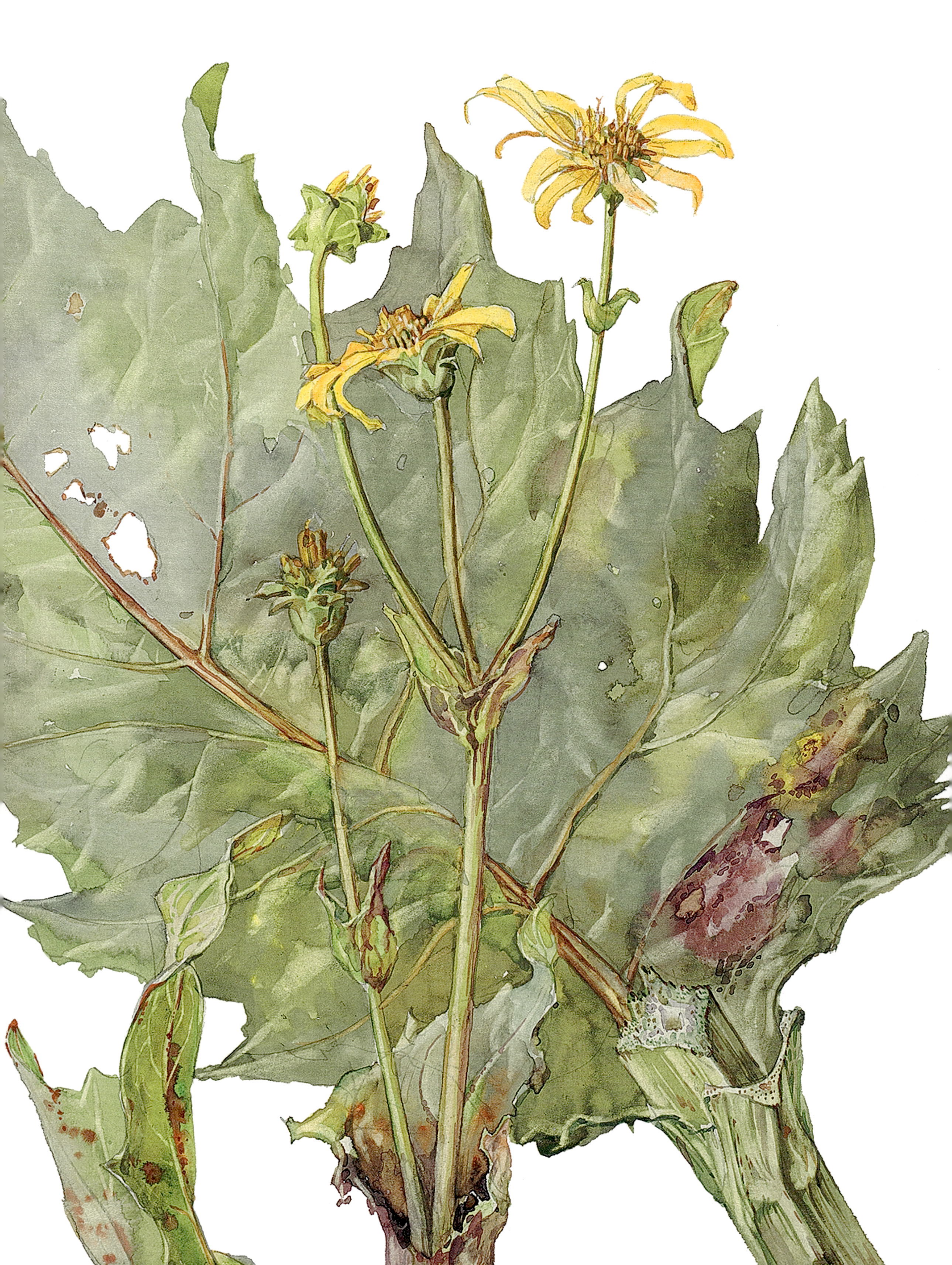

DIRECTOR'S FOREWORD

IT IS A SOURCE OF WONDER to me—as it must be to anyone directing an art or science museum these days—that Andrey Avinoff ran one of the largest natural history museums in the United States (now Carnegie Museum of Natural History in Pittsburgh) and maintained a simultaneous career as a watercolorist and illustrator. Clearly, for him, art and science were compatible disciplines, united by a reverence for nature and the visible world, and elevated by a conception of beauty that could encompass Persian carpets, distribution patterns of Himalayan butterflies, and the scintillating optics of rainbows, bubbles, and flowing water. Even during his lifetime, Avinoff was something of a cult figure, although very few were aware of all the facets of his complex personality, vast intelligence, and wide-ranging interests. It is only in the twenty-first century, with our new access to pre-Soviet-era history and art, and increasing acceptance of homosexuality, that something approaching a complete and integrated view of the man and his art becomes possible.

Andrey Avinoff: In Pursuit of Beauty, the first truly significant exhibition in over fifty years dedicated to Avinoff's work, is the first comprehensive exploration of this lost master of the Russian Silver Age. The champion for this project is Louise Lippincott, curator of fine arts at Carnegie Museum of Art, who has pulled together years of intense research into a stunning exhibition and catalogue. Our hope is that her thoughtful reevaluation of Avinoff will inspire broad interest in his many accomplishments.

The exhibition would not have been possible without the enthusiastic involvement of Avinoff's heirs—Antonia Shoumatoff Foster, Alex Shoumatoff, He Who Stands Firm (Nicholas Avinoff Shoumatoff), and Victoria Ward—who offered works from their collections as well as their knowledge and insight into his legacy. We are also grateful to our colleagues at Carnegie Museum of of Natural History for their spirit of collaboration and for their contribution of numerous specimens and other objects to the exhibition. Our thanks also go to the University Art Gallery, University of Pittsburgh; Hillwood Estate, Museum & Gardens, Washington, D.C.; The Kinsey Institute for Research in Sex, Gender, and Reproduction, Indiana University, Bloomington; and the Smithsonian American Art Museum, Washington, D.C., for their generous loans.

Finally, gratitude is due to our funders. Major support for the exhibition and catalogue has been provided by Dr. Richard and Priscilla Hunt, the Virginia Kaufman Fund, and the Beal Publication Fund. The Heinz Endowments and Allegheny Regional Asset District provide important general operating support, and the museum receives state arts funding support from the Pennsylvania Council on the Arts, a state agency funded by the Commonwealth of Pennsylvania. We deeply appreciate these contributions, which have allowed us to share the story of Andrey Avinoff with the world.

— Lynn Zelevansky
The Henry J. Heinz II Director
Carnegie Museum of Art

ACKNOWLEDGMENTS

THE PRESERVATION OF Andrey Avinoff's legacy has been a lifelong project of the descendants of Avinoff's sister, Elizabeth Shoumatoff: Antonia Shoumatoff Foster (who runs the Andrey Avinoff Foundation and Web site), Alex Shoumatoff, He Who Stands Firm (Nicholas Avinoff Shoumatoff), and Victoria Ward. I am deeply grateful to them for the opportunity to study Avinoff, for opening their homes and collections, for sharing insights about "Uncle," and for suggesting fruitful avenues for research. Their personal accounts of the man convey much that is beyond the scope of conventional scholarship. In addition, this exhibition has temporarily emptied their walls of Avinoff's art.

The intellectual background and structure for this study were developed during an intense three-week Summer Institute sponsored by the National Endowment for the Humanities at the New York Public Library. Edward Kasinec and Robert H. Davis, Jr., led the seminar "America Engages Russia, c. 1880–1930: Studies in Cultural Interaction," and I benefitted immensely from their advice, the knowledge of the presenters, and the feedback of my fellow participants, experienced scholars who taught me constantly. The first version of this study was delivered as a project presentation at the Institute in July 2009.

It has been a pleasure to share my fascination with Avinoff with the following enthusiasts and fellow travelers, whose contributions have been numerous and varied: Mernie Berger, James Cummins, Robert Gangewere, Yelena Harbick, Richard Hunt, Devin Irby, Catherine Johnson-Roehr, Costas Karakatsanis, Janet Kennedy, Rachel Miller, Edgar Munhall, Tracy Myers, John Norman, Kristen Regina, Brian Rohleder, Heather Semple, Kendal Shaber, Graham Shearing, Tom Sokolowski, and Amanda Zehnder. Special thanks are due to colleagues at Carnegie Museum of Natural History who generously walked me through their collections and history during the Avinoff years: Bernadette Callery, Deborah

Harding, Mark Klingler, Ellen McCallie, Cynthia Morton, John Rawlins, Sam Taylor, and Dave Watters.

As usual (and much appreciated, as usual), Carnegie Museum of Art staff has been deeply involved in the development and realization of the exhibition. Two directors, at first, Richard Armstrong, and now, Lynn Zelevansky, supported this curatorial leap into the unknown with their customary courage and open-mindedness. Deputy director Maureen Rolla managed budgets (and, while fellow acting co-director, the entire museum during my absence in New York), and former director of development Renée Pekor provided essential fundraising assistance. Director of exhibitions Sarah Minnaert has taken the tour into her capable hands, while Chris Craychee and the workshop crew ably handled the installation. Monika Tomko, with the assistance of Allison Revello, oversaw the registration process with great care and patience. Dale Luce, preparator, had the critical task of rehousing these delicate works of art for exhibition and future preservation, and head conservator Ellen Baxter provided key guidance. Head of publications Katie Reilly, rights and reproductions coordinator Laurel Mitchell, editor Jane Friedman, and the design and production team of Glue + Paper Workshop worked to ensure that the catalogue lives up to Avinoff's incredibly high standards. Marilyn Russell and her team of educators will introduce visitors to Avinoff's work through imaginative public programs. The fine arts departmental assistants Ayanna Burrus and Akemi May maintained the research files and the checklist, noteworthy examples of both evolution and metamorphosis (often simultaneously). My thanks to them, and the many other colleagues who have contributed as part of their regular duties.

Finally, this catalogue could not have been completed without the assistance of the Pittsburgh blizzard of February 2010, which provided a (mercifully brief) Siberian-style exile ideal for writing. However, flaws that may not be blamed on global warming are entirely the responsibility of the author.

— Louise Lippincott
Curator of Fine Arts
Carnegie Museum of Art

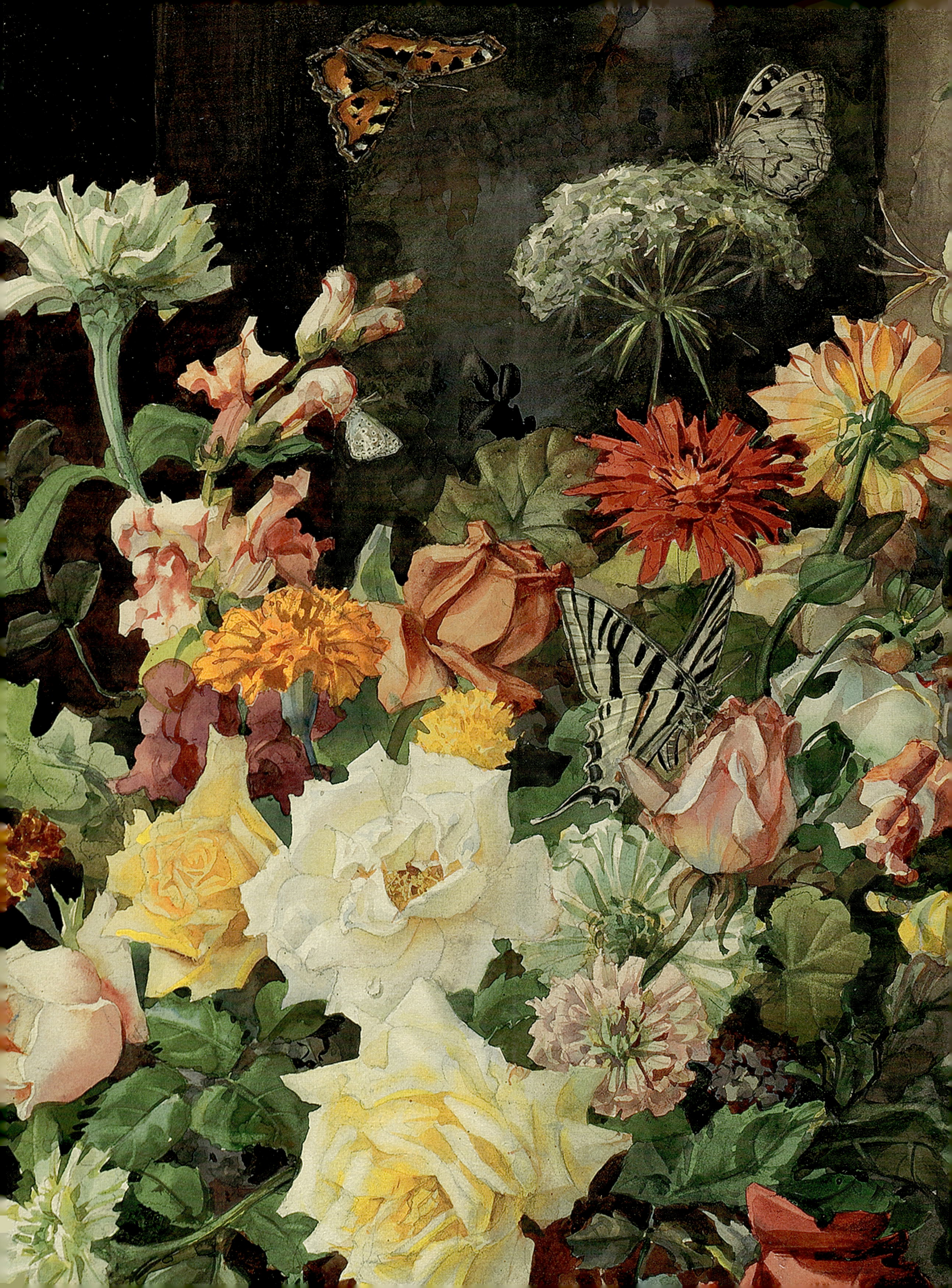

"Beauty will save the world."

—FYODOR DOSTOEVSKY, *THE IDIOT,* 1869[1]

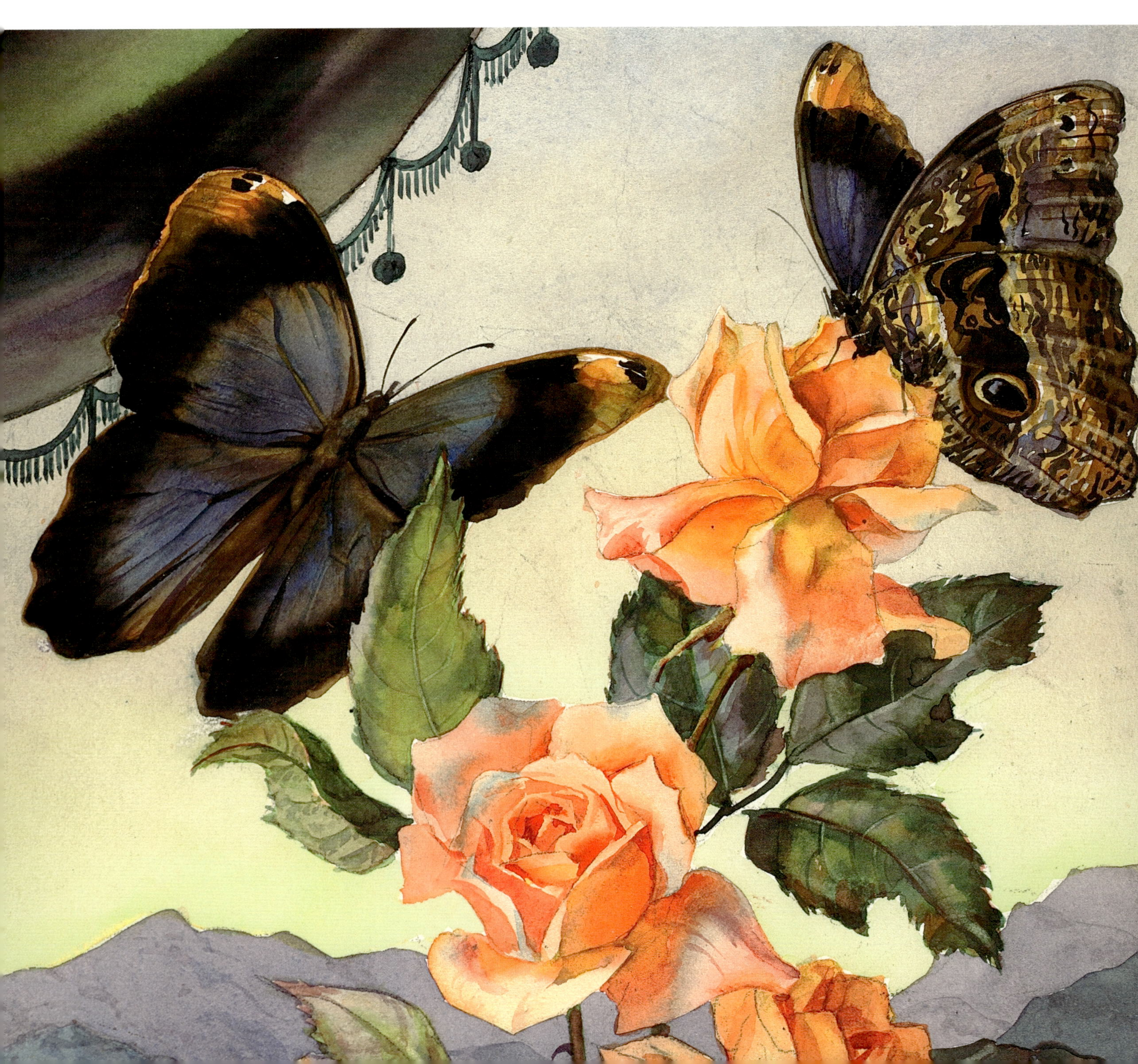

LOUISE LIPPINCOTT

ANDREY AVINOFF IN PURSUIT OF BEAUTY

"BEAUTY WILL SAVE THE WORLD" is the epitaph engraved into Andrey Avinoff's tombstone in Locust Valley Cemetery on Long Island, New York. Avinoff died in New York City on July 16, 1949, at the age of sixty-five, following surgery after months of declining health (figure 1).

There could be no more poignant or apt summation of the spirit of the amazing, brilliant, resilient man who was Andrey Avinoff. Artist, illustrator, entomologist, collector, socialite, admirer of beauty in all its forms, Avinoff lived in a series of worlds lost or destroyed by horror and ugliness: Silver Age St. Petersburg, devastated by World War I and the Russian Revolution; Roaring Twenties America, brought down by the Great Depression; the international peace movement of the 1930s, eroded by Fascism and Communism, and decimated by World War II. The development of the Cold War in his final years ended any hope of reconciliation with his beloved motherland. Avinoff emerged from each of these lost worlds reinvented, but died despairing of the future, having worked tirelessly to improve it.

It is wrong to underestimate Avinoff—painter of butterflies, ballet, orchids, rainbows, soap bubbles, and beautiful young men—as a superficial aesthete skimming above the hard realities of life. His polished manners, aristocratic bearing, and self-deprecating sense of humor all contribute to this impression. Yet, the long lists of his published essays, scientific collections, international committee memberships, and one-man art exhibitions reveal how hard he worked and suggest the intensity of his motivation. As an artist he might have been categorized as an illustrator, but the subjects he illustrated, intimately related to his mystical vision of the interconnectedness of nature, life, and spirit, are of the utmost seriousness. If a man can be both a driven overachiever and an aesthete, he would be Andrey Avinoff.

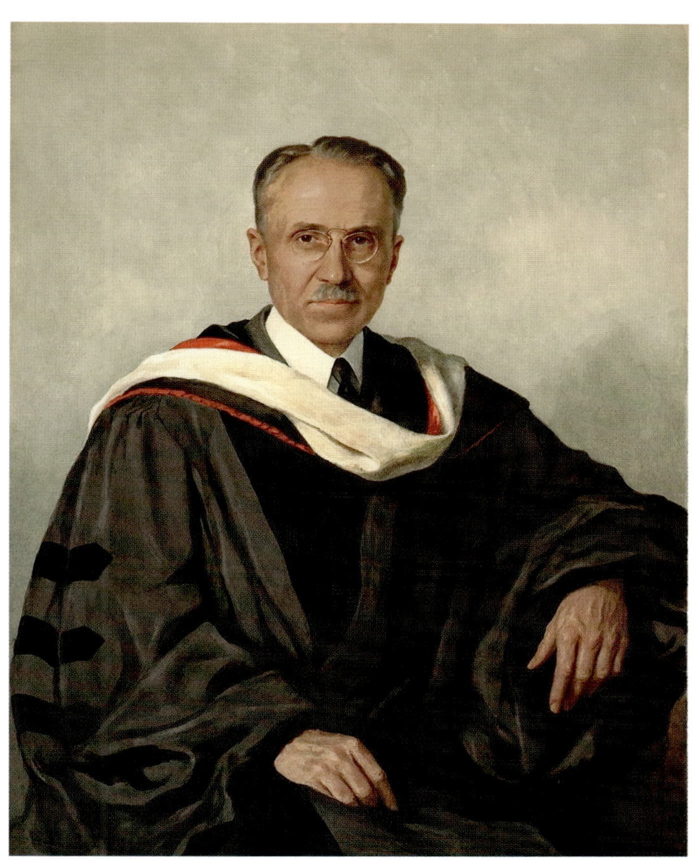

FIGURE 1
Elizabeth Shoumatoff, *Portrait of Andrey Avinoff,* 1943, watercolor on paper, Carnegie Museum of Art, Transfer from Museum Department of Carnegie Institute, 48.21.
Cat. no. 66

Detail of *Talisman Roses,* 1948 (figure 10)

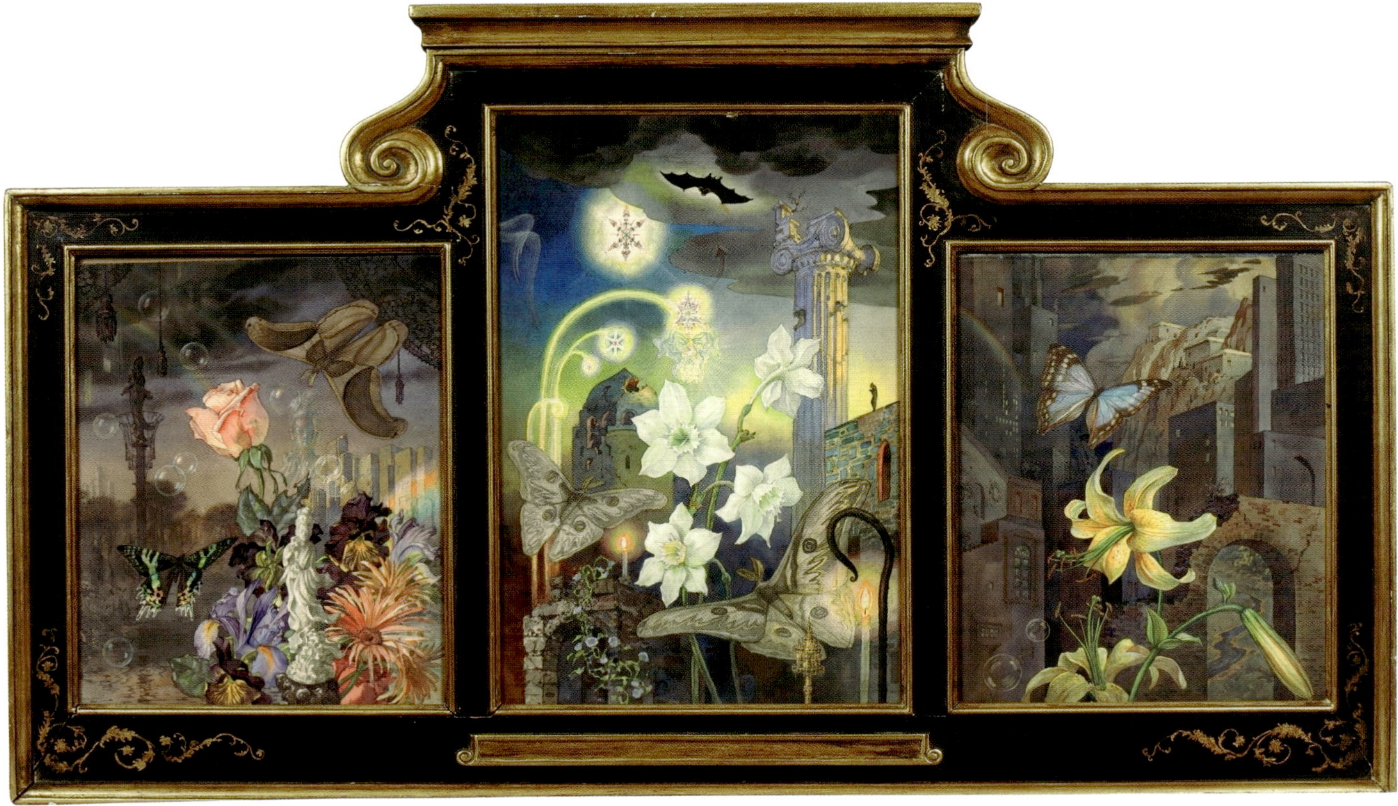

FIGURE 2
The Old Dispensation and the New (The Triptych), three watercolors from 1941 and 1948, framed together in 1951, Carnegie Museum of Art, Heinz Family Fund, 2007.46.1–3. Cat. nos. 34, 51, 52

It's also simplistic to view Avinoff as a sort of cultural dead end. Although he exhibited his paintings at exhibitions alongside Kazimir Malevich and Vassily Kandinsky, towering figures of the early-twentieth-century Russian avant-garde, his elaborate symbolic compositions are the antithesis of modernist abstraction. The posthumous retrospective exhibition held in Pittsburgh in 1953 that was intended to celebrate his achievements unwittingly ended up burying them or otherwise, perhaps inadvertently in some cases, mischaracterizing the artist and his work. Indeed, the pompous title of the show—*An Exhibition of Andrey Avinoff: The Man of Science, Religion, Mysticism, Society, and Fantasy*[2]—gives no hint of Avinoff's identity as a gay Russian émigré artist: an identity that was carefully suppressed by the exhibition organizers, but that played a major role in his creative and intellectual development. The exhibition contained factual inaccuracies as well, hindering an accurate assessment of the man and his work. In one notable instance, three discrete paintings—a 1941 Christmas subject and two 1948 watercolors—were combined into one frame, identified as a single image for that exhibition. The resulting *Triptych* is an incoherent "masterwork" long held to embody Avinoff's mystical philosophy of life (figure 2).[3] Fifty years later, a handful of Carnegie Museum of Art staffers knew Avinoff only as the obscure creator of modest flower paintings such as the c. 1946 watercolor of a potted begonia (figure 3).

FIGURE 3
Begonias, c. 1946, graphite and watercolor on paper, Carnegie Museum of Art, Gift of Mr. and Mrs. John B. Sutton, Jr., 59.54

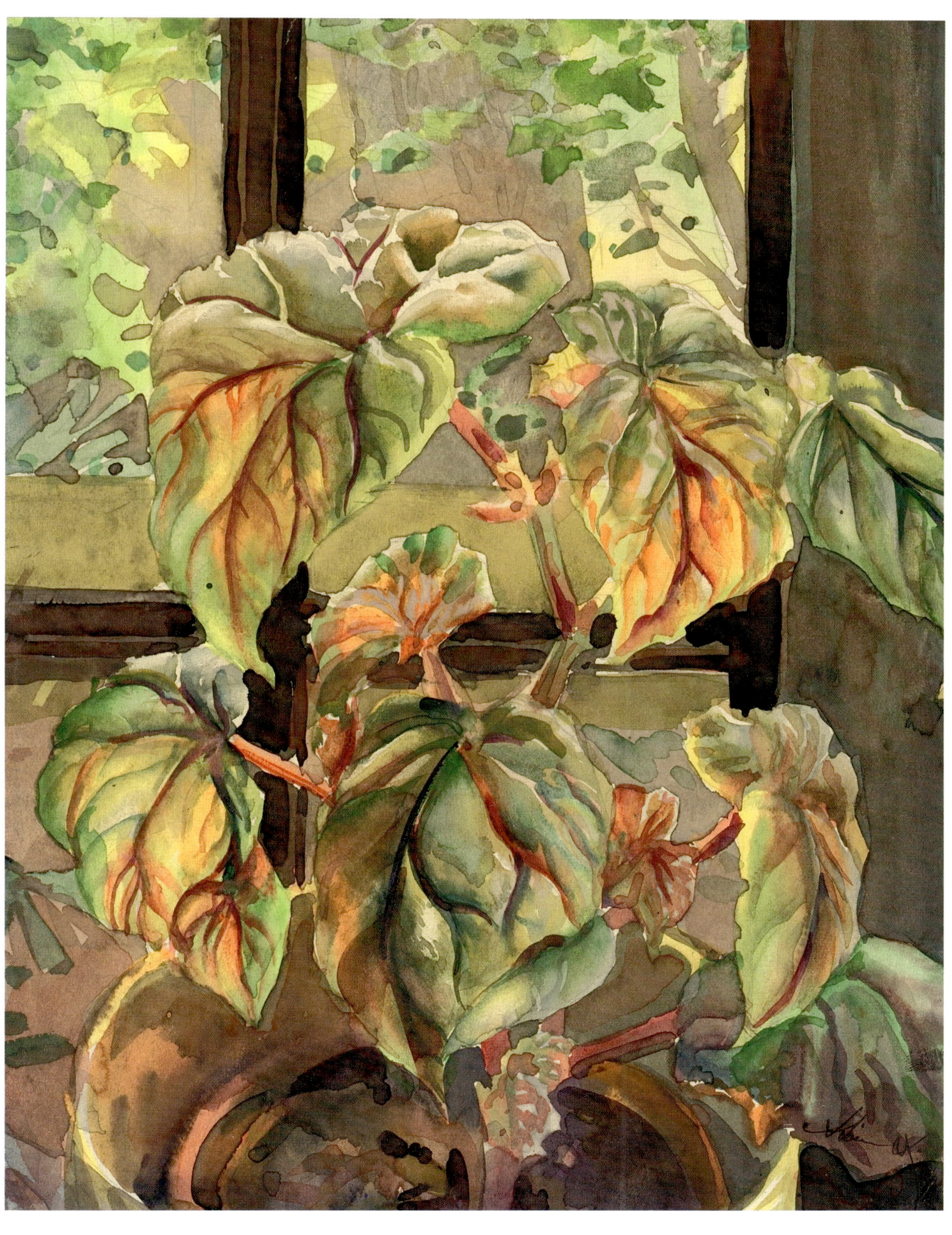

Nonetheless, Avinoff's great-nephews and -nieces, the descendants of his sister, Elizabeth Shoumatoff, continue to revere his memory and recall countless anecdotes about Avinoff's accomplishments, personality, and brilliance (see pp. 83–85). Most of his art, letters, and writings are still with them—an overwhelming inheritance, in many ways. Carnegie Museum of Natural History, where he served as director for nearly twenty years, still houses his legacy: hundreds of thousands of butterflies, an encyclopedic collection of Western Pennsylvania botanical studies, and a T-rex holotype skeleton that, at great expense, was recently morphed into an extremely large, vicious ancestor of the chicken. For many years, boxes of Avinoff's drawings and photographs have sat in darkness at the Kinsey Institute in Bloomington, Indiana—to which Avinoff contributed a significant amount of personal data, artworks, and other materials in the late 1940s—awaiting the researcher with the right interests in Russian history, homosexuality, visual art, or a combination thereof. Avinoff's vast library of Russian art books, a trove of rare and significant publications amassed in the 1920s and 1930s, acquired in 2000 by the Hillwood Estate, Museum & Gardens in Washington, D.C., is only now becoming available to scholars in the field.

These great masses of well-preserved original materials are a godsend for twenty-first-century scholars, whose vision of the twentieth century has been overturned in countless ways. In recent decades, definitions of modernism have expanded considerably beyond the Greenbergian paradigm, with its almost single-minded focus on abstraction and the tools of art-making. The collapse of the Soviet Union has transformed the study of Russian culture, thanks to newfound access to archival and other source materials kept under lock and key for roughly half a century. And the rise of queer studies in academia, combined with the increased tolerance of homosexuality in Western society in general, has eliminated the need for silence and obscurity on this subject. These fields come together—and pertain to Avinoff—in the debate on the impact of Russian exiles on Europe and the United States in the twentieth century. Perhaps even more fascinating because it is still largely unexamined is the extent to which that émigré culture, now being repatriated to the new Russian state, will shape the future of Russia.

As the longstanding barriers between gay and straight, art and science, Soviet and Russian, begin to disintegrate and fall, Andrey Avinoff emerges as an important historical figure whose intriguing body of artwork, multifaceted interests, and equally multifaceted identity—as a gay Russian artist who made it in the very straight world of American science and education, an autocratic European traditionalist who helped create the modern, anything-goes New York art scene—significantly enriches our understanding of twentieth-century art, in all its vitality and complexity.

This study is based on visual images and research sources in the English language, and is focused on Avinoff's contributions to American art and culture. The story of his life in Russia presented herein is therefore sketchy and based on secondary sources; his impact on the natural sciences and museology, now only beginning to be recognized, does not receive comprehensive treatment. The goal of this project has been to separate fact from legend, connect symbol to meaning, and, in the process, arrive at a more accurate assessment of the man and his art. Avinoff's life story is extraordinary in its own right, and is the focus of the first section of this essay. The subsequent sections examine his efforts, through art, to adapt to challenging historical and personal circumstances: his transformation from Russian autocrat to American citizen; his assimilation into Western democratic capitalist culture; his efforts to preserve and disseminate Russian traditions; and, late in life, his dream of creating a new Silver Age of personal freedom and artistic creativity out of the ashes of World War II.

"The versatility of Mr. Avinoff is an international legend."

—EUGENE F. JANUZZI, *PITTSBURGH POST-GAZETTE,* 1949[4]

"He is probably the only man who has ever established, or made an effort to establish, a connection between butterflies and the Russian Revolution."

—GEOFFREY T. HELLMAN, THE *NEW YORKER,* 1948[5]

THE PLAIN FACTS OF AVINOFF'S LIFE are as follows: he was born on February 14, 1884, in Tulchin, a city in what was then southern Russia, but is now part of Ukraine.[6] His father was a lieutenant general in the Russian Imperial Army; his older brother, Nicholas, went on to become an ardent liberal reformer, and his younger sister, Elizabeth, a successful painter. Family sojourns in Tashkent and Samarkand and summer camping expeditions in the Tian Shan (Celestial) Mountains in the wilds of Uzbekistan when he was ten years old had a significant impact on his life. From the beginning, Avinoff was interested in butterflies and art, but he received a conventional elite education culminating in a law degree from Moscow University in 1905. An inheritance from his uncle Serge Avinoff in 1908 allowed him to escape the tedium of government administration with two butterfly-collecting excursions to the Pamir region, Turkestan, India, and Tibet in 1908 and 1912, while he was still in his twenties. He named his most famous lepidopteral discovery *Parnassius autocrator* in tribute to its majestic appearance—or, he would later suggest, as a prophetic homage to Russia's last tsar, Nicholas II.

Following his father's death, in 1911 Avinoff transferred into the service of Nicholas II, initially becoming a gentleman-in-waiting in the Imperial court, then joining the protocol staff in 1913. Upon the outbreak of World War I in 1914, Avinoff, too nearsighted to serve in the military, joined the Russian equivalent of the Red Cross, with which he remained until 1915, when he was sent to the United States as a representative of the All-Russian Zemsky Union to purchase war supplies for the Russian Army. He was back in Russia in 1916 and for most of 1917—an extraordinary period that witnessed the February Revolution, the subsequent installation of the liberal-bourgeois Provisional Government, and Russia's withdrawal from World War I. When he returned to the U.S., this time for good, in September 1917, he did so as a representative of the new Provisional Government, in which his brother Nicholas served as minister, initially in the Department of the Interior and, later, Foreign Affairs.

Avinoff never returned to Russia. Following the Bolshevik Revolution of October 1917, he was joined in New York by his sister, Elizabeth, her husband, Leo Shoumatoff, their children, and his mother; his family anchored his private life until his death in 1949. The 1920s were chaotic, as Avinoff nominally continued in Russian government service, the Provisional Government having been driven into exile shortly after the Bolshevik coup. The family settled in New York state, making a living at first by dairy farming (a disaster), followed by commercial art (Andrey, lucrative), portrait painting (Elizabeth, successful), and business (Leo, with the Sikorsky Aircraft Corporation, until his accidental drowning death in 1930).

Thanks to his reputation as an entomologist, and his connection to B. Preston Clark, a wealthy hawkmoth collector, Avinoff was recommended for a position in the entomology department at Carnegie Museum, Pittsburgh, as early as 1921.[7] In 1923, he felt obliged to decline the museum's offer of a position as assistant curator in the entomology department in order to accept a more lucrative job as an advertising illustrator.[8] However, as Elizabeth Shoumatoff established her portrait-painting career in New York, he was free to accept the museum directorship in 1926. Avinoff achieved much during his nearly twenty-year tenure as director: fostering the growth of the museum's famous collections of insects and dinosaurs, sponsoring the creation of lifelike dioramas for public education and display, capturing specimens in Bermuda and Jamaica, and conducting significant research on evolution, speciation, and biogeography. From 1937 (at the latest) until his death, Avinoff corresponded with that other great lepidopterist of Russia's Silver Age, Vladimir Nabokov, and almost

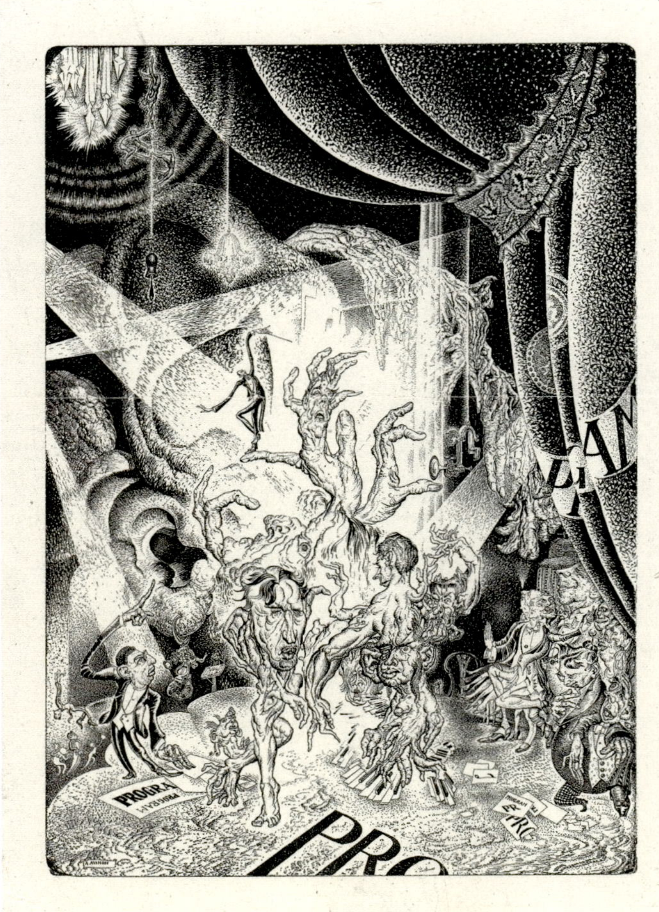

FIGURE 4
Modern Music: Jazz Symphony, c. 1920–1925, photogravure on paper, Antonia Shoumatoff Foster. Cat. no. 12

certainly advised and assisted him in his scientific work at Harvard University and the American Museum of Natural History.

In connection with his scientific work, Avinoff taught scientific illustration and biology at the University of Pittsburgh, served on the Council of the American Association of Museums, chaired the Committee on Museums of Science for the League of Nations, was elected a Fellow of the Entomological Society of America, and was appointed a Trustee of the American Museum of Natural History.

In his free time, he lectured on art history and criticism, joined the committee in charge of staging avant-garde productions for the League of Composers in New York (figure 4), spearheaded the committee to design the Russian Nationality Room at the University of Pittsburgh (see figure 46), served on the board of the Pittsburgh Symphony Orchestra, worked on behalf of the New York–based organization Ballet Associates in America, contributed hundreds of illustrations to various museum publications, and staged two solo exhibitions of his drawings and paintings.[9]

Unknown to all but a select few, Avinoff also led an active gay life and produced a substantial body of homoerotic art, most of which he destroyed immediately following a heart attack in 1945.

Upon retiring from the museum in 1945, Avinoff moved to his sister's mansion in Locust Valley, Long Island, and then persuaded her to move with him to Manhattan in 1948, to adjoining luxury apartments on Fifth Avenue. In New York, he embarked on a career as a full-time painter of still lifes, surrealist landscapes, and botanical illustrations. Over a brief period of four years, while struggling with weak health, he painted more than two hundred compositions and was the subject of eleven one-man shows. The *New Yorker* published a profile on Avinoff titled "Black Tie and Cyanide Jar" in 1948, and *Life* magazine planned a cover story on him for an issue in fall 1949.[10]

In January 1948, Alfred Kinsey published his groundbreaking study *Sexual Behavior in the Human Male.* Upon learning of the forthcoming publication in late 1947, Avinoff broke his decades-long silence about his homosexuality by writing its author a letter of congratulations.[11] The two men developed a close bond (Kinsey had been a noted entomologist prior to his work as a sexologist), and Avinoff became an eager and active contributor to Kinsey's work at the recently founded Institute for Sex Research at Indiana University (now the Kinsey Institute for Research in Sex, Gender, and Reproduction), providing material on his own sexual history and examples of his artistic work. He also introduced Kinsey to the world of gay artists, dancers, musicians, and designers in New York, and confided to Kinsey his dream of "developing eventually some Foundation or Fellowship which would bring together congenial people with similar emotional patterns and kindred esthetic philosophy."[12] At the time of Avinoff's death in July 1949, Avinoff and Kinsey were in the process of collaborating on a history of erotic art, and *Life* magazine had just shot his portrait for its cover.

"My interest in Entomology has been, since my early youth, my love, my passion,—I should say, my fate, and in some ways a tragical fate."

—ANDREY AVINOFF TO J. DOUGLAS STEWART, 1923[13]

"[T]here are glimpses of his secret heart—the butterflies."

—ALAN PRIEST, *ANDREY AVINOFF WATERCOLORS: FLOWERS AND BUTTERFLIES,* 1953[14]

EVERYONE WHO KNEW AVINOFF seems to have been awed by his intelligence and his encyclopedic grasp of esoteric knowledge. His means of relating to the world and to other people was, above all, intellectual. Witty and humorous in several languages (Russian, English, and French), he was a popular figure in the elite social, scientific, and artistic circles in the United States and Europe. He enjoyed company, and formed lasting friendships with kindred spirits, such as the bibliophile and "botanophile" Rachel Hunt. His romantic relationships seem to have been unstable, unequal, and short-lived; in this respect, he may have resembled his older brother, Nicholas, whose wife lamented that their life together could not compete with his higher calling. Avinoff could be warmly engaging with children; his grand-nephews and -nieces remember him today with a mixture of fascination and awe.

Avinoff also seems to have been a canny and sophisticated networker, with political skills matching his intellect. In contrast to Nicholas, Andrey had political stances that were, as he himself admitted, far to the right. He was anti-Semitic, common in Russia but remembered clearly by some Jewish colleagues in Pittsburgh. Like the rest of his family, he was deeply religious, held firmly to Russian Orthodoxy throughout his life, and indulged a mystical streak that shaped his highest ideals and over-the-top symbolic themes.

Despite his traditionalist views, he was in some ways strikingly modern. He took easily to capitalism and democratic citizenship. His cosmopolitan upbringing and facility for languages allowed him to function effectively in the American environment, and unlike many of his fellow émigrés, he wasted little effort on futile campaigns to overthrow the Bolshevik or Soviet regimes. Instead, he sought to preserve and implant in his new home the best that modernist Russian culture had to contribute to Western civilization.

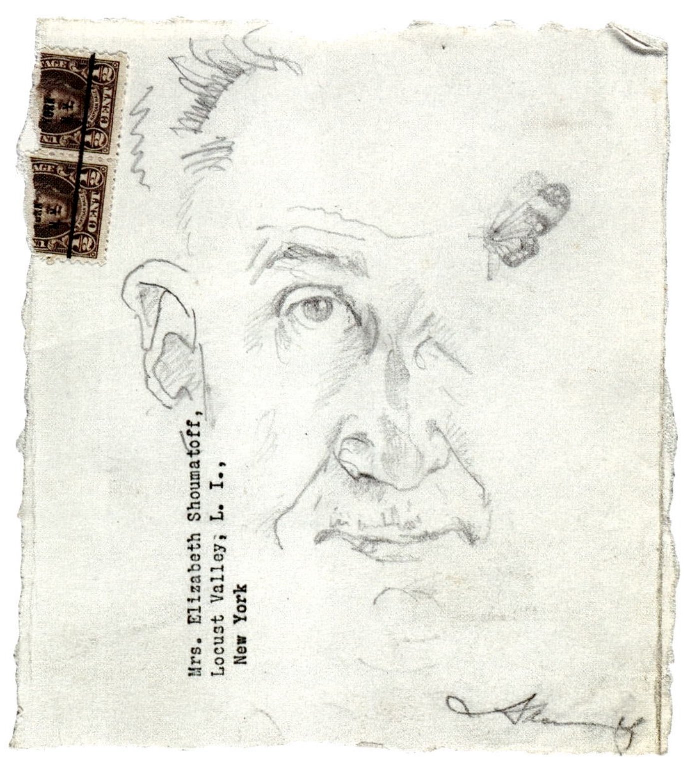

FIGURE 5
Self-Portrait with Butterfly Eye, 1940s, graphite on fragment of envelope, with typescript and stamps, Antonia Shoumatoff Foster. Cat. no. 61

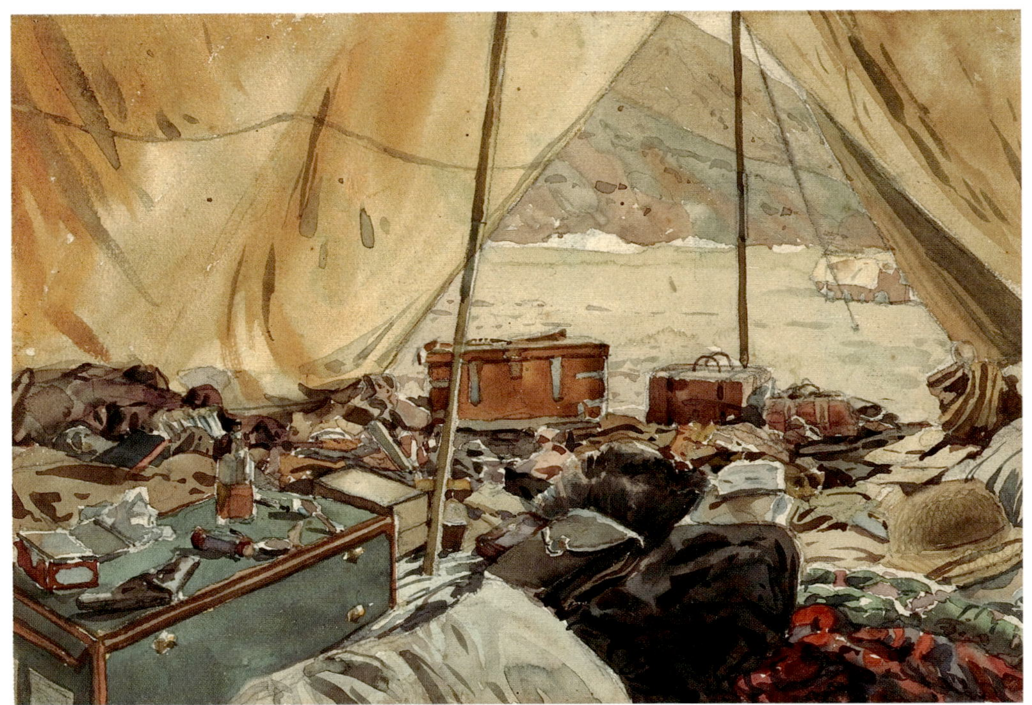

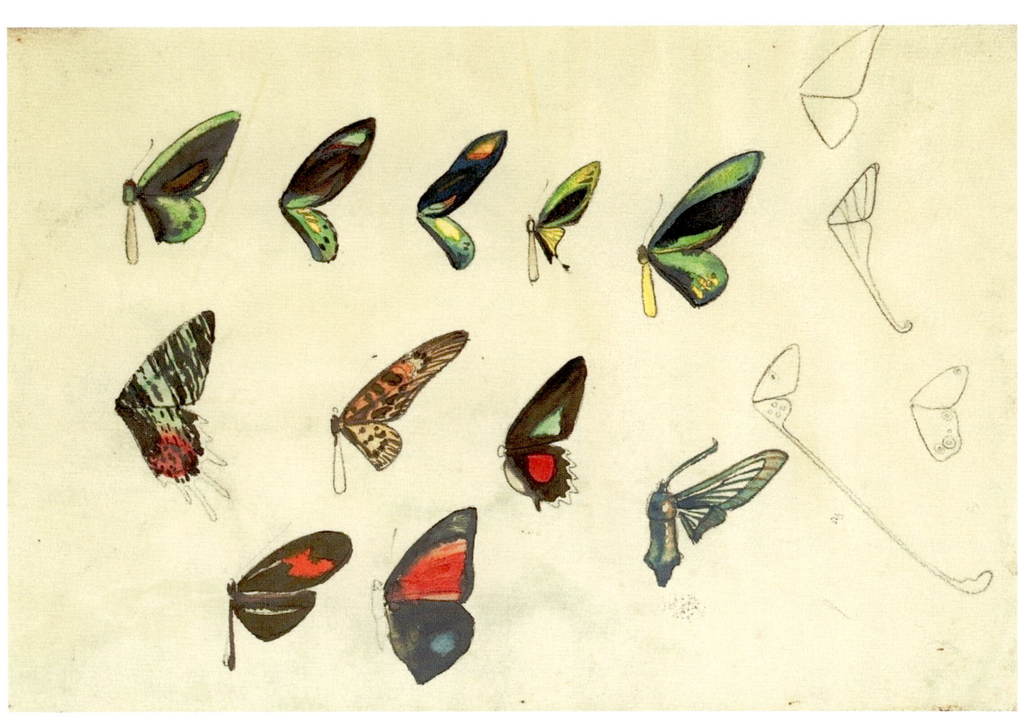

FIGURE 6
Tibet: Camp Scene in the Karakoram at the Foot of the Mountain, 1912, graphite and watercolor on paper, Carnegie Museum of Art, Patrons Art Fund, 2008.12.1. Cat. no. 3

FIGURE 7
Tibet: Studies of Butterfly and Moth Wings, 1912 (verso of figure 6)

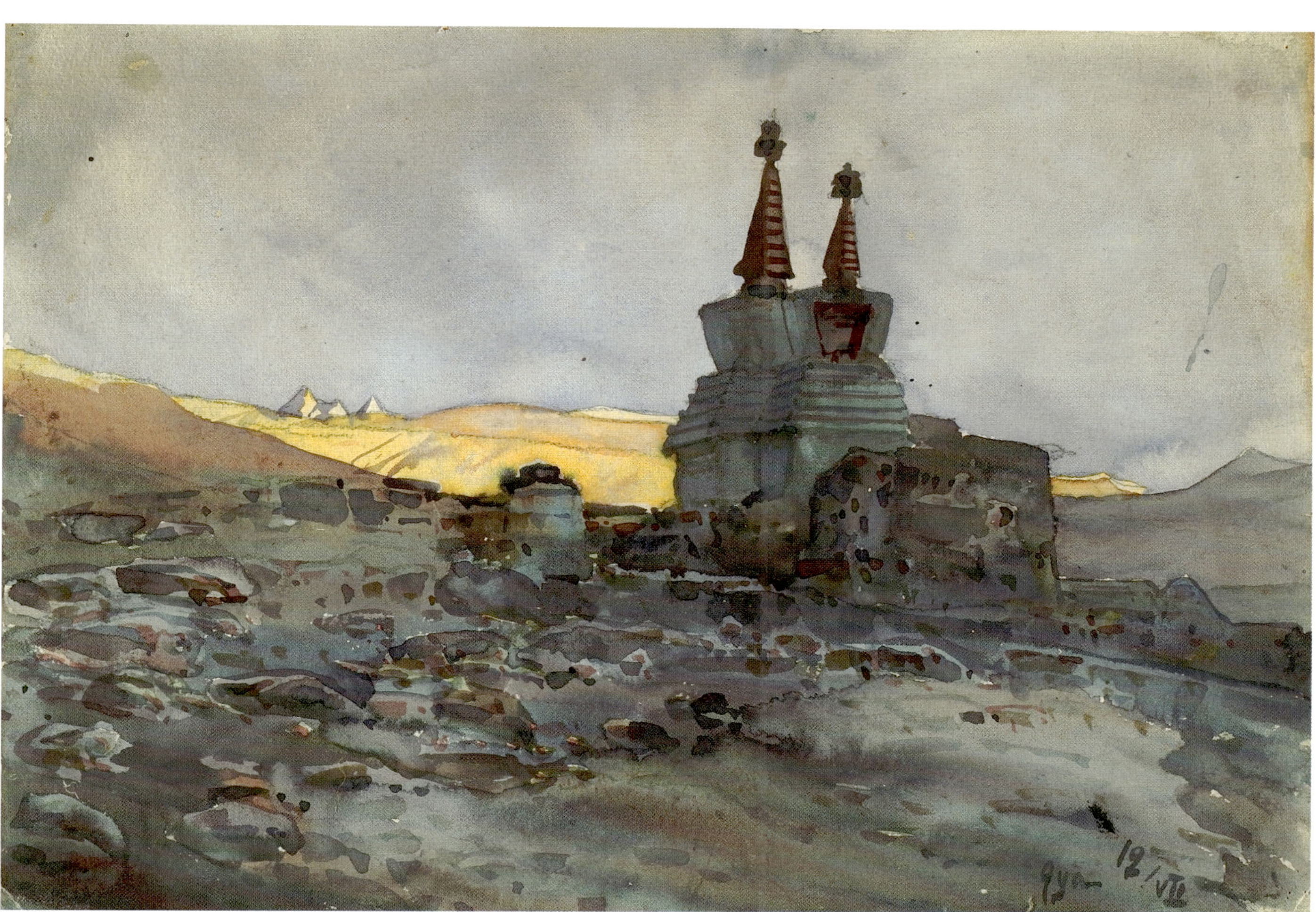

FIGURE 8
Tibet: Monastery in the Mountains, 1912, graphite and watercolor on paper, Carnegie Museum of Art, Patrons Art Fund, 2008.12.3. Cat. no. 5

Andrey Avinoff began his lifelong pursuit of beauty by collecting and painting butterflies. He risked his life and much of his personal fortune to collect these extraordinary insects in some of the world's most dangerous terrains: Russian Turkestan and the Pamir region in 1908, and Kashmir and Tibet in 1912 (figures 6–8). Beyond his own trips, Avinoff helped finance forty-two other such expeditions prior to World War I. By the age of thirty, he had amassed one of the greatest collections of Palearctic butterflies in Europe (80,000 in number), named at least one new species of butterfly (the earlier-cited *Parnassius autocrator*), won the coveted Gold Medal of the Imperial Geographic Society, and published seven articles in three languages on his discoveries.

When Avinoff left Russia for good in 1917, he had to abandon his beloved butterflies as well. What he was able to save—a few favorite specimens, a sheaf of watercolors from the second collecting excursion, and a unique, hand-illustrated copy of an eighteenth-century text on American butterflies (Cat. no. 63)—was symbolic of a lifetime of work. His personal fortune having been lost in the aftermath of the Bolshevik upheaval, butterflies became his profession in the U.S. He worked intermittently in the entomology department of Carnegie Museum of Natural History

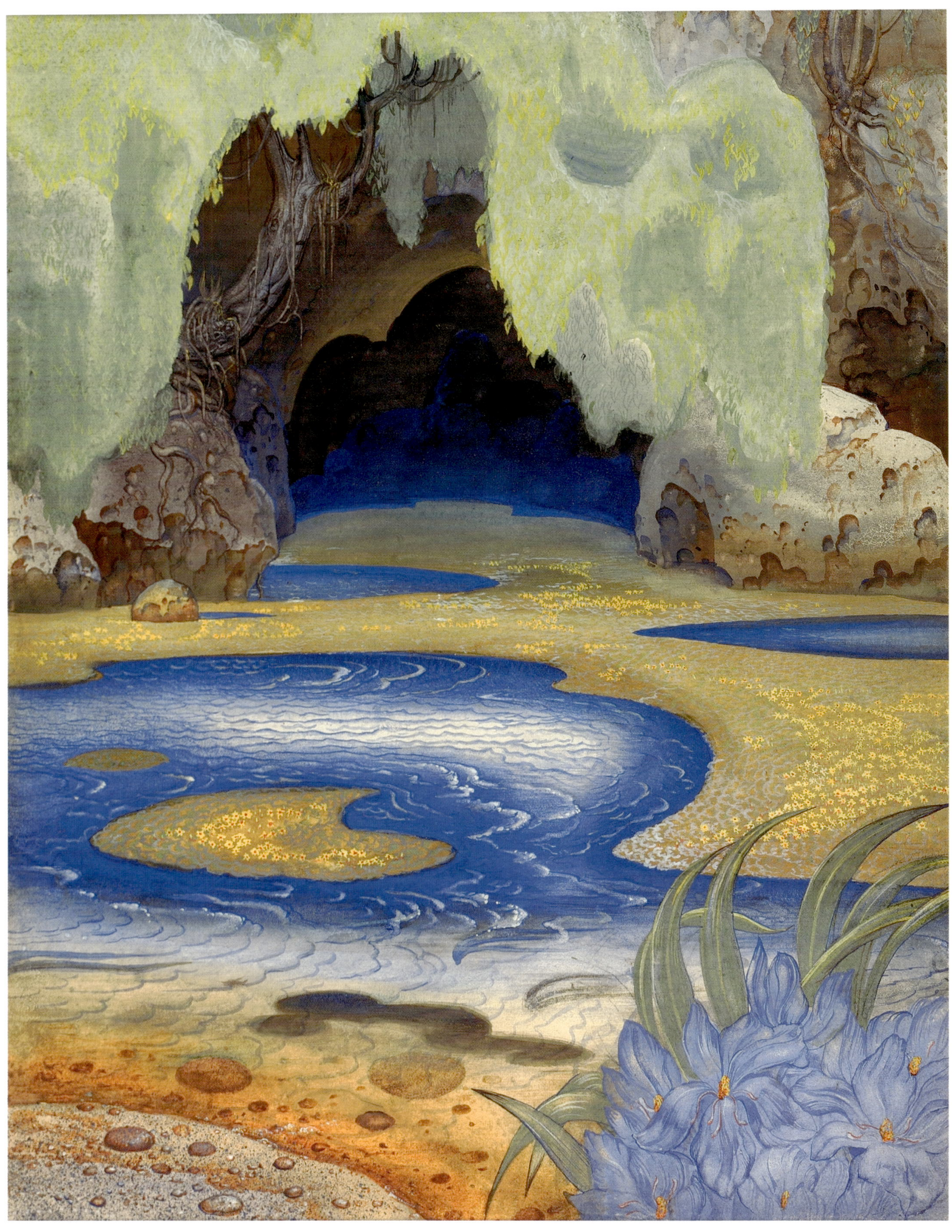

FIGURE 9
Jamaican Landscape: Blue Pool and Iris, 1930s, gouache on card, Antonia Shoumatoff Foster. Cat. no. 29

from 1922 to 1926, struggling to reconcile his love for entomology with his family's need for his presence and financial support in New York. Ultimately, the fit was a good one, for in its first thirty years, the institution had built a distinguished collection and program under the leadership of W. J. Holland and J. Douglas Stewart, whom Avinoff succeeded as director in 1926.

Avinoff continued to pursue butterflies during his tenure as director. As the Palearctic regions of Central Asia, China, and Tibet were no longer accessible due to political and other circumstances, he retained Holland's focus on Latin America and the Caribbean, eventually leading five expeditions through the richly varied terrains of Jamaica (figure 9). In the early 1930s, he arranged with Soviet authorities to catalogue his Russian collection, which had been nationalized following the Revolution. He studied shipments from Leningrad of twenty-five insects at a time, while purchasing comparable specimens and collections for Pittsburgh. Walter Sweadner, a graduate student in biology and subsequent curator of entomology, who joined the museum around that time, brought to Avinoff's project the Western academic background that Avinoff lacked. Together, the two compiled "The Karanasa Butterflies: A Study in Evolution," one of the earliest published studies to convincingly demonstrate the role of geography and ecology in speciation.[15] Even after retiring, Avinoff collected butterflies for the museum with funds raised by selling his artwork: "Flowers [that I paint] turn into butterflies—a welcome transformation and it will enrich the collections of the museum" (figure 10).[16]

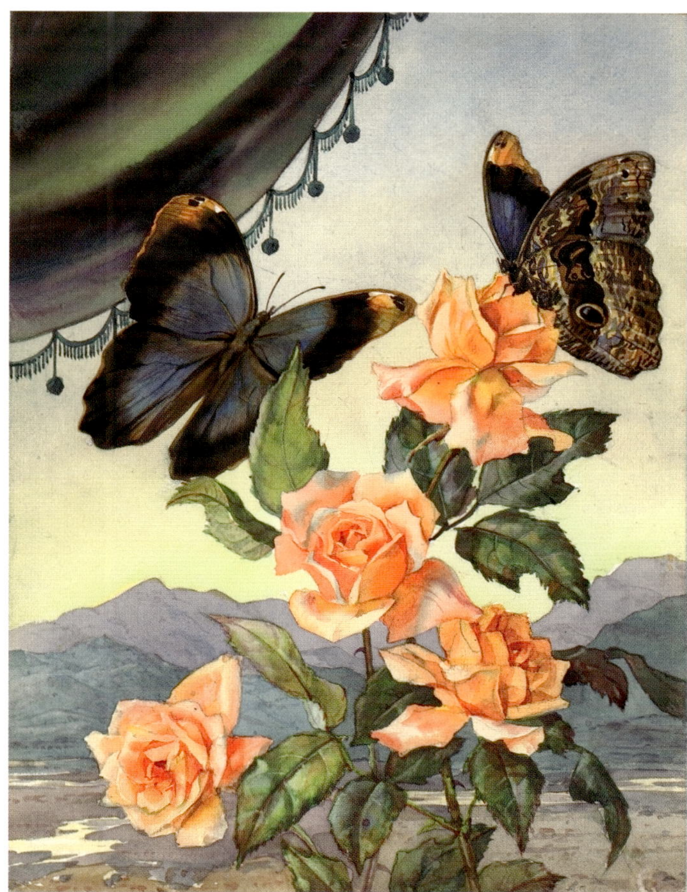

FIGURE 10
Talisman Roses, 1948, graphite and watercolor on pressed paperboard, Victoria Ward. Cat. no. 53

From earliest childhood, Avinoff loved to paint butterflies. Late in life, he wrote in his Artistic Credo, "I always consider butterflies as my main instructor in art."[17] Collecting and cataloguing butterflies is above all a visual exercise that begins with spotting an inconspicuous shape in a tree or bush, following its swooping

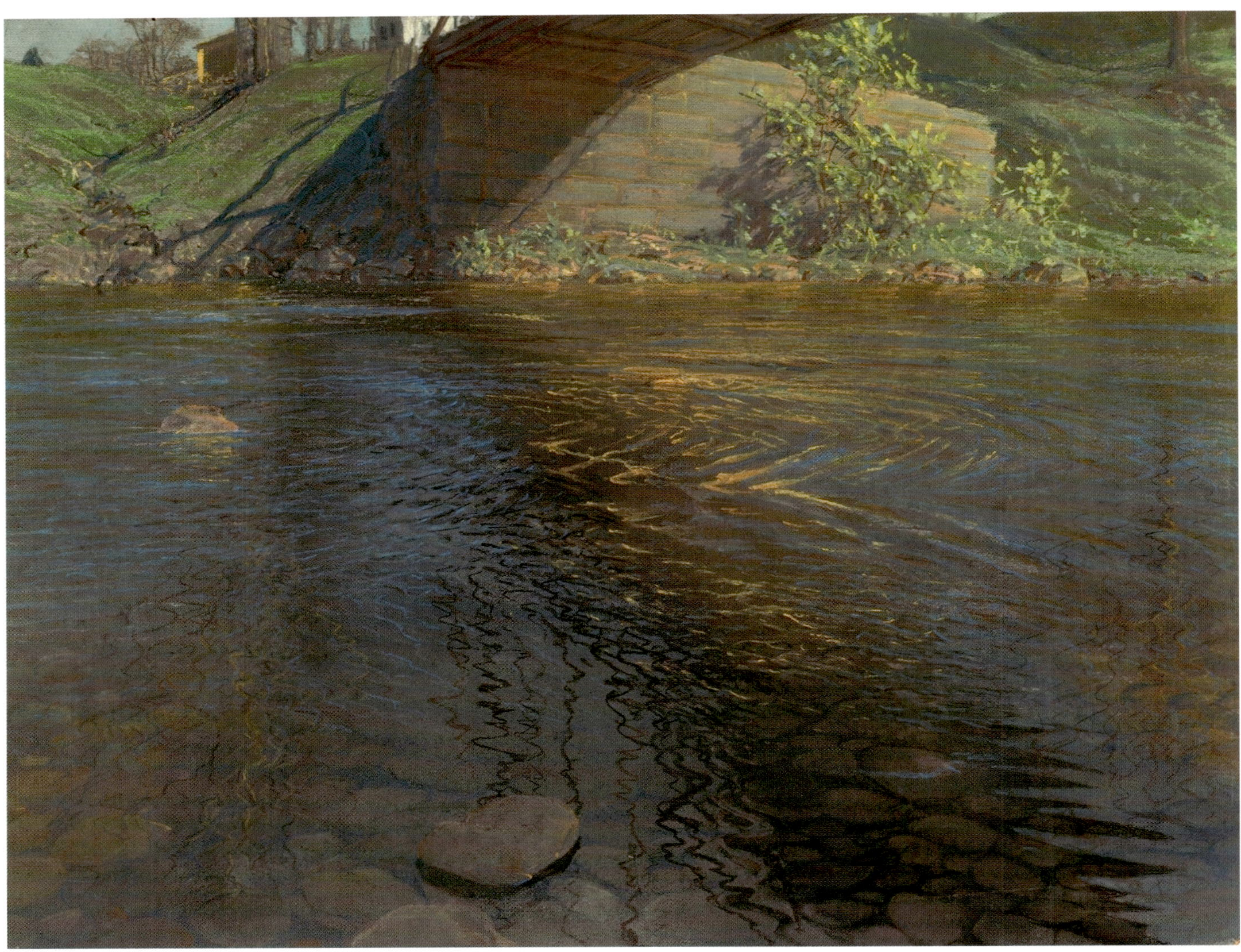

FIGURE 11
The Bridge below Honk Falls at Naponoch, c. 1921, pastel on illustrator's board, Carnegie Museum of Art, Second Century Acquisition Fund, 2007.47. Cat. no. 14

flight, and then patiently studying the tiny body and fragile wings with the help of a microscope. Portraying the color, pattern, form, and detail of resplendent butterfly wings was Avinoff's greatest technical challenge, and it shaped his artistic style, marked by meticulous technique, fanatical observation of appearances, and an obsessive interest in the effects of light on reflective surfaces. The orderly, abstract, yet organic arrangements of color and shape in butterfly wings became his aesthetic ideal, equaled in his mind only by the most beautiful of Persian carpets—both microcosms of a world too complex and varied for a simple method of description. It is safe to say that for Avinoff, the aesthetics of butterfly wings molded his vision of the natural order on a cosmic scale.

Avinoff also possessed a thorough understanding of the animal, depicting each butterfly in its characteristic pose or mode of flight, with antennae, feet, and wings all in the correct positions. Entomologists can usually identify the species and gender of each of Avinoff's subjects, and sometimes even a specific behavior illustrated. However, he painted caterpillars or chrysalises

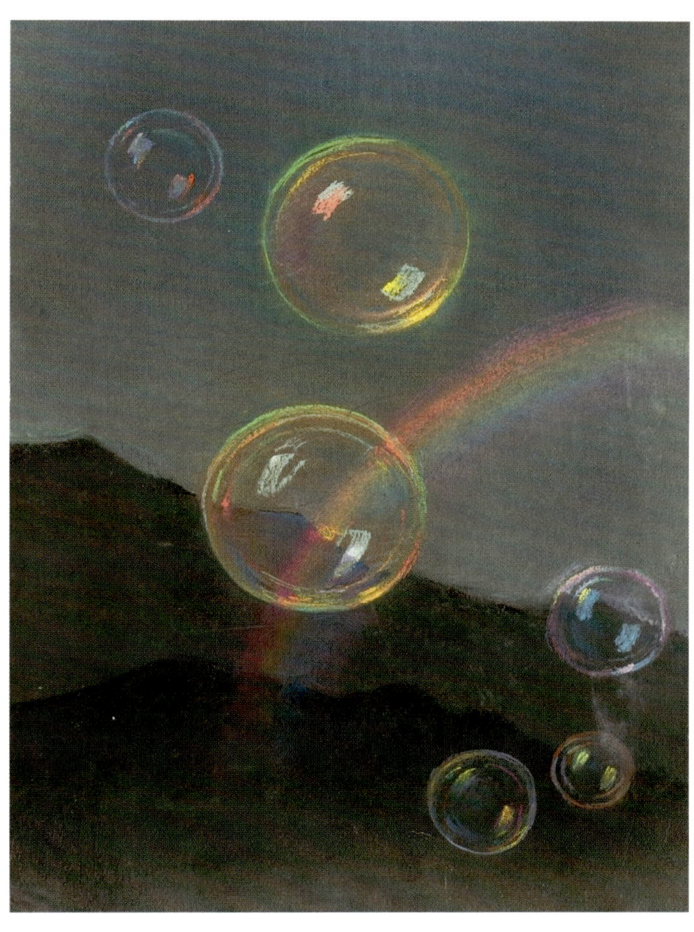

FIGURE 12
Bubbles and Rainbow, c. 1925–1930, pastel on black card, Antonia Shoumatoff Foster. Cat. no. 22

rarely if at all, and none of the insects' preferred foods or habitats; the scientific illustrator's careful record of all the stages of life and details of environment did not engage him. Avinoff's butterflies hover around hothouse bouquets and velvet curtains, rest on architectural plinths, or flutter in front of alien or imaginary vistas—nature's most decorative jewels.

Butterfly aesthetics influenced all of Avinoff's artistic interests. Even modern art could be tolerable if it related to butterflies. To again quote from his Artistic Credo,

> In the modern schools, which leave me cold in comparison with the magnificent achievement of a more spiritual past, I am interested naively in some novel ways of treating luminosities, spectral problems, transparencies and superimposed prismatic reflections, so frequent on the iridescent butterfly wings.[18]

Although it is not clear which modern artworks evoked these thoughts, his love of shiny, translucent, reflective surfaces is consistent throughout his career. Along with butterfly wings, flowing water, gems, jellyfish, and soap bubbles all captured his attention (figures 11–15).

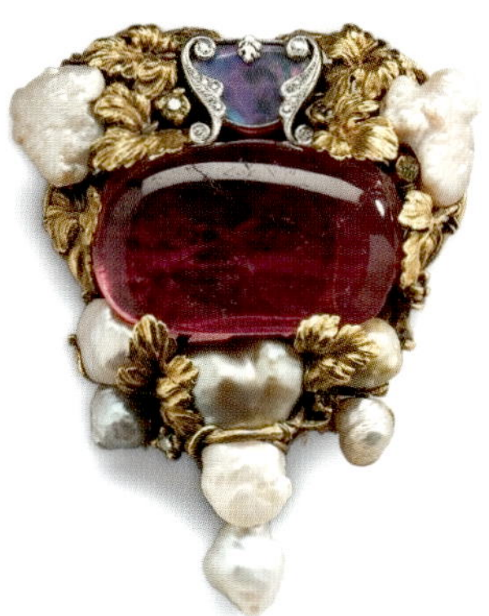

FIGURE 13
Brooch, 1940s, elbaite, opal, pearl, and diamond set in gold and platinum, Carnegie Museum of Natural History. Cat. no. 62

For Avinoff, the visual properties of light's interactions with matter symbolized the unity and interconnectedness of the natural world. His belief was founded in the biological and philosophical theories of the fin-de-siècle, but received its clearest expression in his most original works of art. These can be read as Symbolist fantasies or Surrealist nightmares (depending on their dates), and Avinoff was careful to separate them from his scientific work in public exhibitions. However, in his creative mind, the mid-twentieth-century art/science dichotomy seems not to have existed.

The aptly titled watercolor *Iridescence,* an allusion to the optical property of certain butterfly wings, sheds light on

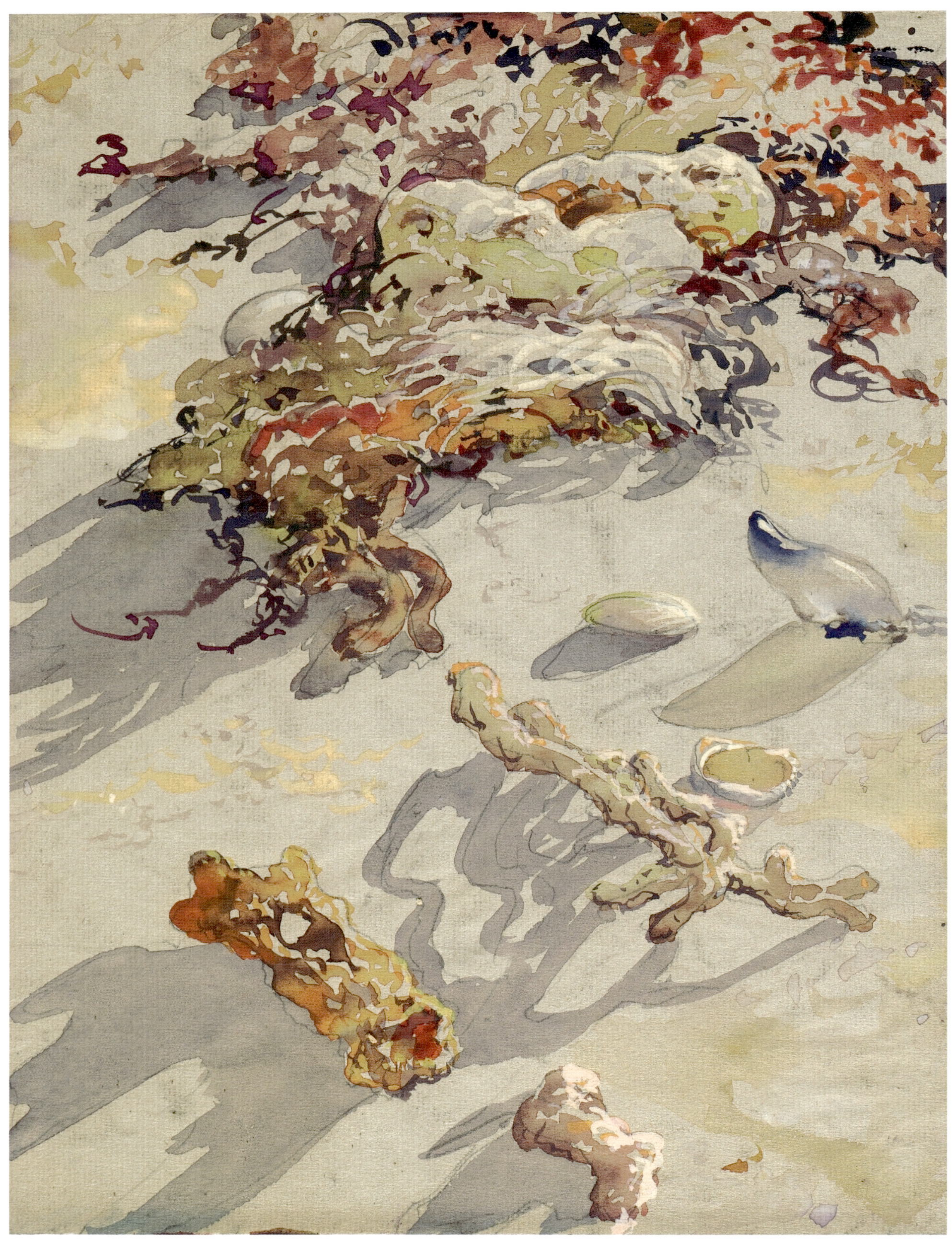

FIGURE 14
Underwater Scene, c. 1946, watercolor on paper, Antonia Shoumatoff Foster. Cat. no. 47

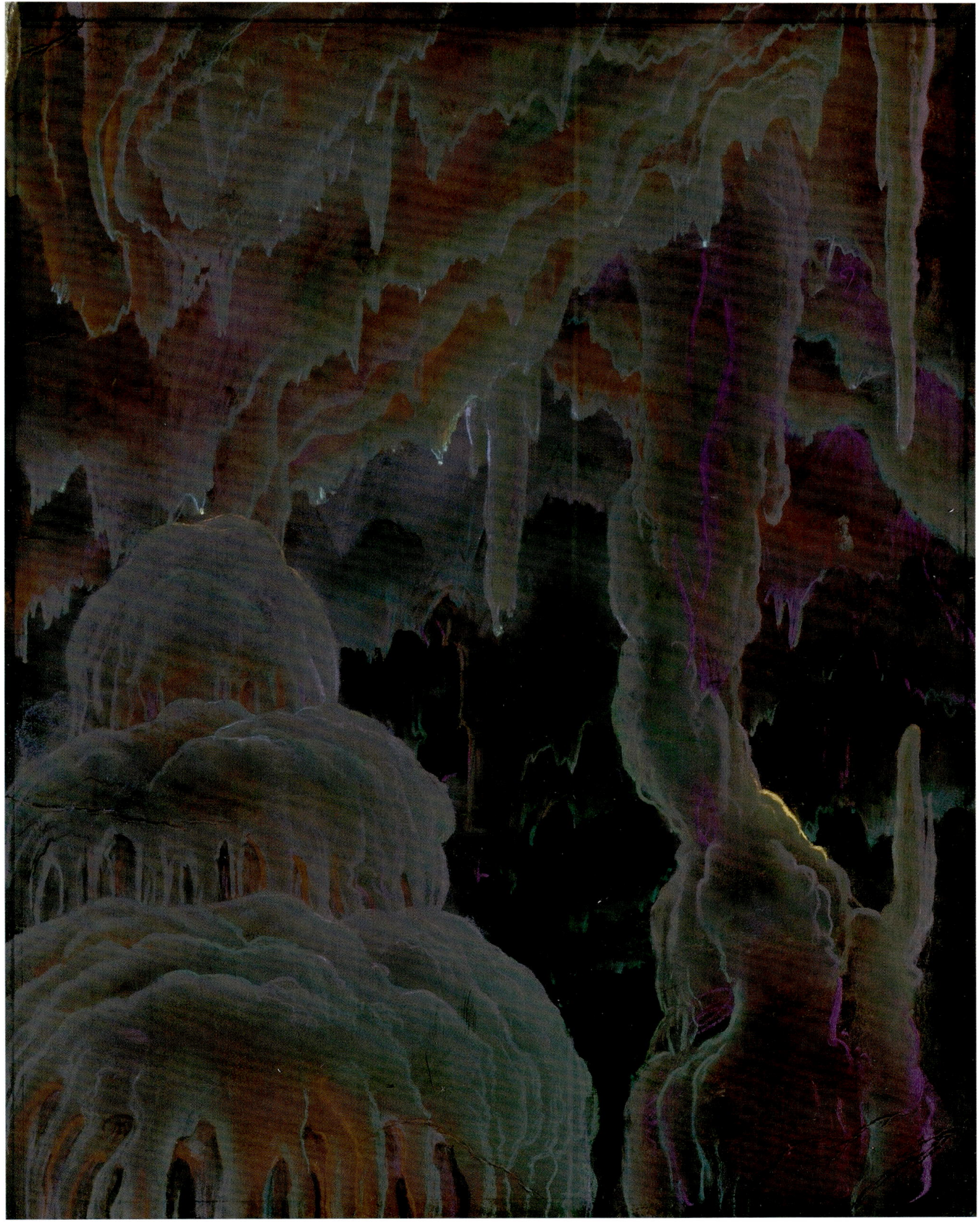

FIGURE 15
Cave Interior, c. 1923, pastel on black paper, Antonia Shoumatoff Foster. Cat. no. 17

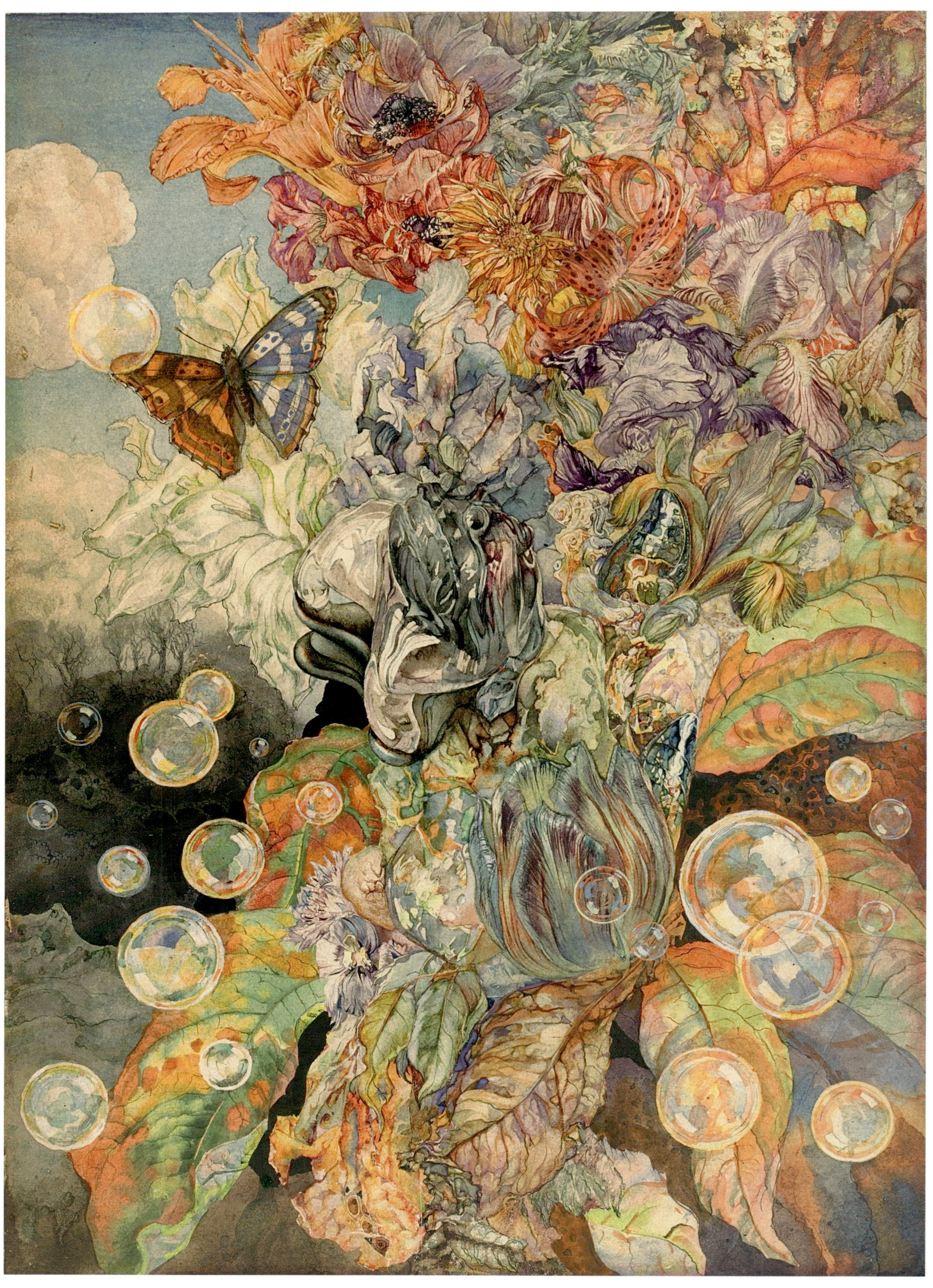

Avinoff's aesthetic theory of nature, life, and his own complex identity (figure 16). He began work on this elaborate composition in 1925, but did not finish it until 1947.[19] Given Avinoff's characteristic working method—drawing outlines in graphite, painting the central motif section by section, and filling in the background last—it seems likely that all but the background was painted in the 1920s. The stylistic resemblance of *Iridescence's* central motif to a painting securely dated to 1916–1917 (see figure 21), and the background's similarity to the bleak landscapes of other paintings from 1948 (see figure 26), support this interpretation. It is significant that Avinoff abandoned work on *Iridescence* around the same period when he began full-time work at Carnegie Museum, and resumed it after he left. One can only speculate as to whether a conflict, perhaps simply one of time, or, more profoundly, about his butterfly symbolism, might have occurred as he changed professions. In subject matter, style, technique, and history of execution, *Iridescence* is about transitions and transformations in nature and in life.

The butterfly depicted in *Iridescence* is famous in entomological circles for the brilliant variable blue sheen on the wings of the male animals (figures 17, 18). The wings themselves are drab black or brown, but in the light they shimmer with a brilliance rivaled by few other species. Because the wings of Avinoff's butterfly are at an angle to each other, each refracts light differently and glows with different colors. In a word, the shimmering wings of *Apatura ilia,* to use its scientific name, connect Avinoff's science to Avinoff's art.[20]

The composition of *Iridescence* is a dazzlingly complex arrangement of organic forms and shifting colors that flow smoothly out from its center to the margins. The central mass is an unintelligible mélange of translucent, glittering, biomorphic shapes that seem to encompass within their fluid borders

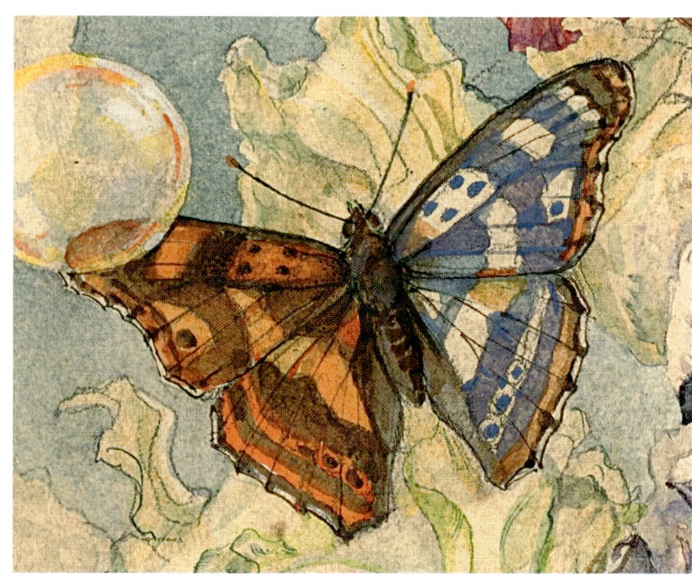

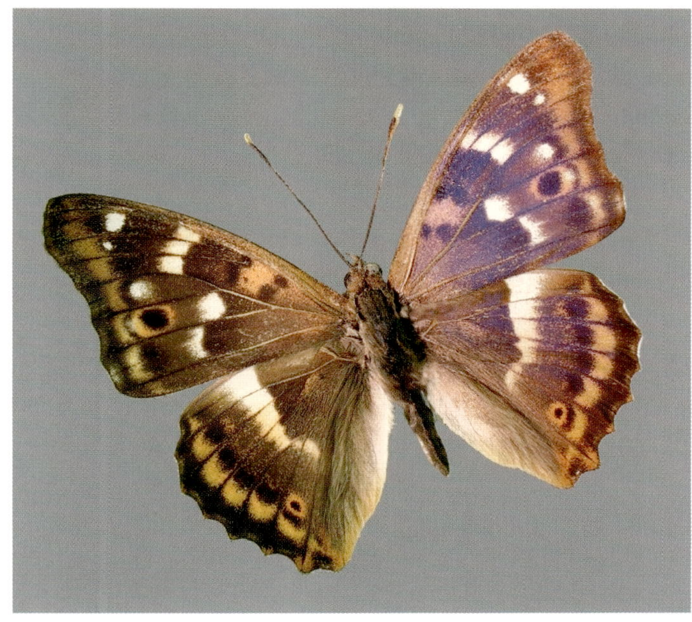

FIGURE 16
Iridescence, 1925/1947, graphite, pen and ink, and watercolor on paper mounted on artist's board, Carnegie Museum of Art, Bequest of Howard Noble, by exchange, and the Margaret M. Vance Fund, 2008.81, Cat. no. 20

FIGURE 17
Detail of *Iridescence,* 1925/1947 (figure 16)

FIGURE 18
Apatura ilia, Carnegie Museum of Natural History, Section of Invertebrate Zoology

and shifting patterns of reflected and refracted light the infinite possibilities of creation. A butterfly (*A. ilia*), flowers, leaves, and bubbles float away from the central mass as if taking flight after taking form. The idea of creation as part of the cycle of life and death is intimated by the withered, decaying leaves in the lower register that give rise to the emerging biomass of flora and fauna.

What Avinoff seems to be articulating in *Iridescence* is the theory, prevalent in European scientific thought circa 1900, that all life developed from protoplasm, "the complex, semifluid, translucent substance that constitutes the living matter of plant and animal cells and manifests the essential life functions of a cell."[21] At the turn of the twentieth century, the mechanism that molds each cell's protoplasm into its final form was not clearly understood: modern genetics did not yet exist; stem cells were unknown; and the role of hormones in growth and development was just emerging in the scientific literature. For a brief historical moment, "protoplasm" was the scientific concept embodying the fundamental mysteries of life. Avinoff represented the potential of protoplasmic material as a swirling spectrum of colors that through some magical, awe-inspiring process could form a butterfly or a flower or a human being.

Iridescence is the last painting in Avinoff's oeuvre to depict this mystical substance. It is also his only painting known to this writer to depict the butterfly chrysalis, in which the lowly caterpillar dissolves into protoplasm before emerging as a new winged creature, a butterfly, embodiment of beauty. By the mid-1920s, the butterfly's metamorphosis could be seen to represent Avinoff's views on life and nature in a manner that was both scientifically up-to-date and poetic.

Metamorphosis, the central mystery of entomology, and one of the secrets of life, has endowed the fragile butterfly with a metaphoric power unique in the animal kingdom. In Christian thought, metamorphosis represents resurrection or rebirth. Avinoff conflated the pagan, Christian, and modern outlooks on the butterfly with his own theory of beauty in a remarkable fable that he developed late one night with a friend, the Episcopalian bishop Austin Pardue, who copyrighted it in 1946 with the title *He Lives.*[22]

In the fable, a caterpillar creeps along in life, lost and uncomprehending amid a welter of unpleasant and chaotic sensations generated by its immediate surroundings. Entering a period of oblivion, it sleeps. Awakening, escorted by a brilliantly colored guide, it lifts itself up into the air, and, from newfound heights, it looks down and sees, for the first time, the elaborate patterns of the Persian carpet on which it lives. Avinoff's fable adds a new twist to traditional symbolism; in acquiring wings, his butterfly acquires the ability to see and understand beauties invisible to the earthbound that ultimately reconcile it to its continuing existence. It's not hard to imagine this butterfly as a metaphorical Avinoff self-portrait.

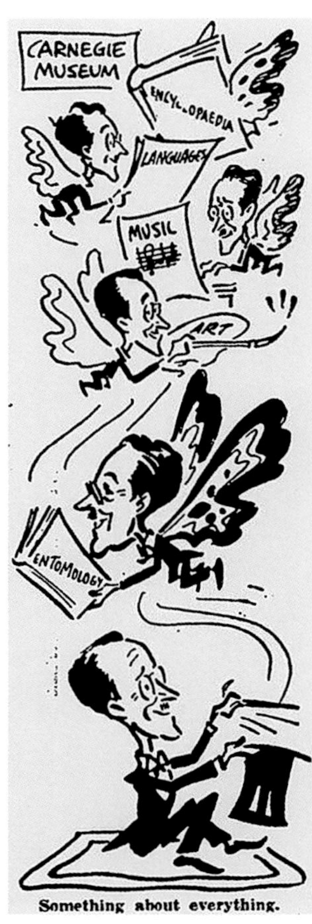

FIGURE 19
Unknown artist, *"Something about everything,"* 1936, illustration to "Avinoff: The Expert Amateur," *Pittsburgh Post-Gazette*, December 12, 1936

One night in 1927, Avinoff happily attired himself in butterfly costume for a fancy Pittsburgh soirée.[23] On December 12, 1936, the *Pittsburgh Post-Gazette* caricatured him flitting on beautiful wings among art, science, music, and languages (figure 19). The 1948 *New Yorker* article "Black Tie and Cyanide Jar" cemented his public image as social butterfly/butterfly collector. As for Avinoff, he seems to have tolerated if not encouraged this superficial view of himself as an elegant lightweight, whose pursuit of beauty focused on debutantes, even going so far as to suggest to the *New Yorker* writer that his heart attack was the result of excessive socializing on behalf of Carnegie Museum.[24] But the autobiographical nature of Avinoff's major butterfly paintings, and their deeply personal meaning, remained private and disguised. Thus, in the definitive 1953 retrospective exhibition, *Iridescence* was described as a charming Victorian fantasy and its title given as *The Chrysalis: Passage of the Flight of Time* (no. 65), while the *Triptych*—the earlier discussed assemblage of three separate works—was subtitled *The Old Dispensation and the New,* with no explanation whatsoever (no. 67).

Apatura ilia's luminous wings reflect not only Avinoff's scientific and spiritual views of the world, but also his politics. *A. ilia* is native to Eastern Europe, Russia, and northern China—essentially the purview of the early-twentieth-century Russian Empire. The butterfly's popular name, "Lesser Purple Emperor," evokes a host of imperial rulers, from Julius Caesar to Tsar Nicholas II. After 1917, this butterfly's life cycle of metamorphosis and rebirth represented the hopes and dreams of exiled Russians eking out new lives in Europe and the United States.

The notion that butterflies can outlast empires was an idea common among Avinoff's circle of literary friends. Haniel Long, until 1929 an English professor at Carnegie Mellon University, Pittsburgh, expressed this concept in a poem from the 1920s that resonates with all of Avinoff's major butterfly compositions:

> There will be butterflies,
> There will be summer skies
> And flowers upthrust,
> When all that Caesar bids,
> And all the pyramids
> Are dust.
>
> There will be gaudy wings
> Over the bones of things,
> And never grief:
> Who says that summer skies,
> Who says that butterflies,
> Are brief?[25]

Beauty will save the world when empires crumble. It could be the story of Avinoff's life.

"As an example of successful assimilation, Dr. Andrey Avinoff . . . stands high among czarist émigrés in this country."

—GEOFFREY T. HELLMAN, THE *NEW YORKER,* 1948[26]

AVINOFF'S TRANSITION FROM SUBJECT of the moribund Russian Empire to citizen of the United States was a metamorphosis as fundamental as that of the butterfly. As he adapted from old world to new, Avinoff seems to have reconfigured his own protoplasm into a new arrangement of outward surfaces and internal processes appropriate for the American cultural environment. In some ways, he could be said to have turned himself inside out, as elements of his private life in Russia became features of his American public persona. He was in the chrysalis, so to speak, from 1915, when he first departed Russia for New York, to September 10, 1928, when he swore the oath of citizenship in Pittsburgh.

On April 3, 1915, Andre [*sic*] Avinoff arrived in New York for the first time, on board the *Kristianafjord* from Bergen, Norway.[27] Giving the French spelling of his name, as an elite Russian would do, he listed his profession as lawyer, and his address as Furstadtskaja 43, Petrograd. His mother lived at the same address. He was part of a group of Russian civil engineers on a mission to purchase war supplies. According to family histories, he spent his first night in New York attending a meeting of the New York Entomological Society, where (according to the *New York Times*) Dr. Frank E. Lutz spoke on "Origins and Distribution of West Indian Spiders" at 8:15 p.m.[28] Records of his business dealings are not known, although he may have visited Pittsburgh in order to buy steel.[29] Toward the end of his sojourn in April 1916, he attended a performance by the Ballets Russes that featured Vaslav Nijinsky in *Spectre de la Rose*, followed by a backstage meeting with the dancer that Avinoff would never forget (figure 20). He returned to Russia in 1916 and was present for the liberal revolution of February 1917, in which the tsar was overthrown and a provisional government installed. His older brother, Nicholas, was charged with drafting a constitution for the new government, and Andrey retreated to the relative safety of a provincial government post as Marshal of the Nobility in Ukraine.

Avinoff returned to the United States on October 11, 1917, on board the *Ecuador,* landing in San Francisco.[30] His first name is spelled "Andrew" on the passenger list, his profession is jurist, and his next of kin in Russia is no longer his mother but his

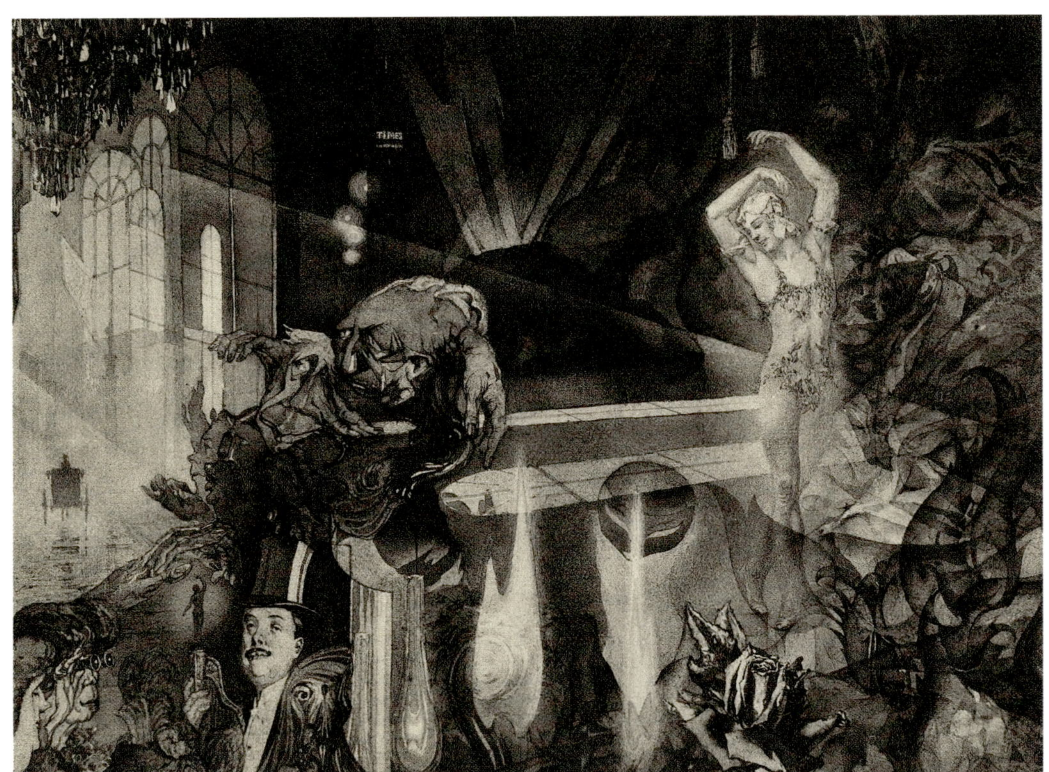

FIGURE 20
Reminiscences of the Ballet ("Spectre de la Rose"), 1916, watercolor on paper, location unknown

FIGURE 21
Reminiscences of the House in Russia, 1916–1917, watercolor on paper mounted on card, Victoria Ward. Cat. no. 9

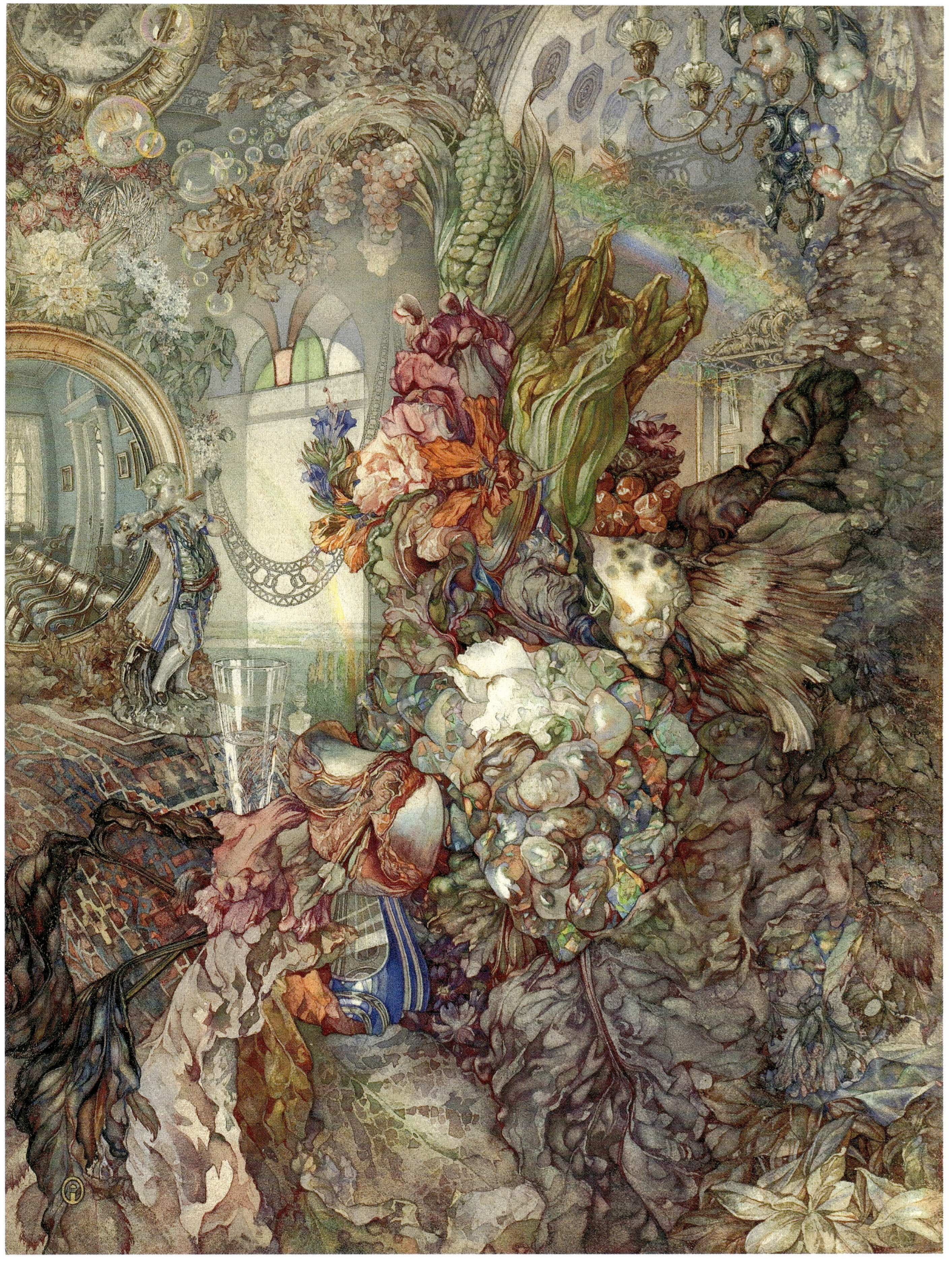

FIGURE 23
Memories (unfinished), 1949, graphite and watercolor on Whatman drawing board, Antonia Shoumatoff Foster. Cat. no. 58

older brother, "Nicolas Avinoff, Asst. Minister of Foreign Affairs, Petrograd." Avinoff had traveled eastward over the recently completed Trans-Siberian Railway, via Japan, and his assignment was to terminate the Russian war contracts initiated in 1915, a process that would drag on into the 1920s.[31] On this trip, he brought an album of eighteenth-century watercolors of rare American lepidoptera, his drawings from the Tibetan journey of 1912, and a glorious painting of the family house in Ukraine, along with suitcases full of rubles. His arrival preceded Russia's long-anticipated second revolution, the Bolshevik coup, by just a few weeks. Two months later, his sister, her family, and his mother arrived in New York via the same route.

Avinoff painted *Reminiscences of the House in Russia* in the interlude between his first and second trips to the United States (figure 21). The family estate at Shideyevo, near Poltava in Ukraine, represented home for Avinoff no matter where he lived. It is the subject of *Reminiscences,* his most beautiful painting, and it would continue to appear in his landscapes until his death in 1949 (figure 23). These landscapes are invariably sunny—the house, which belonged to his mother's family, served as a summer residence; the family wintered elsewhere, while Andrey attended schools in Kiev and Moscow. Shideyevo housed the family art collections—paintings, Persian rugs, books, and icons—and its gardens hosted the first butterflies for his collections. According to Andrey's sister-in-law, Marie Avinoff, who first saw the family in residence there in 1906, "there was a riotous abundance of furniture, china, and valuable bibelots, as well as fine works of art collected by my mother-in-law's father."[32] Something of that riotous atmosphere is captured in *Reminiscences,* where mirrors, swags, champagne glasses, vistas, jewels, rainbows, bubbles, moldings, and cornices float in a dream-like space enveloped in radiant light. The abstract geometry of a richly patterned oriental carpet flows and merges with the veined and crackled surface of a dying leaf: art and nature unified by a single aesthetic. A Meissen porcelain flute player serenades a central, jewel-like, protoplasmic mass, whose swirling energy generates an ear of American corn and a shimmering turkey gizzard (figure 22), as well as brilliant flowers and withered vegetation.

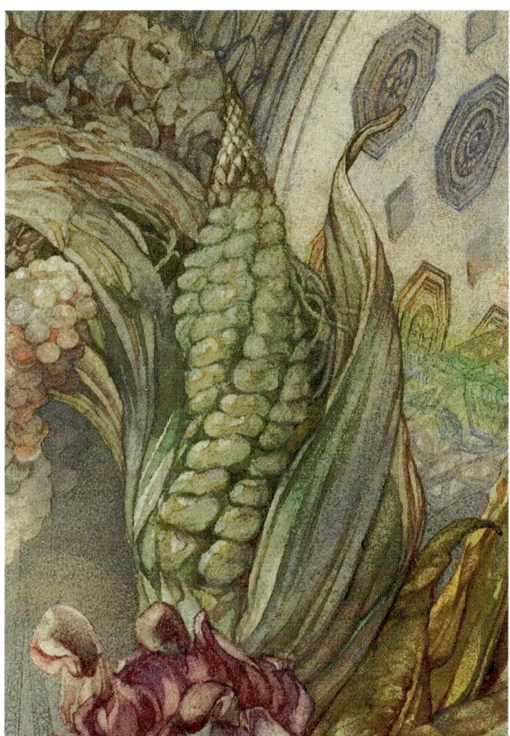

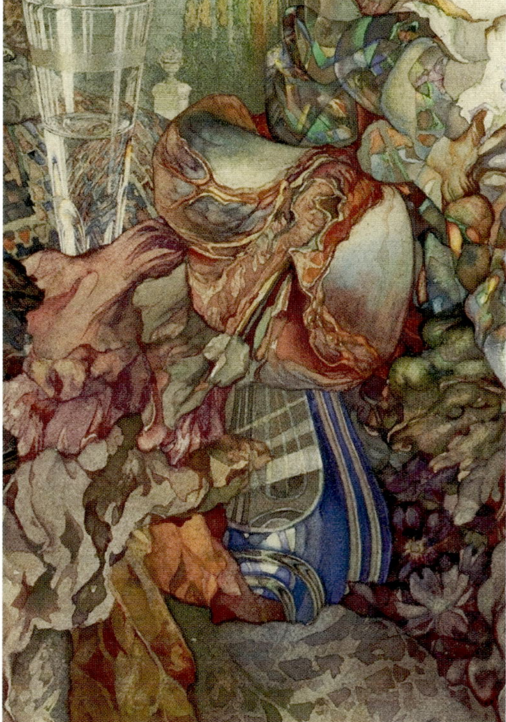

FIGURE 22
Details of *Reminiscences of the House in Russia* (figure 21)

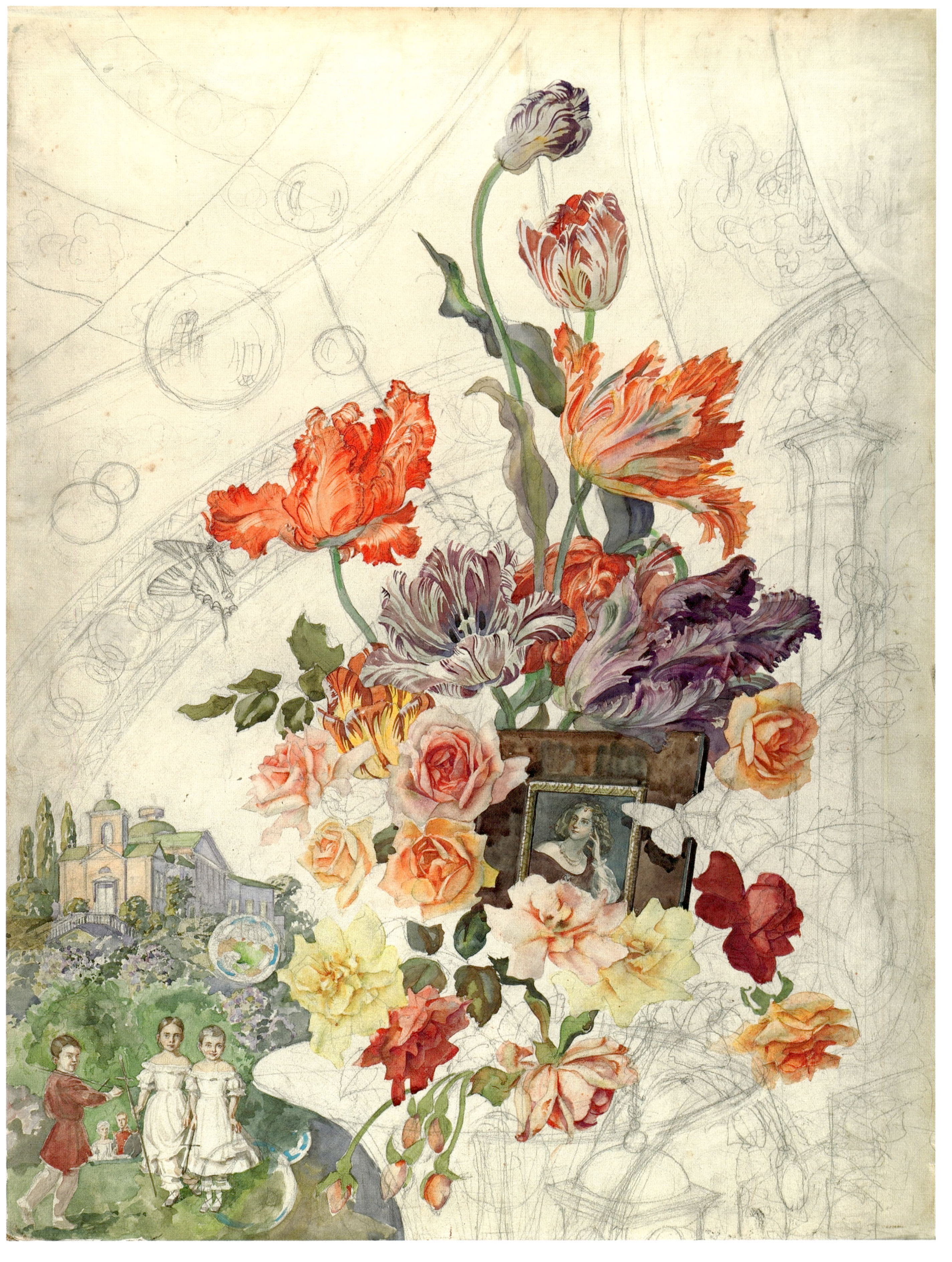

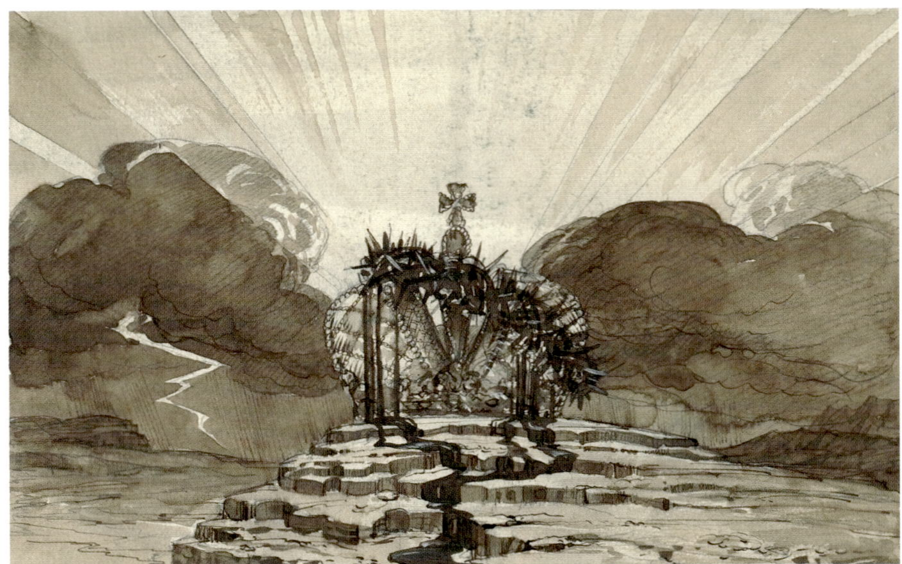

FIGURE 24
Tsar's Crown and Crown of Thorns in Stormy Landscape, c. 1917, graphite, pen and ink, and ink wash heightened with white on paper, Antonia Shoumatoff Foster. Cat. no. 10

The American symbolism of corn and turkey suggests that Avinoff may have already been envisioning life in the United States. If so, it connects the magical experience of his childhood home with an equally magical dream of reshaping Russian protoplasm into an American form. That this dream had a nightmarish counterpart is suggested by *Nightmare of Faces,* of 1915 (figure 25). Based on an actual dream, and probably responding to the horrors of World War I, its hideous distortions anticipate the Surrealist movement of the 1920s and 1930s. However, *Reminiscences* presents a vision of life that is mystical, exuberant, all-embracing, ephemeral, and sensual—Andrey Avinoff's Russian soul. One can only speculate as to whether this image of transition is also political, alluding to hopes for the American-style democratic liberal reforms advocated by Nicholas Avinoff and others in the Provisional Government of February through October 1917. The destruction of the house in 1919 was devastating; its loss severed the family's ties to the land, obliterated the gardens and furnishings that had enriched their lives, and wiped out the family history and accomplishments embodied in its many collections.

Avinoff's third arrival in the United States occurred in 1919. He had left New York in December 1918 on a ship to Liverpool, England, part of a twelve-man mission led by Prince George Lvoff bound for the Russian embassy in Paris.[33] The prince, deposed head of the exiled Provisional Government, had been invited to observe the Versailles Peace Conference on behalf of the Russian people, now engulfed in horrific civil war as Bolsheviks struggled against Whites for control of the country (figure 24). Avinoff served as translator for the voluble prince. He returned from a frustrating three-month stay in Paris on board *La Touraine,* on February 19, 1919.[34] Occupation: jurist. Last Russian address: none. Next of kin in Russia: none. His parting from his homeland was viewed as a betrayal in the nascent Soviet Union; when Nicholas's wife, Marie, mentioned Andrey's name while pleading for her husband's release from prison, People's Commissar for Justice Nikolai Krylenko responded: "That White vermin!"[35] Many years later, when Fiske Kimball, the longtime head of the Philadelphia Museum of Art, asked Avinoff whether it were true that he had served the Russian tsar, he was able to joke, "Yes it is true; and if I were to go back there now, I should be elevated to a still higher position—by the aid of a necktie!"[36] Nicholas Avinoff had refused to leave Russia; after his seventh and final arrest in November 1937, he became one of the many to disappear amid the horrors of the Stalinist purges.

The loss of Andrey Avinoff's Russian home and homeland forced the creation of a new, American identity. Avinoff accomplished this on paper on September 10, 1928, the day he became a U.S. citizen.[37] Avinoff's American homes were nothing like the one he had left behind in Russia. The family moved from a boarding house on the Upper West Side of Manhattan, to a dairy farm in the Catskills, to substantial suburban properties on Long Island. Avinoff lived in rented rooms while in Pittsburgh, with a brief interlude in a small stone house that he built himself in ritzy, rural Fox Chapel, but sold almost immediately.[38] Following his heart attack, he moved back in with his sister on Long Island and from there to a luxury apartment in Manhattan. Despite their varying appeal, none of these residences could replace the magical world of Shideyevo.

The contrast between *Reminiscences of the House in Russia* and a similar work painted in 1948 underscores the contrast between his dreams of 1916 and the realities he encountered in the United States (figure 26). The latter painting depicts a single blue butterfly (scientific name: *Morpho aega*), two bubbles, and yellow lilies set in front of a stormy, jumbled architectural landscape.[39] Behind the flower and butterfly, a crumbling gateway

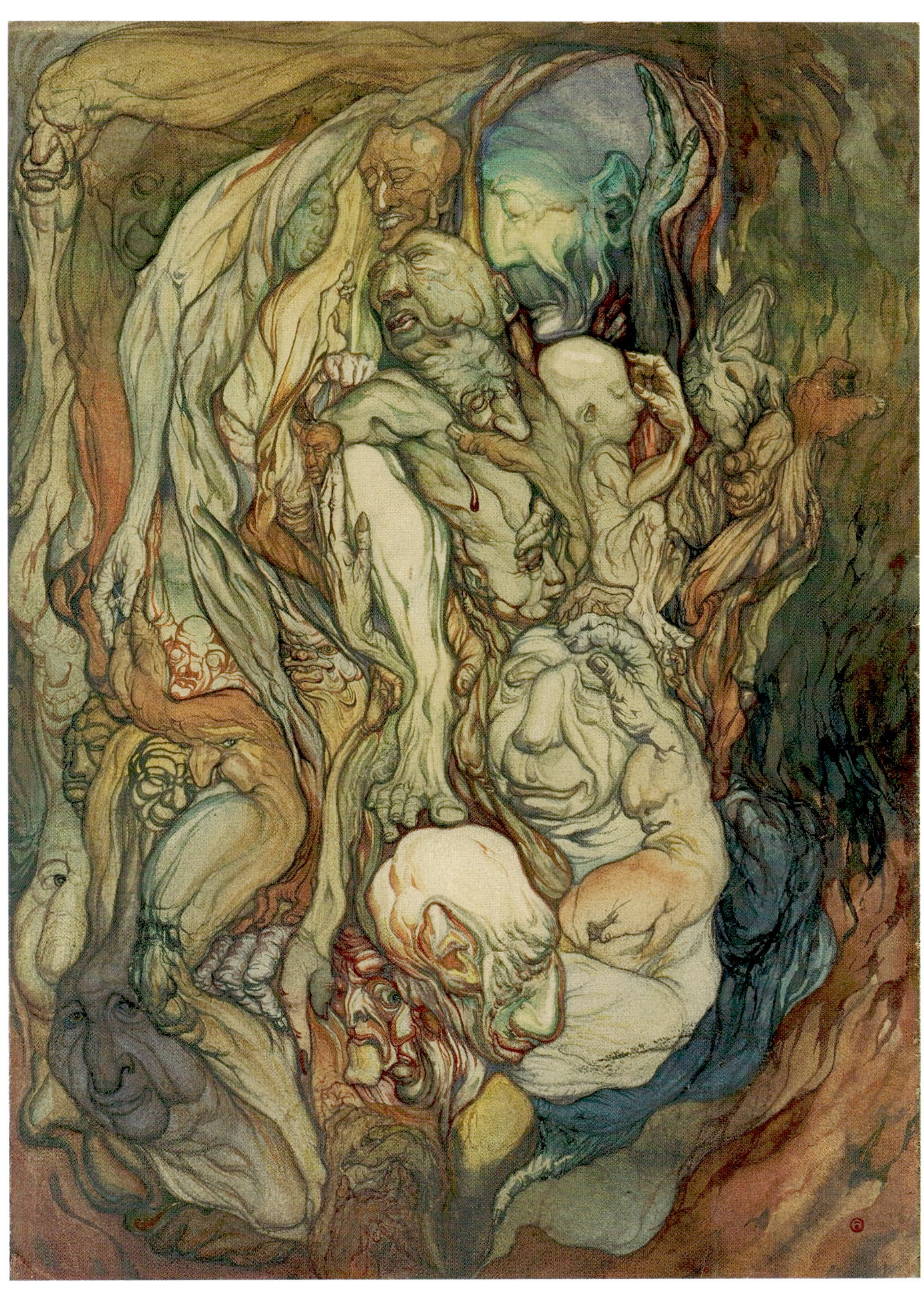

FIGURE 25
Nightmare of Faces, 1915, graphite and watercolor with ink and chalk on paper, Carnegie Museum of Art, Gift of He Who Stands Firm (Nicholas Avinoff Shoumatoff), 2007.50.4. Cat. no. 7

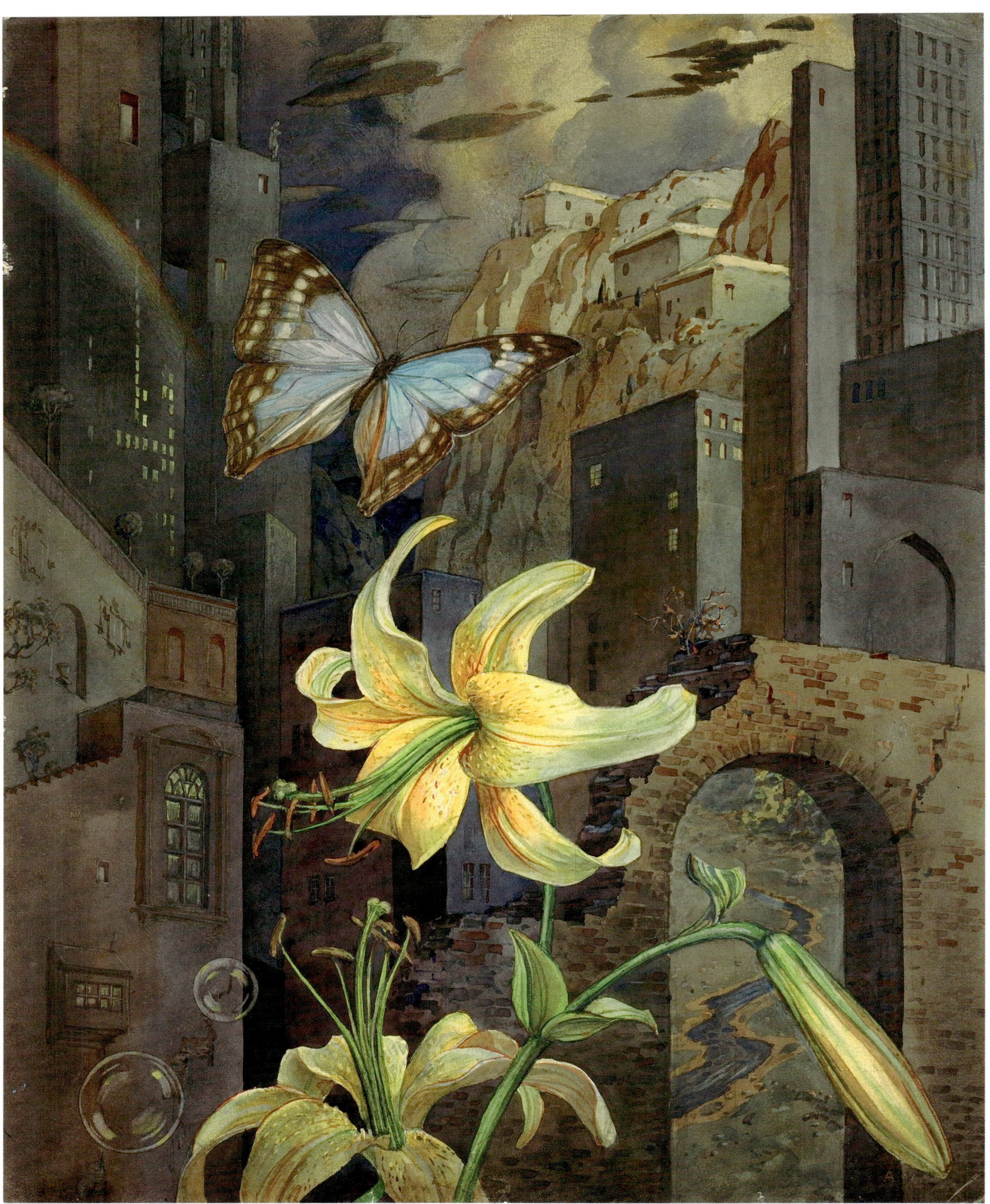

FIGURE 26
Morpho: Remembrance of Things Past, 1948, graphite and watercolor on paper mounted on paperboard, Carnegie Museum of Art, Heinz Family Fund, 2007.46.2. Cat. no. 52

frames a barren landscape with a river (of life?). It looks eastward past New York skyscrapers, to a Russian Orthodox church, then further east to the river's origin near the cliff-top lamaseries of Tibet. The scintillating light effects of *Iridescence* persist in Avinoff's choice of another highly reflective blue butterfly, bubbles, stained glass, and a rainbow, supplemented by the yellow glow of electric light dimly echoing the Tibetan sunshine. On a photograph of the watercolor Avinoff provided to Alfred Kinsey in 1949, he dated the work to 1948 and gave it its title: *Morpho: Remembrance of Things Past.*[40] Although the protoplasm of *Reminiscences* and *Iridescence* has disappeared, the shape-shifting symbolism continues in the central figure of *M. aega*, whose scientific name translates to "metamorphosis." In this painting, we're seeing Avinoff's autobiography.

Some psychologists compare the magnitude of adjustments an émigré must make to the basic developmental stages of infancy, childhood, adolescence, and adulthood.[41] For Avinoff to picture his life story as a series of developmental stages linked to transitions from east to west, past to present, makes sense: childhood in Ukraine, adolescence in Uzbekistan and Central Asia, early adulthood in Russia, and this final stage in the United States. Like a caterpillar, he would shed the old form in order to move on to each new phase of existence. His Russian legal and administrative expertise was obsolete after 1917, although the glamour of his association with the tsarist court lingered on in royalty-obsessed America. Since his most marketable skills were his knowledge of various languages and his draftsmanship, during the 1920s he morphed from poverty-stricken Russian bureaucrat into well-connected commercial illustrator-cum-society portrait painter.

His transition from old world to new appears first in his work for Frank Seaman's New York advertising agency. For example, around 1923 Avinoff conjured up landscapes from his past evoking Samarkand and Tibet as backdrops for his new American present—beautifully packaged offerings of Colgate's Cashmere Bouquet perfume and soap (figure 27). To someone familiar with Avinoff's personal history, the juxtaposition of the austere, spiritual landscapes of the Asian steppe and the luxury consumer goods of modern America seems either painful or hilarious. But to the uninitiated, the images create seamless, Maxfield Parrish–type fantasies of sights, smells, and sensations redolent

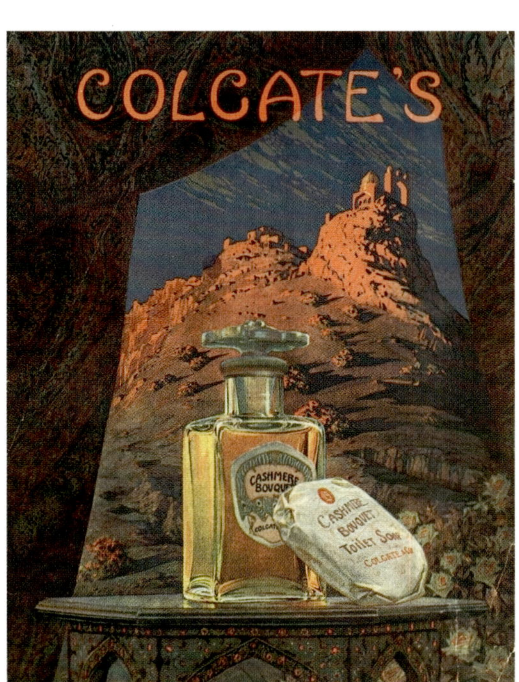

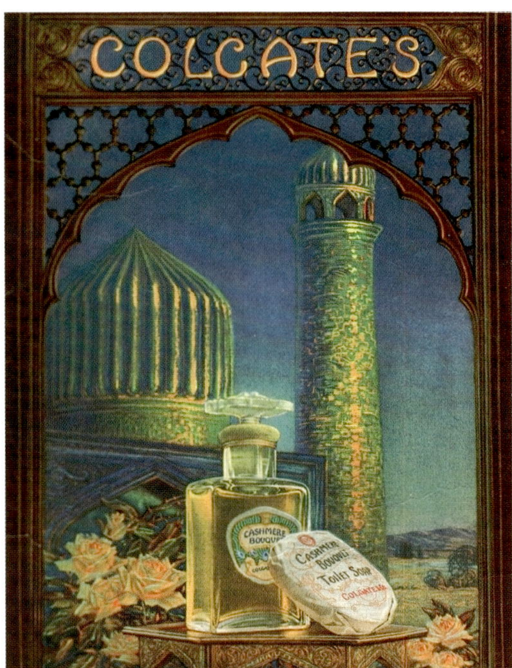

FIGURE 27
Tear sheets showing advertisements for Colgate's Cashmere Bouquet, c. 1923, photo offset lithographs on paper, Antonia Shoumatoff Foster. Cat. no. 25

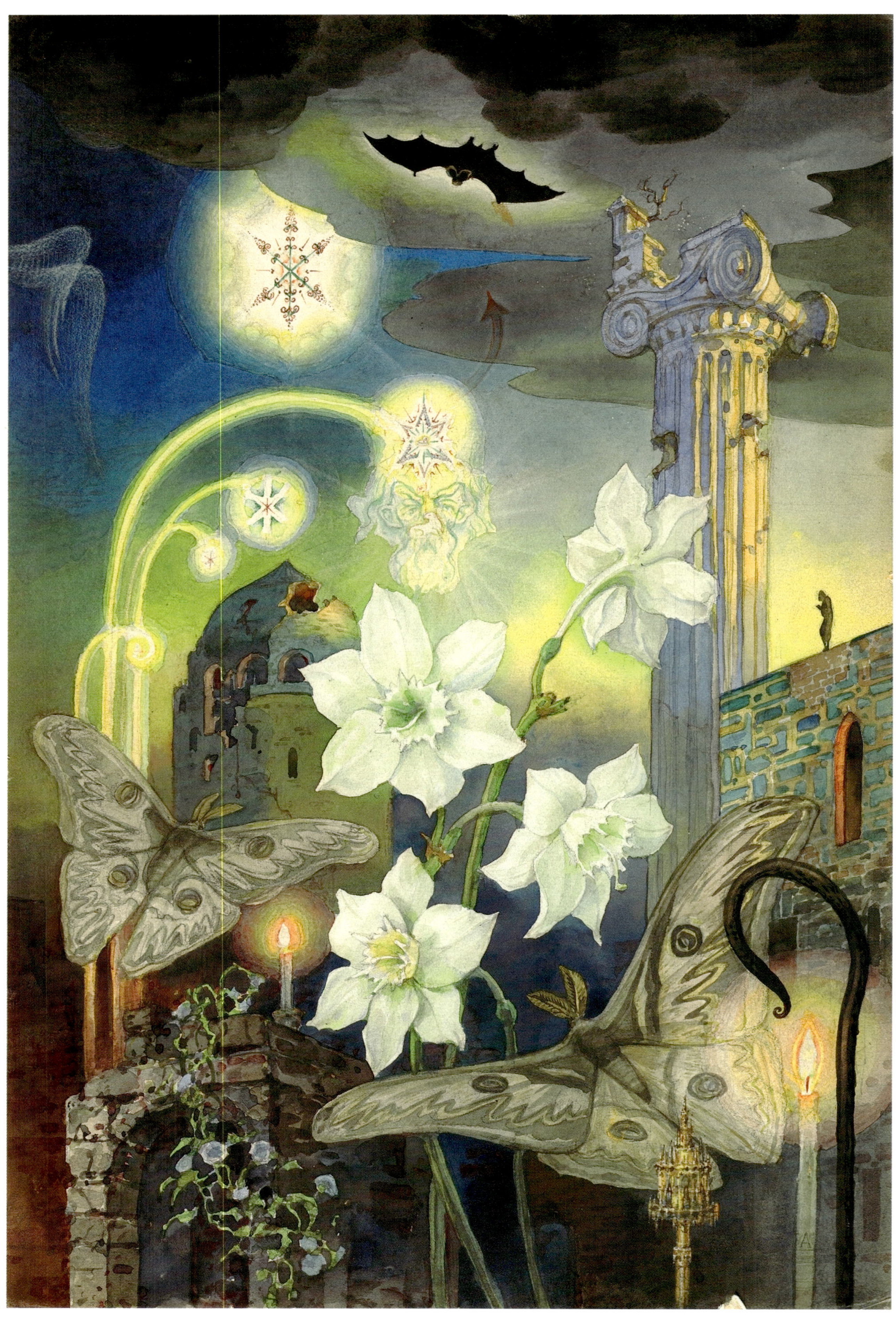

FIGURE 28
Star of Bethlehem, 1941, graphite and watercolor on Whatman drawing board, Carnegie Museum of Art, Heinz Family Fund, 2007.46.1.
Cat. no. 34

of the exotic East but conveniently attainable at nearby department stores. Sharing a copy of the ads with Alfred Kinsey in 1948, Avinoff proudly recalled winning a prize at the *Third Annual Advertising Art Exhibition* in 1924.[42] He also had steady work from Johns-Manville, an American manufacturer of asbestos shingles and building supplies, as well as a brief fling with Chevrolet. In 1930, he designed the winged *S* logo for Sikorsky helicopters, still in use today.

These advertisements ended up playing an important role in Avinoff's transition to American life. He utilized the basic compositional device of the Colgate's ads, a life-size representation of the "product" in front of a symbolic and association-rich landscape backdrop, for zoological dioramas in Carnegie Museum of Natural History and his major paintings of the 1930s and 1940s. For example, his 1941 *Star of Bethlehem* repeats the composition of one of the Colgate's advertisements, with an exotic dome and column in the background and two stalks of Star of Bethlehem flowers replacing the perfume bottle and soap packet (figure 28). The inspiration for this elaborate painting was probably twofold: a Pittsburgh debutante's corsage, which Avinoff borrowed after a party in order to paint the Star of Bethlehem flowers in it, and John Greenleaf Whittier's 1830 poem of the same name (figure 29).[43] The poem describes a Christian wanderer meditating among the Moslem tombs of Persia (Avinoff depicts the Mausoleum of Tamerlane on the left, and a column from the Mausoleum of Halicarnassus on the right) and despairing of his mission in this pagan wilderness, until the sight of some symbolic star-flowers restores his hope and faith.

Then there is the set of drawings of "Imaginary Houses," ten literary-architectural fantasies published by *Country Life* magazine in 1924.[44] In these stylistically varied drawings, Avinoff designed homes for best-selling American authors and/or their fictional characters (figure 30). The most impressive, a mansion for Booth Tarkington, appeared with the accompanying text by Avinoff:

> In such a house as this might dwell Booth Tarkington of "The Magnificent Ambersons." A stately dream of opulence, governed by good taste. A dwelling indeed that poor Dan Olyphant, the hero of Mr. Tarkington's new novel, "The Midlander," might well have dreamed of, and one no less pleasing to the critical taste of his brother, the conservative Harlan.[45]

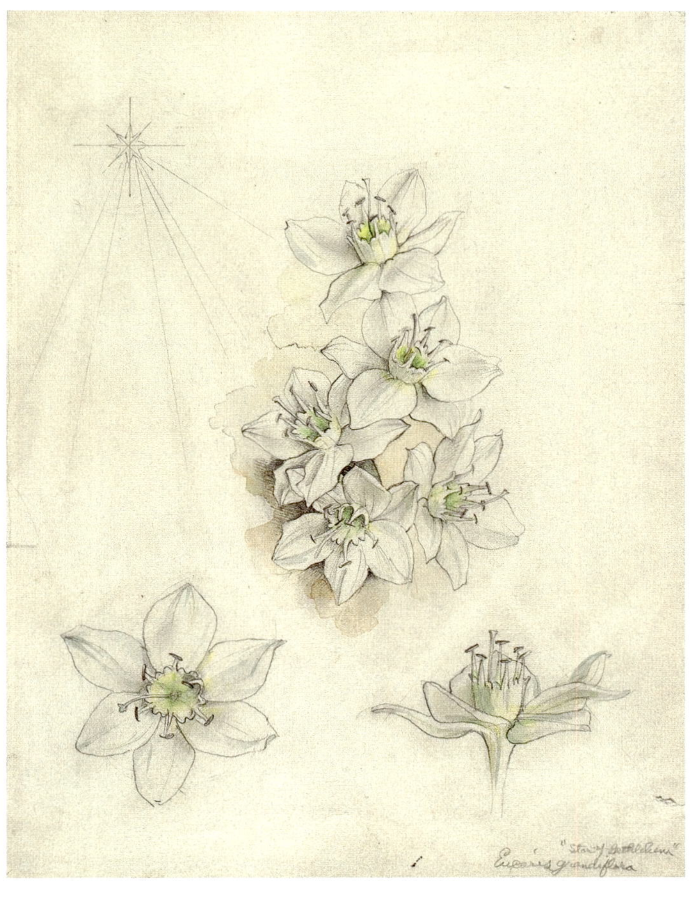

FIGURE 29
Star of Bethlehem, 1941, graphite and watercolor on paper, Carnegie Museum of Art, Gift of Mary Murtland Berger, 2007.67.
Cat. no. 33

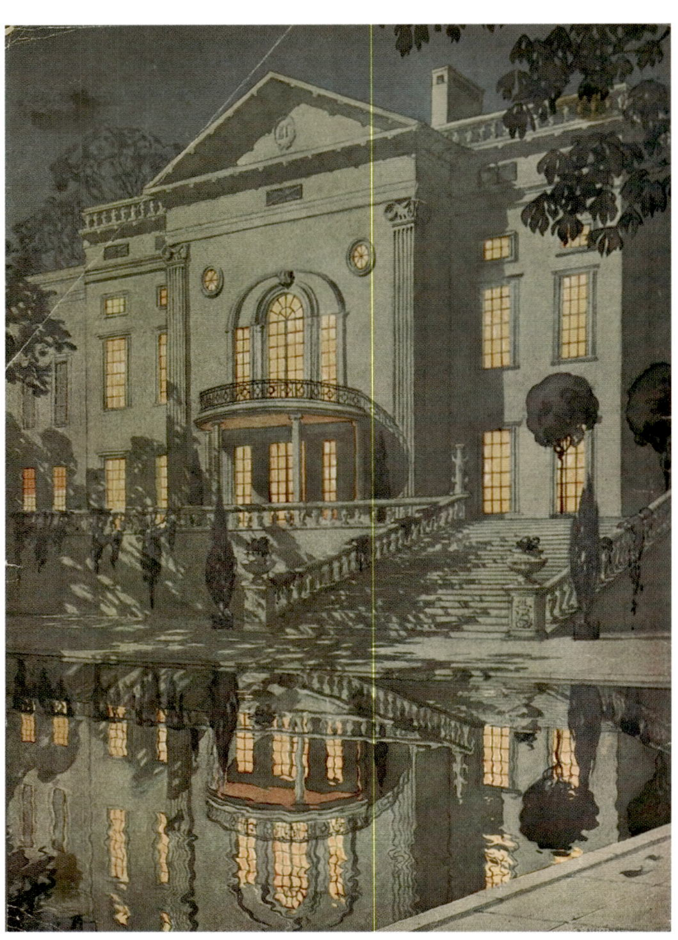

FIGURE 30
Imaginary House for Booth Tarkington, 1924, photo offset lithograph published in Thomas L. Masson, "Ten Houses for Ten Authors: Paintings and Sketches by Andrew Avinoff," *Country Life* 45 (April 1924). Antonia Shoumatoff Foster

Avinoff also designed fantasy homes for Edith Wharton, Zane Grey, and F. Scott Fitzgerald.

With no named commercial sponsor, the "Imaginary Houses" seem to have been Avinoff's American-style effort at commercial self-promotion. They are uncharacteristically signed with his full name printed clearly and distinctly at lower right, and the fulsome paragraphs showcase his sophisticated knowledge of American culture, such as it was. Yet as with the Cashmere Bouquet ads, there is the underlying poignancy or strangeness: in this case, a homeless exile dreaming up homes for famous people he did not know, or for literary characters who never existed.

In the 1920s, professional portrait painting was another lucrative occupation with social benefits. Both Andrey and his sister, Elizabeth, had been well instructed in miniature painting and watercolor by their English governess, a Miss Whishaw, during their childhoods. When Marie Avinoff first met Andrey in 1906, his room at Shideyevo was a morass of art supplies and butterflies pinned on walls and curtains, and she recalled him telling his mother that despite the mess, "I've actually done quite a lot. Yesterday I finished this miniature on ivory, and today I've written a paper for the entomological society."[46] Avinoff told Kinsey that in 1924–1925 he was selling children's watercolor and pastel portraits for $100 each, while Elizabeth did even better, meeting her clients in a studio at the Plaza Hotel en route to a career as a society painter that would last until the 1970s (see figure 1).[47] He was making so much money that he was forced to decline Carnegie Museum's offers of jobs in its entomology department in 1923 and 1925.[48] As late as 1927, after Avinoff had accepted the directorship of the museum, he was decorating Manhattan sitting rooms with Chinese fantasy landscapes and exhibiting paintings in a private home in the Hamptons.[49] Andrey's and Elizabeth's careers were mutually beneficial: in the 1930s and 1940s, Elizabeth painted Pittsburgh millionaires to whom she had been introduced by Andrey, and Andrey, in turn, sometimes joined her on painting expeditions to the rich and famous, including President Franklin Roosevelt.

From commercial illustration and portraiture, Avinoff eventually moved into the realm of flower painting. A stint in botanical illustration for Carnegie Museum got him started. As the Great Depression and World War II limited funds and travel,

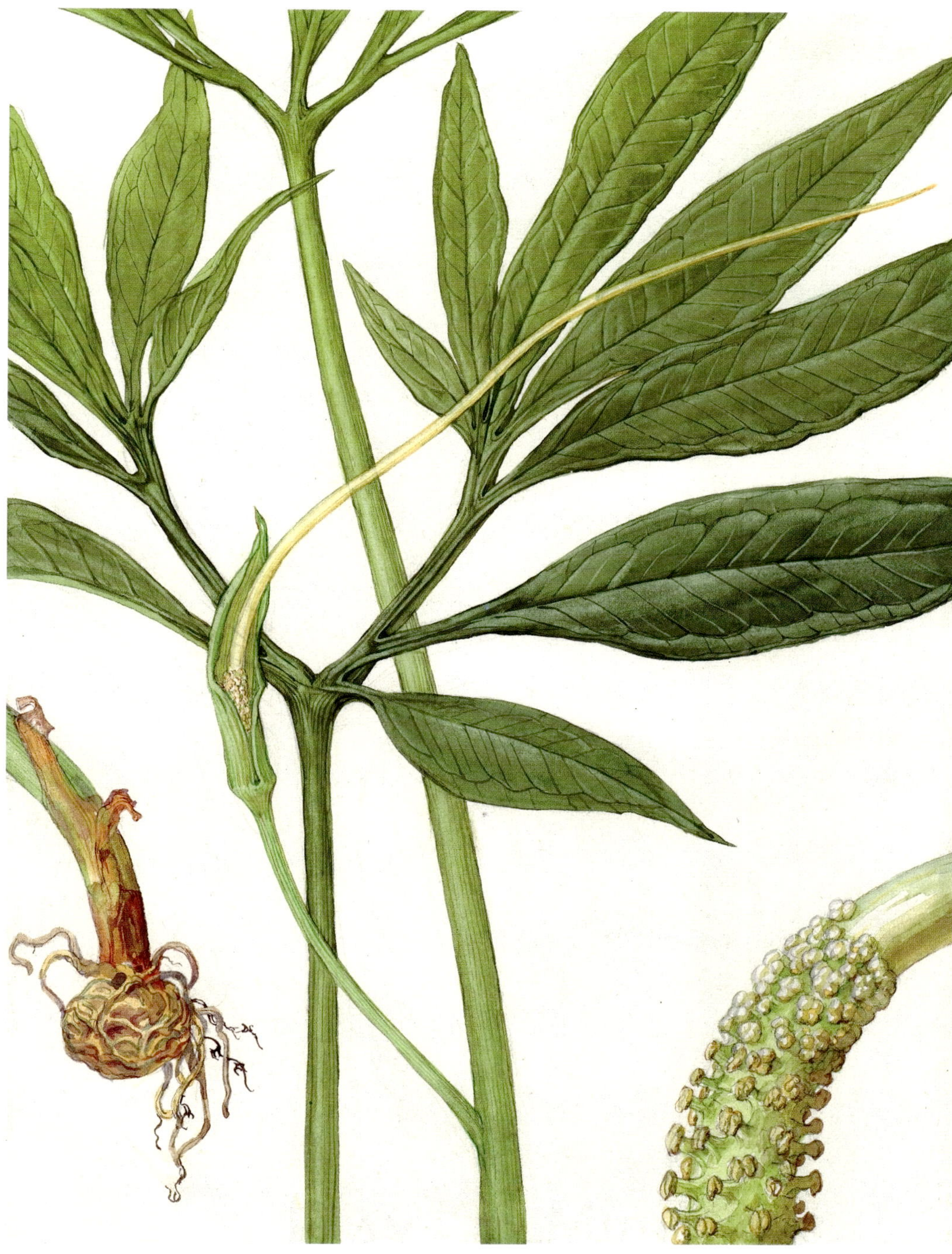

FIGURE 31
Green Dragon, plate 7 from *Wild Flowers of Western Pennsylvania and the Upper Ohio Basin,* 1941–1943, graphite and watercolor on paper, Carnegie Museum of Natural History, Section of Anthropology, Natural History Art Collection, 36.423. Cat. no. 35

the botany curator O. E. Jennings began an encyclopedic collection of regional flora that Avinoff proposed to illustrate, turning a dry scholarly project into an opulent production. Avinoff's 450-odd watercolor illustrations for the two-volume publication *Wild Flowers of Western Pennsylvania and the Upper Ohio Basin,* executed for the most part between 1941 and 1943, are brilliant for their technical accomplishment as well as their scientific accuracy (figures 31–36). The project rapidly expanded into the galleries of the museum with the creation of a set of full-scale dioramas incorporating many of the flowers in the book. Although scientific in nature, the dioramas are composed like fine landscape paintings, and include painted backdrops by museum artist Ottmar von Fuehrer (figure 37). The project resumed after 1945, as Avinoff wrote to a friend in Pittsburgh in November 1948: "Jennings just sent me two miserable looking blades of grass to be glorified into separate plates!"[50]

The *Wild Flower* subjects, painted in the field or from freshly collected specimens, are miracles of spontaneity and precision. Although these illustrations earned Avinoff nothing in monetary terms (in fact, he gave all rights to the museum), they did bolster his professional status as a scientific naturalist and thereby furthered his career.

FIGURE 32

Coral Root & Lady's Tresses, plate 45 from *Wild Flowers of Western Pennsylvania and the Upper Ohio Basin,* 1941–1943, graphite and watercolor on paper, Carnegie Museum of Natural History, Section of Anthropology, Natural History Art Collection, 36,423. Cat. no. 37

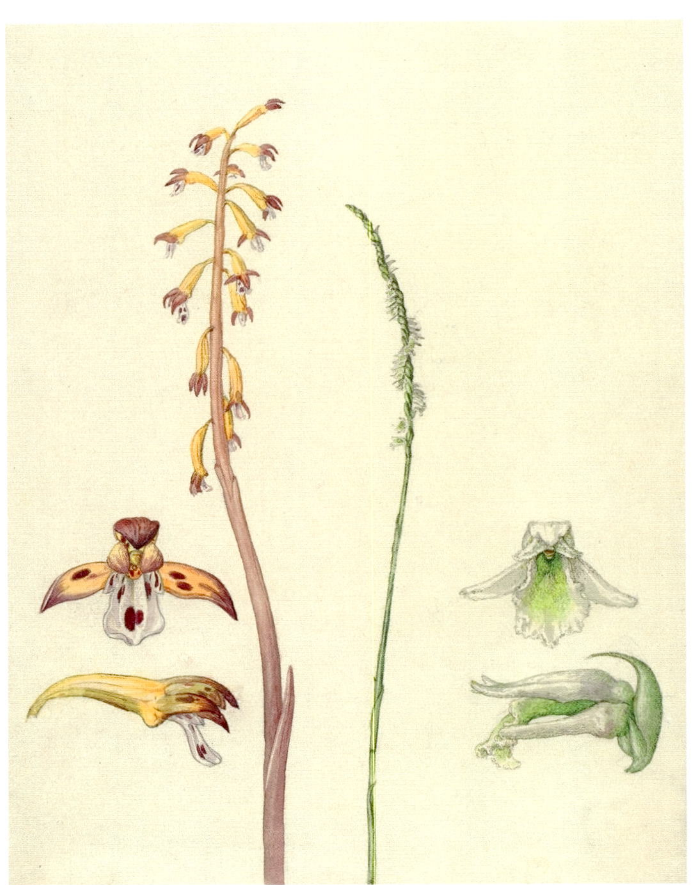

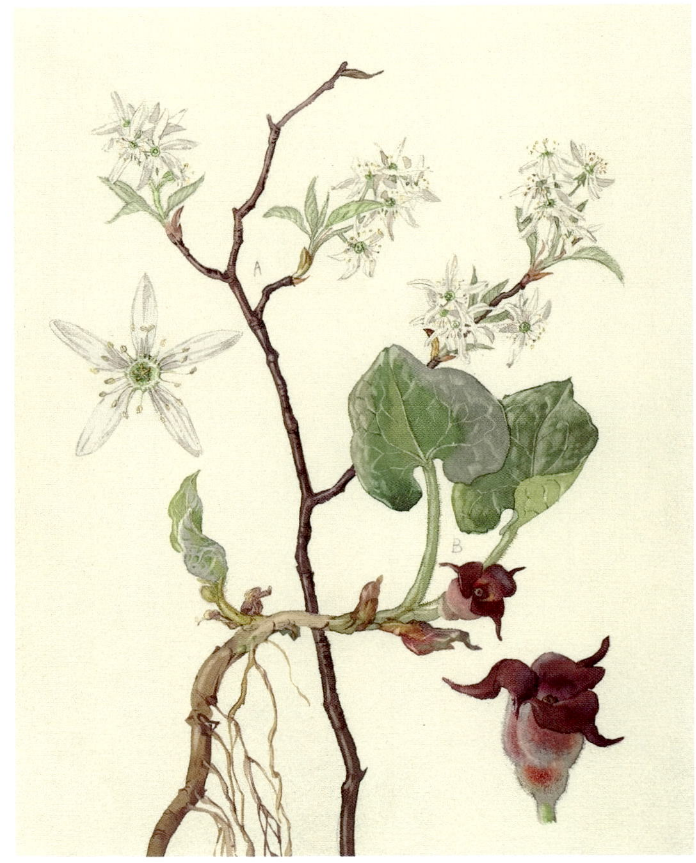

FIGURE 33

Juneberry and Ginger, plate 47 from *Wild Flowers of Western Pennsylvania and the Upper Ohio Basin,* 1941–1943, graphite and watercolor on paper, Carnegie Museum of Natural History, Section of Anthropology, Natural History Art Collection, 36,423. Cat. no. 38

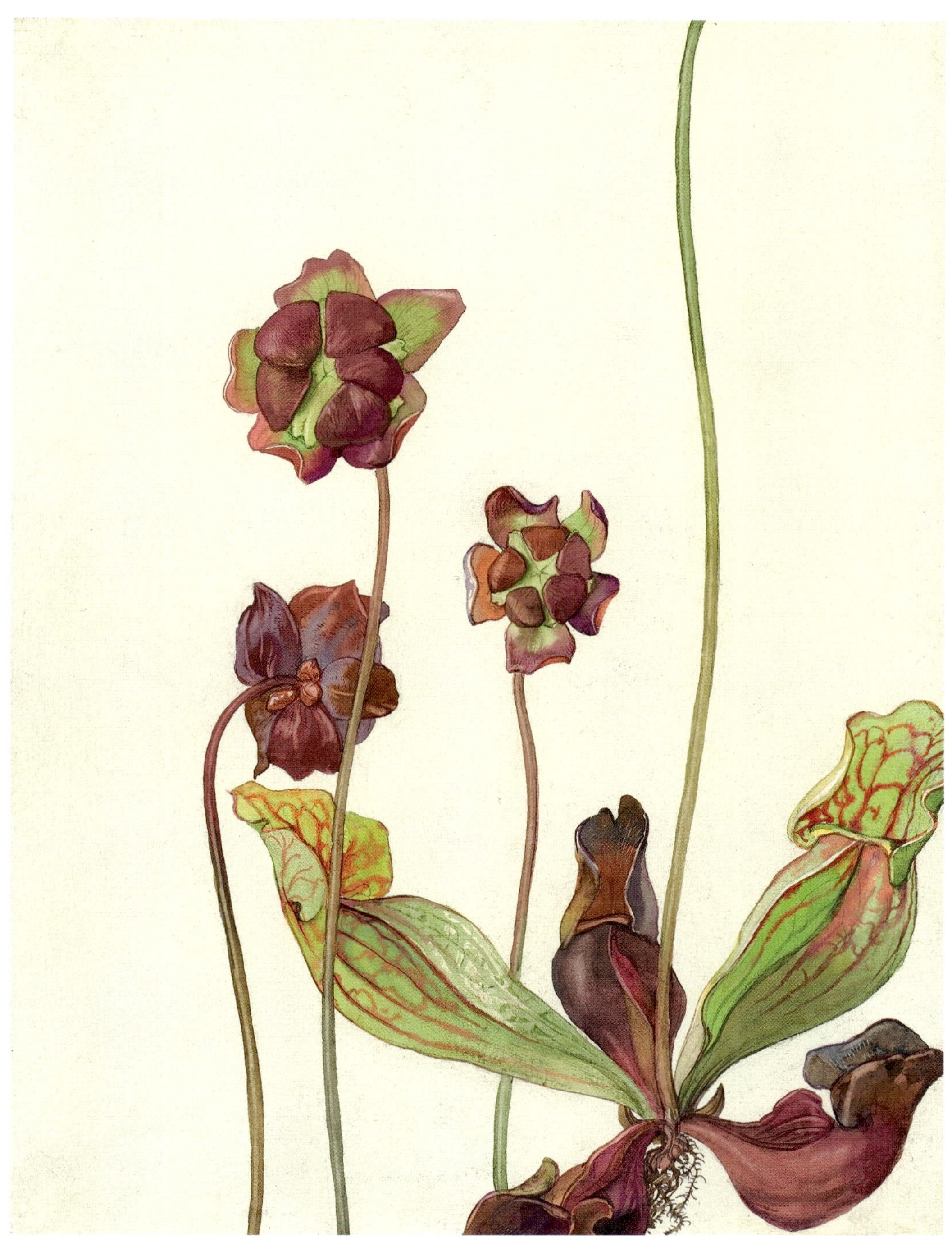

FIGURE 34
Pitcher Plant, plate 72 from *Wild Flowers of Western Pennsylvania and the Upper Ohio Basin,* 1941–1943, graphite and watercolor on paper, Carnegie Museum of Natural History, Section of Anthropology, Natural History Art Collection, 36,423. Cat. no. 39

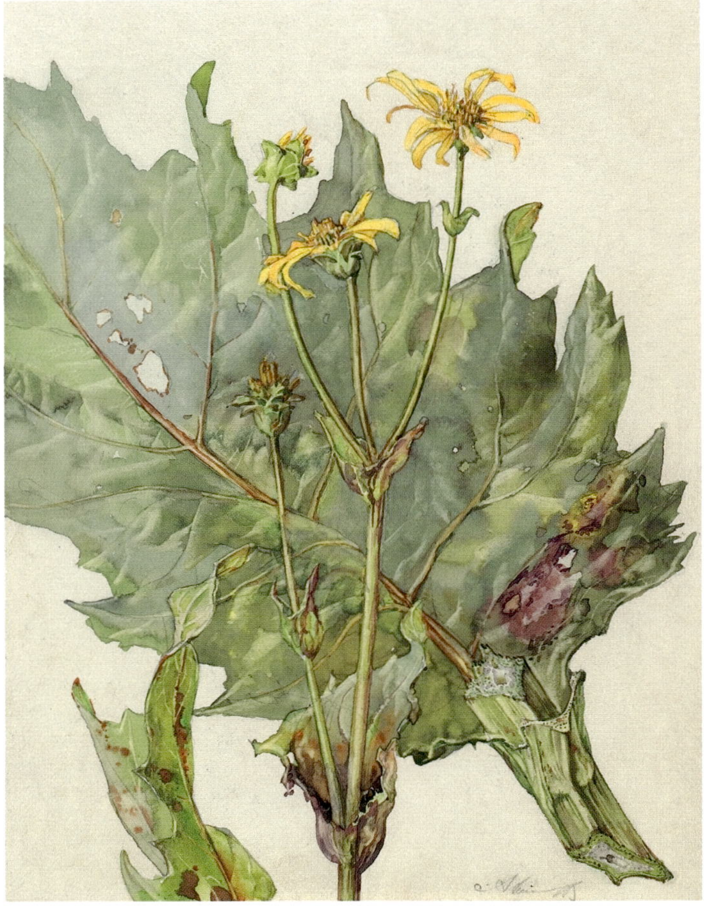

FIGURE 35

Cup Plant, plate 182 from *Wild Flowers of Western Pennsylvania and the Upper Ohio Basin,* 1941–1943, graphite and watercolor on paper, Carnegie Museum of Natural History, Section of Anthropology, Natural History Art Collection, 36,423. Cat. no. 40

FIGURE 36

Wake Robin, plate 28 from *Wild Flowers of Western Pennsylvania and the Upper Ohio Basin,* 1941–1943, graphite and watercolor on paper, Carnegie Museum of Natural History, Section of Anthropology, Natural History Art Collection, 36,423. Cat. no. 36

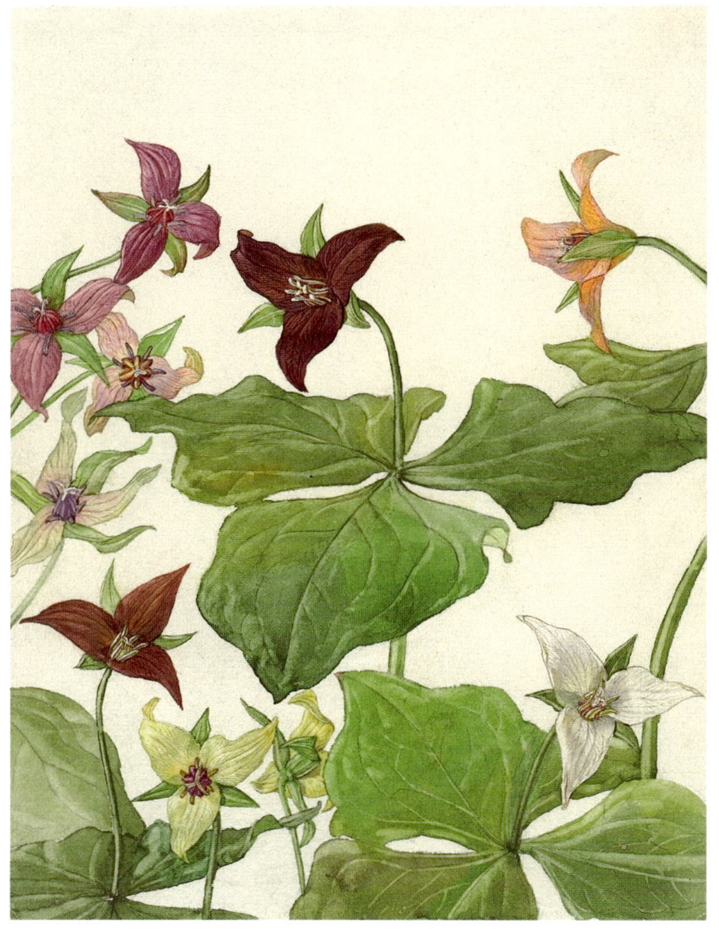

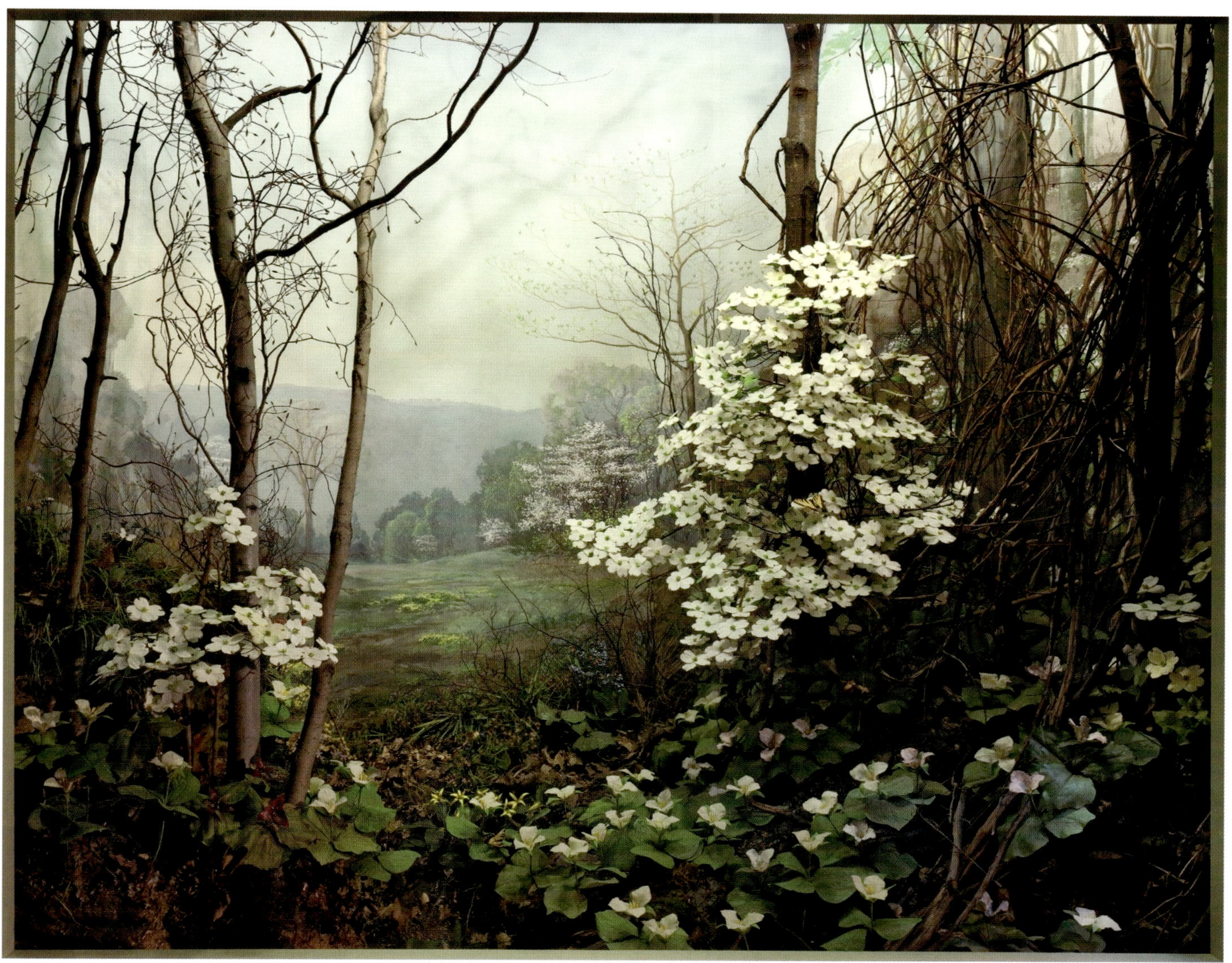

FIGURE 37
Ottmar F. and Hanna von Fuehrer, *Pennsylvania Spring Flora,* c. 1940–1945, diorama, Carnegie Museum of Natural History, Section of Botany, Presented by the Garden Club of Allegheny County

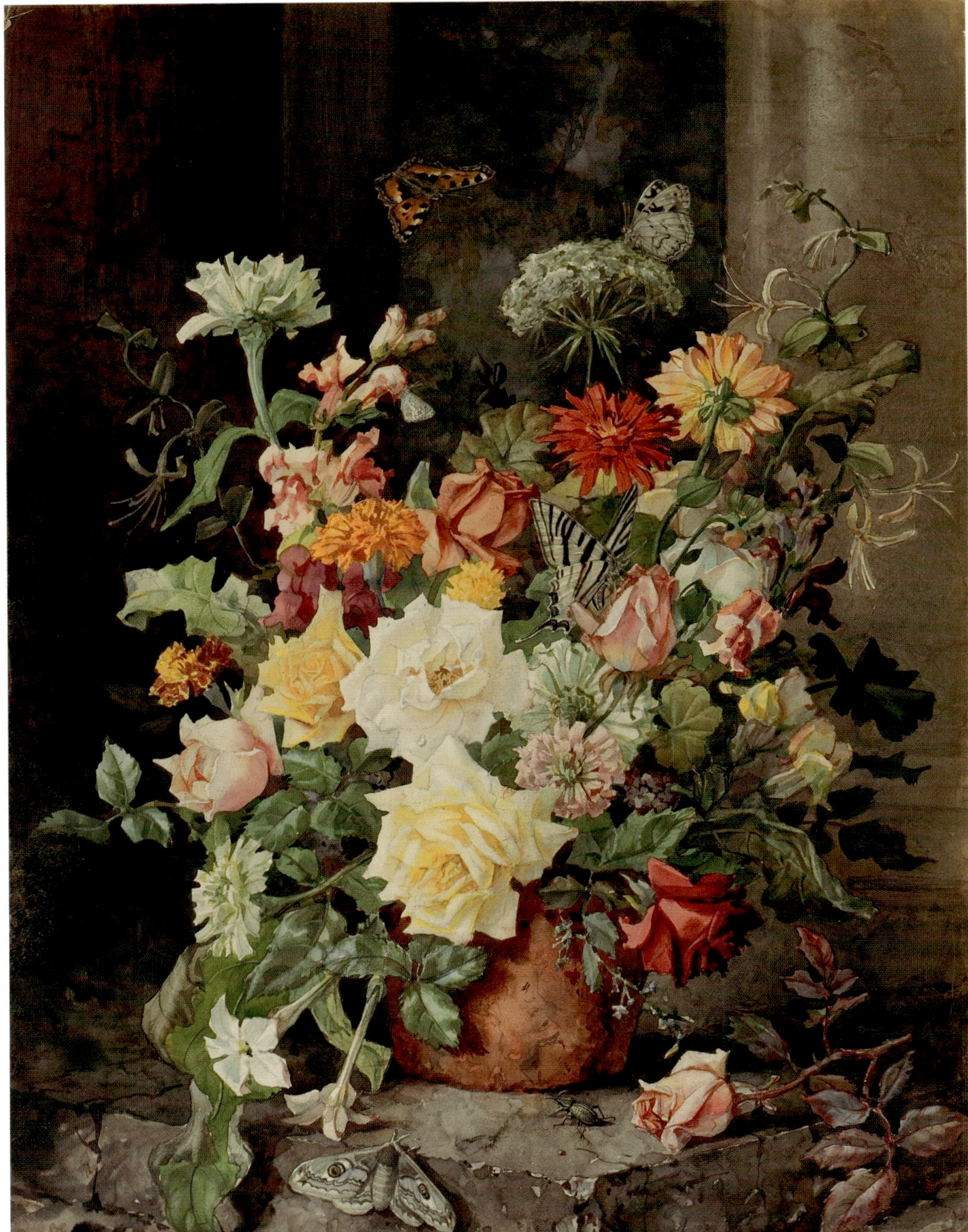

FIGURE 38
Dutch Bouquet, 1948, watercolor on paper mounted on Whatman board, Victoria Ward. Cat. no. 50

The move from scientific illustration to decorative flower painting may have been encouraged by Avinoff's good friend Rachel Hunt, whose famous collection of illustrated botanical books provides the basis of the Hunt Botanical Library at Carnegie Mellon University. They met shortly after Avinoff arrived in Pittsburgh, and she and her husband were among the "butterflies" attending the 1927 costume party. Avinoff shared her admiration for the great botanical painters of the past, particularly the eighteenth-century Dutchman Jan van Huysum and the early-nineteenth-century French artist Pierre Joseph Redouté. If the *Wild Flowers* can be seen as a sort of American homage to Redouté, Avinoff's "Dutch Bouquets" of the late 1940s are imitations of Van Huysum down to the stone plinths and attendant butterflies (figure 38). They Americanize Van Huysum by pairing bouquets of American flora and lepidoptera unknown to the Dutchman with arrangements of traditional European blooms, sometimes visited by Emperor butterflies.

Avinoff's other botanical works of the 1940s also derive from historical models, notably the bouquets in landscape settings that relate to John Thornton's scientifically oriented classic,

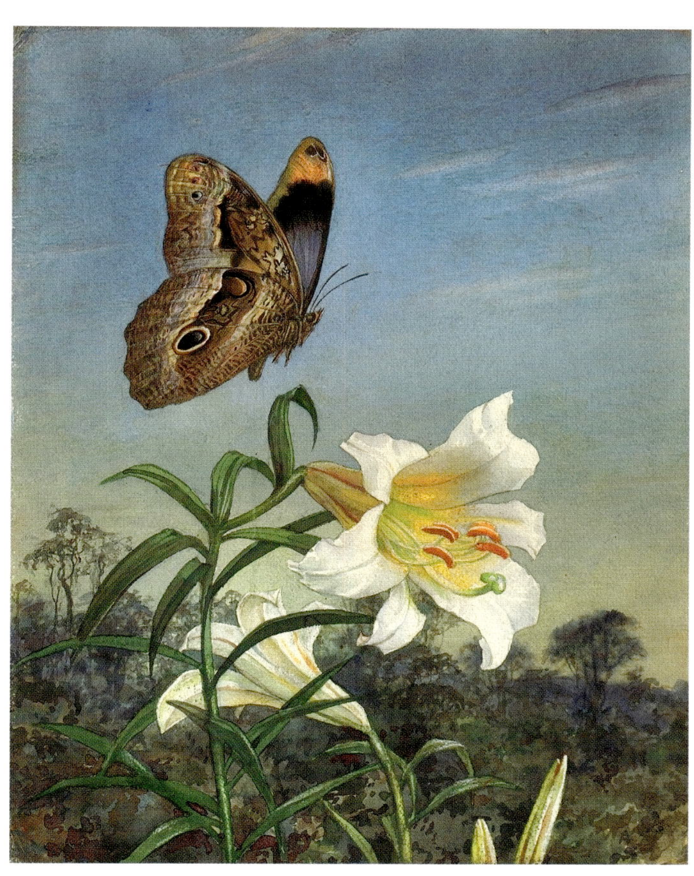

FIGURE 39
White Lilies and Caligo Butterfly, 1947, watercolor on pressed paperboard, Victoria Ward. Cat. no. 49

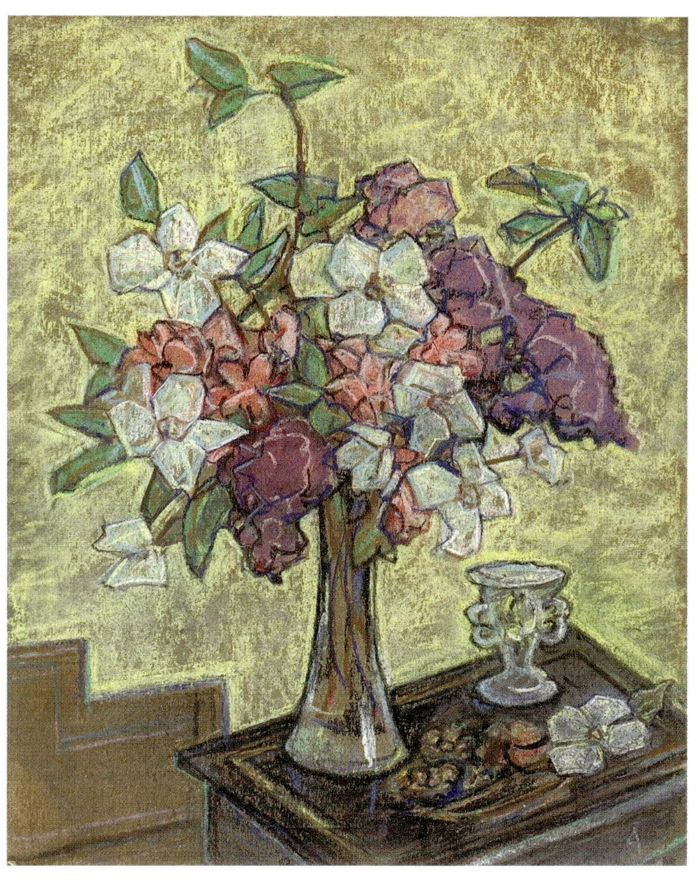

FIGURE 40
Spring Flowers, Manner of Vincent van Gogh, 1948–1949, pastel on card, Victoria Ward. Cat. no. 57

The Temple of Flora (figure 39).[51] His final series, a stunning set of portraits of unique or rare orchid hybrids, combines his strengths: sharp observation of individual characteristics, seemingly effortless technique, and marvelously organic, abstract compositions with a weird beauty all their own (figures 41–43). When he was so inclined, and in order to vary his market, he also painted flowers in imitation of Odilon Redon, Vincent van Gogh, and Henri Matisse (figure 40). By 1948, these works had become so well known that he had to explain:

> my pictorial tastes are not entirely vegetative. It is true that since my early days I was fond of painting flowers occasionally, but at none of the shows in Russia, England and this country where I had some paintings on view did I have any flower paintings shown. . . before last year.[52]

Avinoff sold his *Dutch Bouquets* and *Temple of Flora* landscapes at public exhibitions and through the art dealer Knoedler & Company in New York. Surviving price lists reveal high prices for his flower paintings, with a roster of buyers that reads like a Who's Who of East Coast society.[53]

In all of his commercial work—advertisements and magazine illustrations, society portraits and decorative botanical paintings—Avinoff adapted elements from his Russian past to the new realities of American life. To most American observers, this was a complete metamorphosis—in the words of *New Yorker* columnist Geoffrey Hellman, he had "assimilated." But every butterfly retains vestiges of its previous life stages, and Avinoff was no exception. One must therefore ask, "What happened to his 'Russian-ness' in America?"

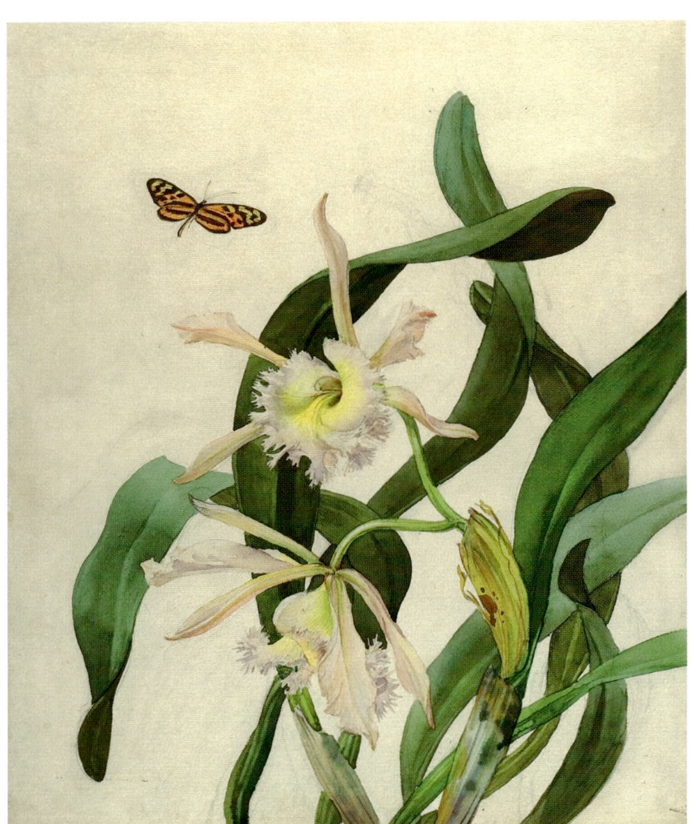

FIGURE 41
Orchid with Butterfly, 1948–1949, graphite and watercolor on Whatman board, Victoria Ward. Cat. no. 54

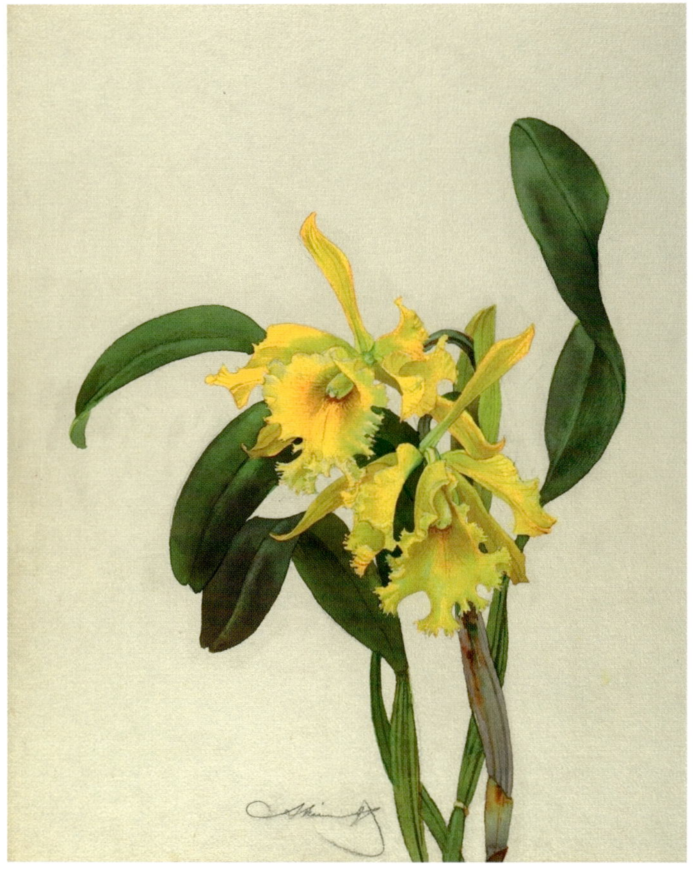

FIGURE 42
Yellow Orchid, 1948–1949, graphite and watercolor on paper, Victoria Ward. Cat. no. 56

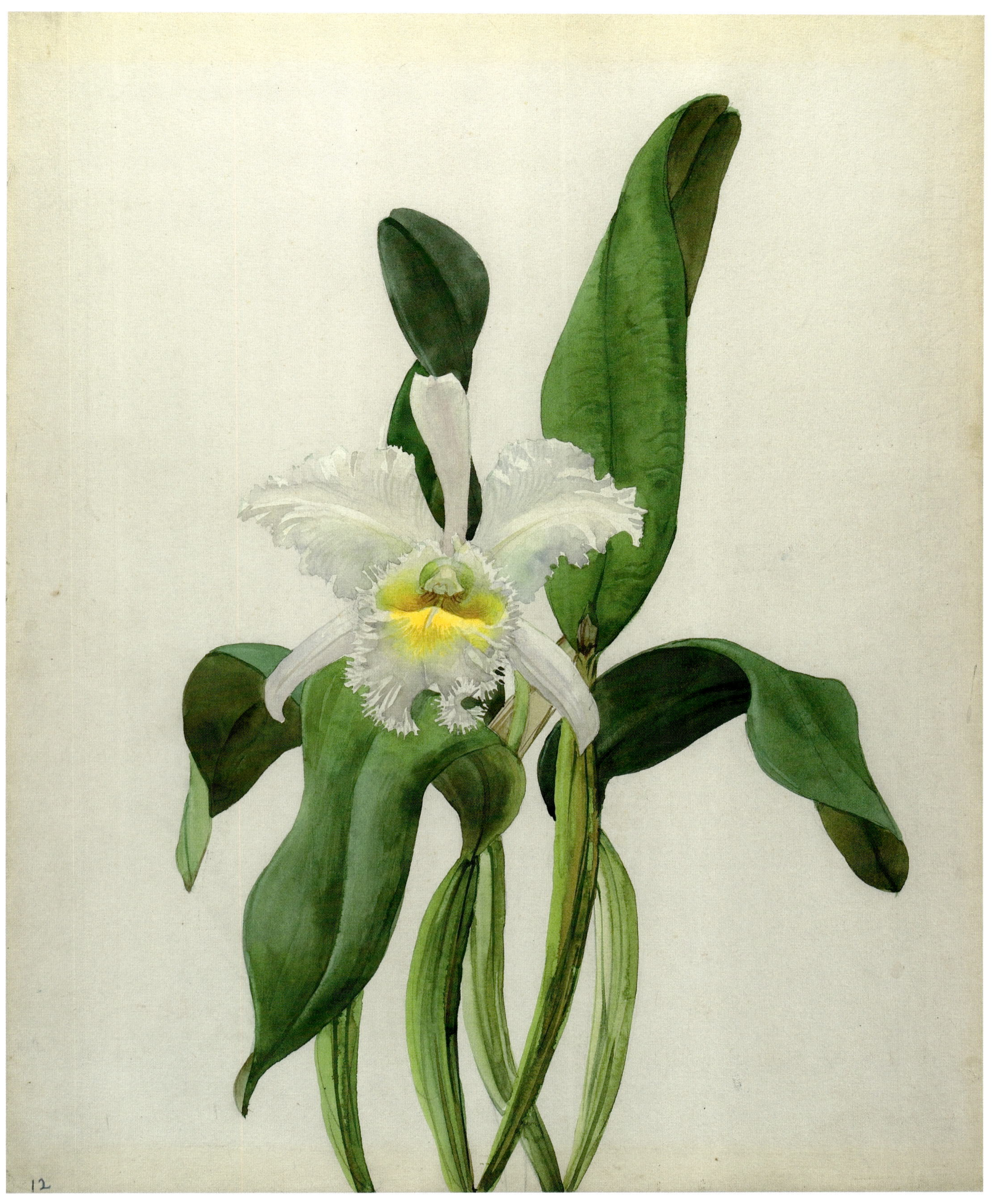

FIGURE 43
White Orchid, 1948–1949, graphite and watercolor on paper mounted on pressed paperboard, Victoria Ward. Cat. no. 55

"The best way to understand the nature and the soul of the Russian people is through the sympathetic study of their creative efforts exemplified by painting, architecture, literature, and music."

—ANDREY AVINOFF, [INTRODUCTION TO AN EXHIBITION OF RUSSIAN ART], 1943[54]

SOME ELEMENTS OF AVINOFF'S PAST could not be stripped of personal associations and repackaged to support his American lifestyle, his family, or his day job at Carnegie Museum. His cultural heritage, Orthodox religion, and homosexuality were as intrinsic to his personality as his love of butterflies and artistic talent, but they did not conform to the scientific, Protestant, capitalist values of his new country. If his Russian identity were to survive the transition to America, its manifestations had to be translated into forms adapted to the new environment.

The story of Avinoff's watercolor illustrations to Mikhail Lermontov's poem *The Demon* is a case in point. *The Demon* is one of Russia's great Romantic poems, and it was a favorite subject of nineteenth- and early-twentieth-century Russian painters—Mikhail Vrubel's great Symbolist paintings of the hero Demon being the most famous.[55] Set in the mountainous Caucasus region, it is the tale of a fallen angel drawn to earth by the beauty of a young woman's dance; enamored, he arranges for the death of her betrothed and seduces her; she dies. A guardian angel rescues her soul, the demon spins into outer darkness—and another legend is added to the wild storehouse of Caucasian mythology. Avinoff's six or more *Demon* watercolors date to the mid-1920s and represent specific moments in the poem. They amount to a visual translation of the Russian masterpiece. One scene depicts the Demon disdaining two visions of the human world, the one dark and turbulent, the other sunny and peaceful (part 1, stanzas 3 and 4) (figure 45). In another illustration, the Demon watches Tamara's fateful dance and is unable to turn away (part 1, stanza 9) (figure 44). Russian viewers would have instantly recognized the subject, and appreciated the subtlety of Avinoff's bubble imagery symbolizing the transparent lens through which the Demon views the human world, the permeable boundary between the angelic and human spheres, and the ephemerality of earthly life in a universe of cosmic eternities.

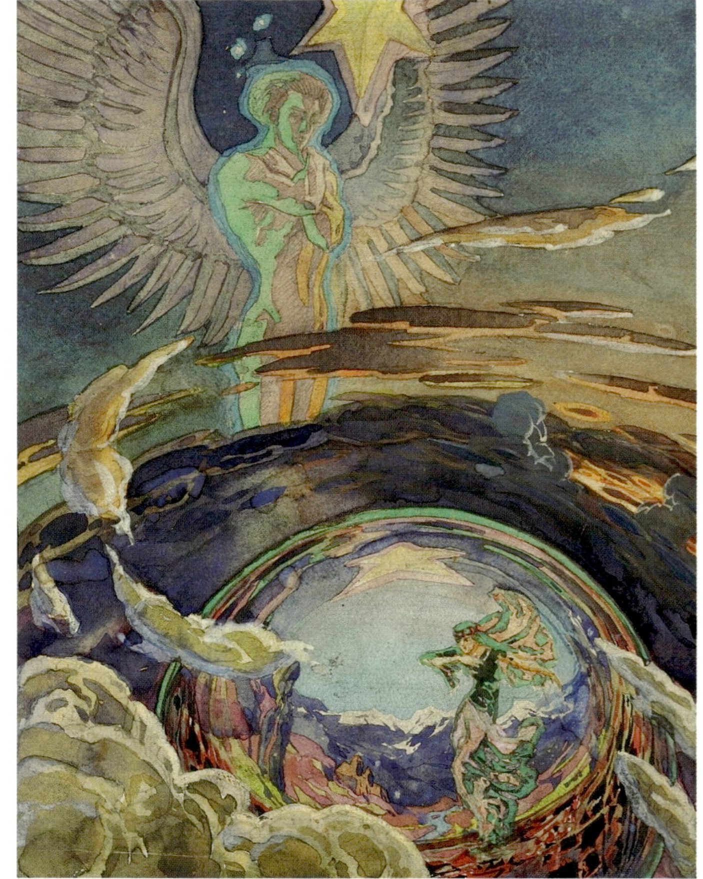

FIGURE 44
Lermontov's Demon, part 1, stanza 9, c. 1924, graphite and watercolor on paper, Antonia Shoumatoff Foster. Cat. no. 19

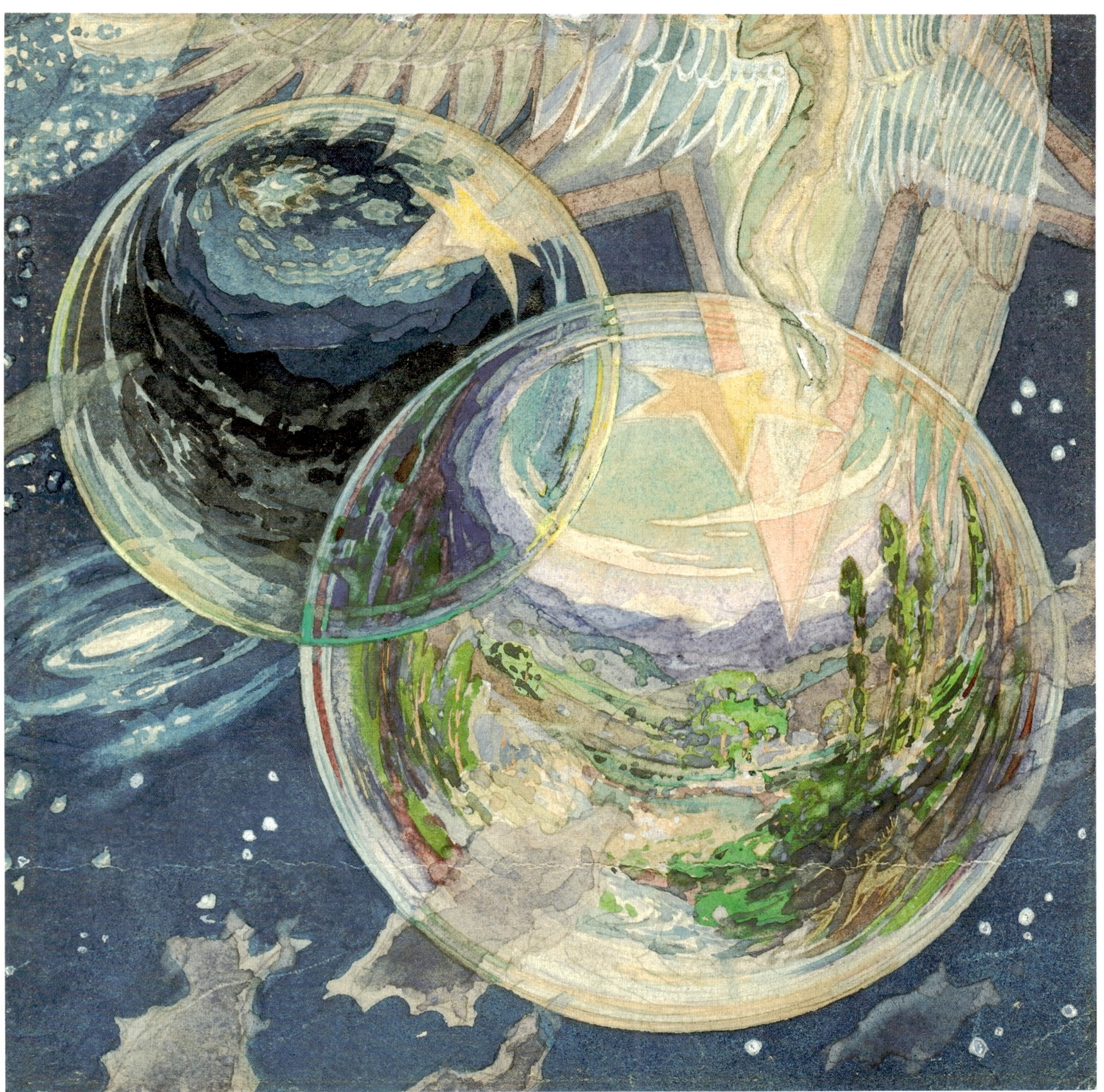

FIGURE 45
Lermontov's Demon, part 1, stanzas 3–4,
c. 1924, watercolor on paper, Victoria Ward. Cat. no. 18

FIGURE 46
The Russian Room, c. 1938–1944, watercolor on paper, University Art Gallery, University of Pittsburgh, 72.1.250.49. Cat. no. 28

Americans didn't get it. Although *The Demon* had been translated into English in the nineteenth century, it was by no means standard fare for American readers. Avinoff showed the illustrations only once, at a small exhibition at the College of Fine Arts at Carnegie Institute of Technology (now Carnegie Mellon University), under the title *Caucasian Saga*, relegating it to the picturesque world of the folk tale. *Pittsburgh Sun-Telegraph* reviewer Penelope Redd interpreted the images as "a group of metaphysical visualizations of the Christian beliefs in vivid symbols. The firmament peopled by stars, planets, angels and archangels moving in their allotted courses."[56] Quite possibly, Avinoff's highly personal *Sketch for the Last Judgment* may have been one of the works in this group (figure 47). If Redd's misreading was typical of the American response, Avinoff's attempt to create a visual translation of the poem had failed. No one corrected her, and Elizabeth Shoumatoff included only one tersely titled *Illustration for Lermontov's Demon* (no. 59) in the 1953 Pittsburgh exhibition in the section on Mysticism. Clearly, Americans weren't ready for a story of illicit, demonic love and seduction, where the author's and illustrator's sympathies lay with the tortured soul of the fallen angel, rather than his innocent, powerless victim.

Avinoff's most successful effort at translating Russian culture for Americans was his design for the "Russian Room," one of the famous Nationality Rooms, or classrooms, at the University of Pittsburgh (figure 46). Housed in the monumental Cathedral of Learning constructed at the center of the university's campus in the 1930s, the Nationality Rooms simulate traditional ethnic interiors, with special emphasis on the cultures of origin of the city's immigrant population. Avinoff described the Nationality Rooms as the university's "unwritten curriculum. . . [which] can be defined no more than the fragrance of a flower can be defined; but it is as real."[57] His surviving correspondence in the archives of the University of Pittsburgh suggests that he, university chancellor John Bowman, and Ruth Crawford Mitchell were the driving forces behind the entire project from its inception in the late 1920s. Avinoff chaired the committee of displaced Russian, Ukrainian, and Carpatho-Russian individuals and groups that organized and funded the room, and he designed the room and its contents himself. Begun in 1933, the room opened on July 8, 1938. "Into the design of the Russian room Dr. Avinoff has put his knowledge of Russian art forms and his devotion to the spirit of old Russia," wrote John Bowman in 1947.[58] Some parts of the room were inspired by Avinoff's grandmother's folk songs "got into forms which are beautiful."[59] The tapestry of St. George is also an Avinoff design, while the icon in the corner of the room is his copy of the family icon lost in the aftermath of the Bolshevik Revolution.

The Russian Room is another eerie Avinoff meditation on the subject of home. Unlike the baroque fantasia of the house at Shideyevo, this memory of Russia features austere designs dating back to antiquity and incorporating motifs from remote provinces. In so doing, it connects Russian folk art to ancient European and Asian sources, and to the almost universal symbolism of the tree of life. This was also the view of Russian culture most palatable to early-twentieth-century Americans, who found these "simple" peasant forms more consistent with the "simple" culture of American democracy. Significantly, the American Room in the Cathedral of Learning is a homespun colonial interior.

Bowman and Avinoff both dreamed—as did many in the years between the wars—of peaceful coexistence for the warring, struggling, antagonistic peoples both within the United States and in the world at large. Writing about the University of Pittsburgh project, Avinoff reiterated his belief that beauty would transcend language by speaking directly to the human eye, mind, and heart, thus satisfying the universal hope for peaceful understanding; he concluded, "The Russian mystic Dostoievsky, in words forever genuine, said: 'Beauty will save the world.'"[60]

The idealistic, universalizing vision of the Nationality Rooms appears in other Avinoff undertakings of the 1930s. In 1932, he became chairman of the Committee on Museums of Science for the League of Nations, and in 1936, he addressed the American Association of Museums' annual meeting on the topic of "Cooperation in the Museum Field." He dreamed of turning all the world's museums into one gigantic consortium of knowledge—a "universalium."[61] On a much smaller scale, he was practicing what he preached by working with Soviet museum authorities to catalogue his pre-Revolutionary butterfly collection, still in the Soviet Union. In all of these ambitious public projects, he seems to have been pursuing common ground and mutual understanding on an international level, and he seems to have believed that museums

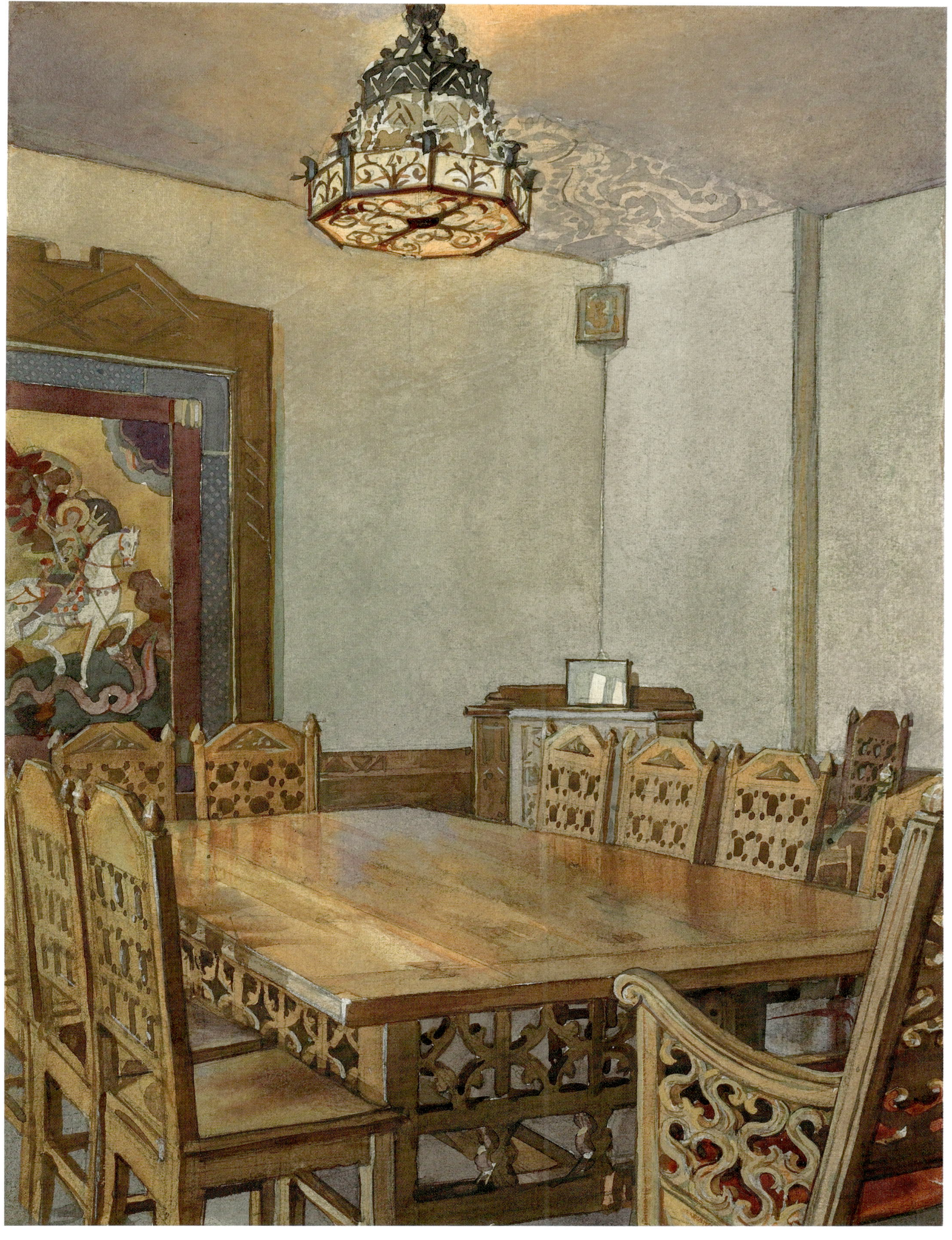

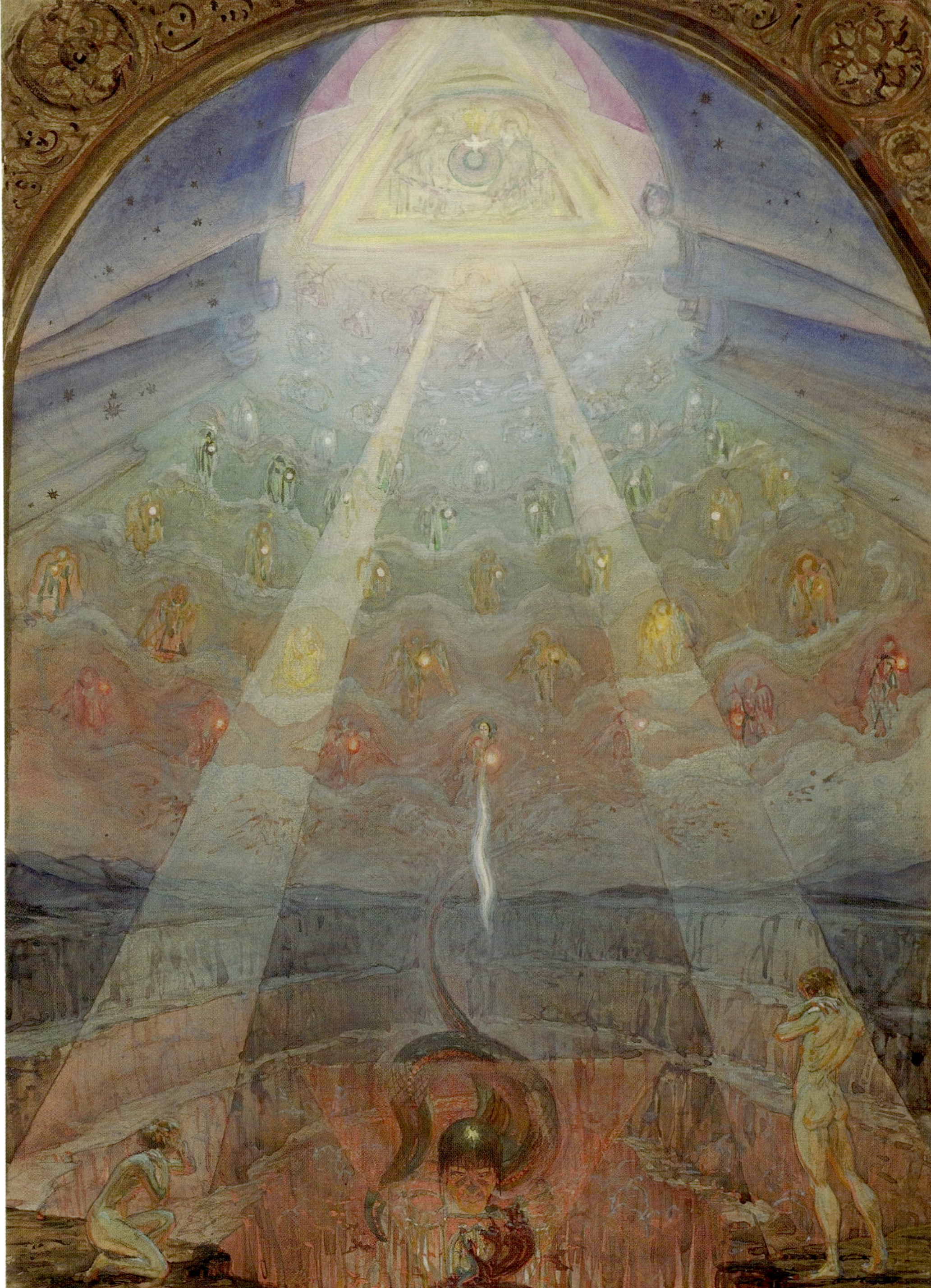

FIGURE 47
Sketch for the Last Judgment, c. 1920–1925, graphite and watercolor heightened with white and gold on paper mounted on board, Antonia Shoumatoff Foster. Cat. no. 13

communicating universally through visual experience could unite humanity in the face of political disruption, economic dislocation, and impending war. For Andrey Avinoff, the complex patterns and colors of the Persian carpet of human civilization could encompass all knowledge and all beliefs.

These hopes were brutally dashed with the outbreak of World War II. Avinoff was one of many distinguished signers of a statement of protest against the Soviet invasion of Finland of November 30, 1939.[62] Soon after the invasion, the Soviet Union was expelled from the League of Nations, international trade and travel ceased amid the escalation of the war, and collaboration on museum projects became impossible.

Where Avinoff could not translate, he could collect and preserve. The Bolshevik government's massive confiscations of church and aristocratic property, followed by Stalin's disastrous five-year economic plans, led to a flood of Russian exports to

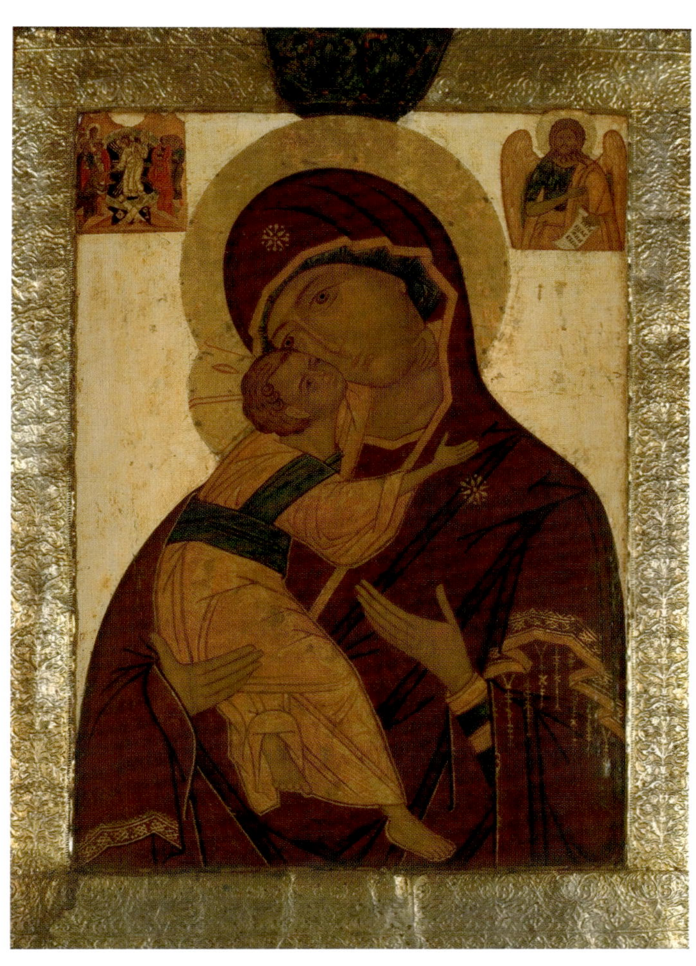

FIGURE 48
Russian, 19th century, *The Mother of God Vladimirskaya,* 19th century in the style of 16th century, tempera and gilding on gesso on panel, Carnegie Museum of Art, Gift of O. John Anderson in memory of Mr. and Mrs. George Hann, 80.63.1. Cat. no. 64

Europe and the United States throughout the 1920s and 1930s. These were the years of the great Soviet art sales, when everything from Old Master paintings to Fabergé eggs were sold to raise funds to pay for Soviet industrialization—"Treasures into Tractors," in the memorable title of a recent book.[63] From this flood of exports, Avinoff bought books. Beginning in 1931, working with New York book dealers representing the Soviet authorities, he built an important collection of Russian books on art, architecture, culture, and history, forming what was to become the best private library on Russian art in the U.S.[64] His collection, now preserved in the library of the Hillwood Estate, Museum & Gardens, includes rare limited editions and at least one unique survival, an early-twentieth-century facsimile of an illustrated medieval Apocalypse in Old Church Slavonic (see figure 55). This library, combined with his former access to the great pre-Revolutionary art collections, made him a leading authority on traditional Russian art in the U.S.

As the author of the catalogue of the 1944 exhibition of George Rice Hann's famous collection of Russian icons, Avinoff contributed to the meteoric rise and equally spectacular fall of icon collecting in the U.S. (figure 48). George Hann, a pioneer of national commercial air travel in the 1920s, and a resident of the exclusive Pittsburgh suburb of Sewickley, acquired a major collection of Russian icons around 1935. He seems to have worked through an agent (not Avinoff), who was buying from Soviet sources such as Antikvariat, the official outlet for Soviet government sales. No one has ever explained the motivation for Hann's sudden interest in Russian art, which became a lifelong collecting passion. The date of his first meeting with Avinoff is also unknown, as is the question of whether their friendship motivated Hann's collection, or resulted from it. In 1938, Hann remodeled his estate to showcase his icons, and in 1944, he agreed to lend 102 icons and 149 decorative objects to Carnegie Institute for a major exhibition, *Russian Icons and Objects of Ecclesiastical and Decorative Arts from the Collection of George R. Hann.*[65] Smaller exhibitions comprising only icons from the collection would travel to museums in Columbus, Ohio; Indianapolis; and Syracuse, New York. Avinoff agreed to catalogue the works in the Pittsburgh exhibition and write the catalogue introduction; the epigraph of this section comes from his typed remarks for the show's opening in Pittsburgh.

The exhibition was a critical success, and the Hann collection would be considered one of the finest and most important groups of icons outside the Soviet Union for nearly four decades.[66] Avinoff became a leading American authority on the subject, lecturing at the Baltimore Museum of Art in 1942 and the Metropolitan Museum of Art in New York in April 1944. In July 1943, President Roosevelt thanked Avinoff for providing "memoranda on the two religious paintings given to me by Ambassador [Joseph E.] Davies," the two paintings in question presumably icons.[67] Davies, the U.S. ambassador to the Soviet Union from 1936 to 1938 (and the third husband of Marjorie Merriwhether Post, whose collections of Russian and French art comprise the holdings of Hillwood Museum), also collected icons, along with Socialist Realist paintings. Public interest in icons was high during the war years as Americans sought better understanding of their Soviet ally, and as the entrepreneurial efforts of Antikvariat, Armand and Victor Hammer, and other dealers flooded the American market with glitzy Russian treasures. The two-dimensionality, formal stylization, and spirituality of icon painting also appealed to advanced modernist tastes, ultimately leading to the elevation of the genre from the realm of decorative and applied arts to the category of fine arts and paintings in American art museums.

After George Hann died in 1979, the 1980 sale of his collection at Christie's, New York, was one of the art world's most hotly anticipated events. The Christie's cataloguers consulted Avinoff's 1944 catalogue for their descriptions of lots in the sale—indeed, some of the attributions and dates came straight from Avinoff. The Hann icons broke all existing records for prices in this area, with several lots doubling the previous record of $75,000. Shortly after the sale, however, the émigré Soviet art restorer Vladimir Teteriatnikov denounced almost the entire icon collection as consisting of modern fakes and copies. By credibly tracing the origins of these hallowed masterpieces to a Soviet campaign to copy, restore, and dump thousands of confiscated icons, Teteriatnikov devastated the international market for Russian icons, while also destroying Avinoff's credibility as an icon expert.

Lost amid the uproar and scandal was Teteriatnikov's appraisal of Avinoff's connoisseurship, which sheds considerable light on Avinoff's conception of his Russian art heritage. Teteriatnikov noted that in the first half of the twentieth century, "a consciously cultivated mystical approach to Russian art first appeared," an approach adopted by Avinoff, who viewed the icon as "an eloquent and characteristic manifestation of the spiritual quest and artistic ideas of the Russian people."[68] Teteriatnikov recognized that Avinoff's visual analysis of the Hann icons was based on comparisons between the Hann paintings and illustrations from books printed for the most part before 1900 that did not document the activities of the twentieth-century icon industry. Avinoff had accepted at face value the date and provenance details on the labels affixed to the icons, and based attributions on iconography and style—subject matter, composition, and the painted surface. Teteriatnikov characterized Avinoff's connoisseurship as the work of a brilliant, diligent amateur of scientific mindset with no access to other originals for comparison and limited awareness of the structural components of icon painting, and who (out of necessity) placed undue reliance on printed books.

Regarding the story from the vantage point of the twenty-first century, it is one of many examples of how changing standards in art conservation and museum connoisseurship affect evaluations of works of art, especially those from remote times and places. What stands out now for the purposes of this study is the extent to which Avinoff's methods and assumptions for cataloguing icons parallel those he employed in cataloguing butterflies. The icons, like the butterflies, arrived with printed labels concerning geographical origins and collecting data (indeed, many of the icons bore Tretyakov Gallery labels, the gold standard for icon collections), which Avinoff did not question. He looked at icons and butterflies for pattern, coloration, and resemblance to type specimens (the famous icons in the books in his library) in order to make identifications. However, he was unable to dissect the icons in the way that entomologists dissect butterflies, and in this lay the basis for many of the dating and attribution errors in the 1944 Hann catalogue.

"I bow to scientific fact until five o'clock. After that I may have other ideas."

—ANDREY AVINOFF TO NICHOLAS SHOUMATOFF[69]

"The white powder uranium, in its twins—235 and 238—descends like the 'pale' fourth horseman of the Apocalypse at this fateful hour. . . Might it not be an echo of the forbidden daring of the Lost Atlantis, foreshadowing the visions of the Apocalypse, strangely—two themes that always seemed to be ominously linked." —ANDREY AVINOFF TO RACHEL HUNT, 1945[70]

THE CHRISTIAN VISION OF THE APOCALYPSE and the classical myth of Atlantis are about cataclysmic destruction of corrupted human civilizations. Fire and brimstone. Earthquakes, volcanoes, and tidal waves. To which one could now add, Little Boy and Fat Man.

The year 1945, for Andrey Avinoff, was Apocalypse and Atlantis, and Hiroshima and Nagasaki all rolled into one. The year started out well. The Allied forces in Europe were slowly gaining the upper hand over the Germans, and at the Yalta Conference in February 1945, Roosevelt, Churchill, and Stalin met to discuss the future of Europe. Avinoff wrote, "I should have obtained the signature of the three big wigs in Yalta. How well I remember the courtly palaces of the Emperor—Livadia and Massandra!. . . I presume the meeting was held in Livadia."[71] Then on April 16, 1945, Avinoff suffered the heart attack that suddenly ended his career as museum director and man-about-town. Soon afterward, he destroyed about 150 of his homoerotic paintings and drawings, as he "did not want to leave after me to my sister such sort of things."[72] He would refer later to this event as his "holocaust."[73] He retired from Carnegie Museum and moved to Hidden Hollow, Elizabeth Shoumatoff's house in Locust Valley, Long Island, to recuperate.

The German surrender in May 1945 was followed by the bombing of Hiroshima and Nagasaki in August, and by Japan's surrender in September. But for Avinoff, the cataclysmic event of this period would be the appearance of Alfred Kinsey's *Sexual Behavior in the Human Male* (1948). After learning about the forthcoming publication of this groundbreaking sex study, Avinoff came out of the closet like a butterfly out of its chrysalis in a letter to Kinsey himself, dated December 14, 1947.

> Let me introduce myself. I am a fellow entomologist. . . I read about your forthcoming book in the last issue of 47, and am very interested to know when it will appear. . . My observations on the artistic and theatrical world of Old Russia—including poets and writers—makes me think whether there are some parallels with conditions in this country. I hope you will excuse this letter from a stranger.[74]

In the "Old Russia" referenced in this letter to America's most controversial sex researcher, homosexual behavior had been, relative to elsewhere, an accepted aspect of male life in elite society.[75] Several of the Grand Dukes, including Grand Duke Nicholas Mikhailovitch (who had advised Avinoff before his 1912 expedition) were openly gay or bisexual; the Russian bathhouses supported a flourishing gay culture; and many of the chief protagonists of Russian Silver Age art and literature—including Serge Diaghilev and Vaslav Nijinsky—hid neither their sexual orientation nor their relationships with other men. The most visible, flamboyant, unapologetic, and influential member of this extraordinary culture was the Russian Silver Age poet and writer Mikhail Kuzmin.

The evidence linking Avinoff to Kuzmin is at present circumstantial and is primarily to be found in Avinoff's homoerotic art. In 1906, the poet published a short romantic novel, *Wings,* that told the story of an older man seducing a younger one—a typical turn-of-the-century romance except for the fact that the lovers are male. However tame the story line may appear today, the notoriety surrounding the book made it an immediate best seller. The key line in the book describes the rapturous process of discovering one's true sexual identity: "And the people saw that every sort of beauty, every sort of love was from the gods, and they became free and bold, and they grew wings."[76] In 1917, along with *Reminiscences of the House in Russia,* Avinoff salvaged a little painting with the discreet title *Cretan Motif* (figure 49). The work's survival indicates its importance to him. It depicts a lithe, muscular male nude wrestling a giant snake in an archaic

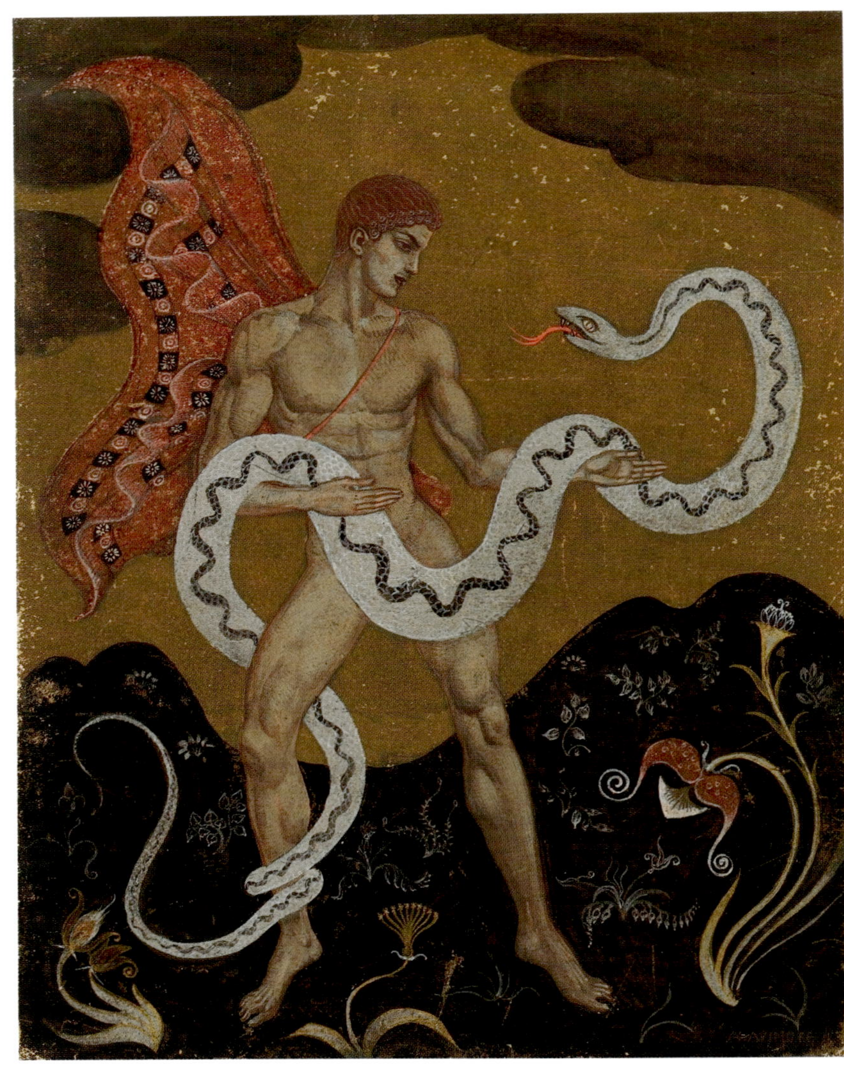

FIGURE 49
Cretan Motif, c. 1911–1915, tempera on Bainbridge illustration board, Antonia Shoumatoff Foster. Cat. no. 1

landscape with gilded sky. The young man's billowing cloak is shaped and dotted like the wing of a giant butterfly. The allusion to Crete, a gay paradise in fin-de-siècle thinking, underscores the symbolism.

Kuzmin's powerful blend of sexuality, aestheticism, and traditional religion—he didn't see these as mutually exclusive or conflicting—turns up in *He Lives,* the fable Avinoff co-authored with Austin Pardue. From the perspective of *Wings,* the caterpillar's metamorphosis and flight of discovery—guided by a mentor with brilliant yellow wings—is as much a sexual voyage as a spiritual one. And the achievement of understanding, serenity, and acceptance through sexuality, beauty, and spirituality was a Russian Silver Age dream—one that Avinoff kept throughout his life. Other Kuzmin influences appear in Avinoff's early paintings: for example, a small group of exquisite "Persian-style" paintings (figure 50) that evoke the decadence of Kuzmin's St. Petersburg club, the "Tavern of Hafiz," and an important image (c. 1920s, private collection) of the archangel St. Michael corresponding to Kuzmin's "Guide," an angelic figure and heavenly warrior leading the uninitiated to love in Kuzmin's 1906 volume of poems, *Nets.*[77] The most spectacular and explicit likely reference to Kuzmin in Avinoff's art would come in 1948, in his poster-boy portrait of a fully aroused young paratrooper in leather jacket (and nothing else), haloed by fluttering penises, and titled *WINGS.*[78]

The other key thinker in Avinoff's sexual and intellectual evolution was the Viennese writer Otto Weininger. Weininger's *Geschlecht und Charakter* (Sex and Character) was published in German in 1903, and like *Wings* it became a notorious best seller, in this case finding a vast European readership for its multiple editions in many languages, including English and French.[79] Andrey's brother, Nicholas, certainly knew the book, as his wife, Marie, referred to it: "He [Nicholas] reminded me of Weininger's theory that every human being possessed both masculine and feminine genes in varying degrees."[80] This difficult and complex, albeit not always coherent, treatise articulates three concepts that Avinoff seems to have adopted: that masculinity and femininity

FIGURE 50

"Persian" St. Francis, c. 1925, gouache on card, He Who Stands Firm (Nicholas Avinoff Shoumatoff). Cat. no. 21

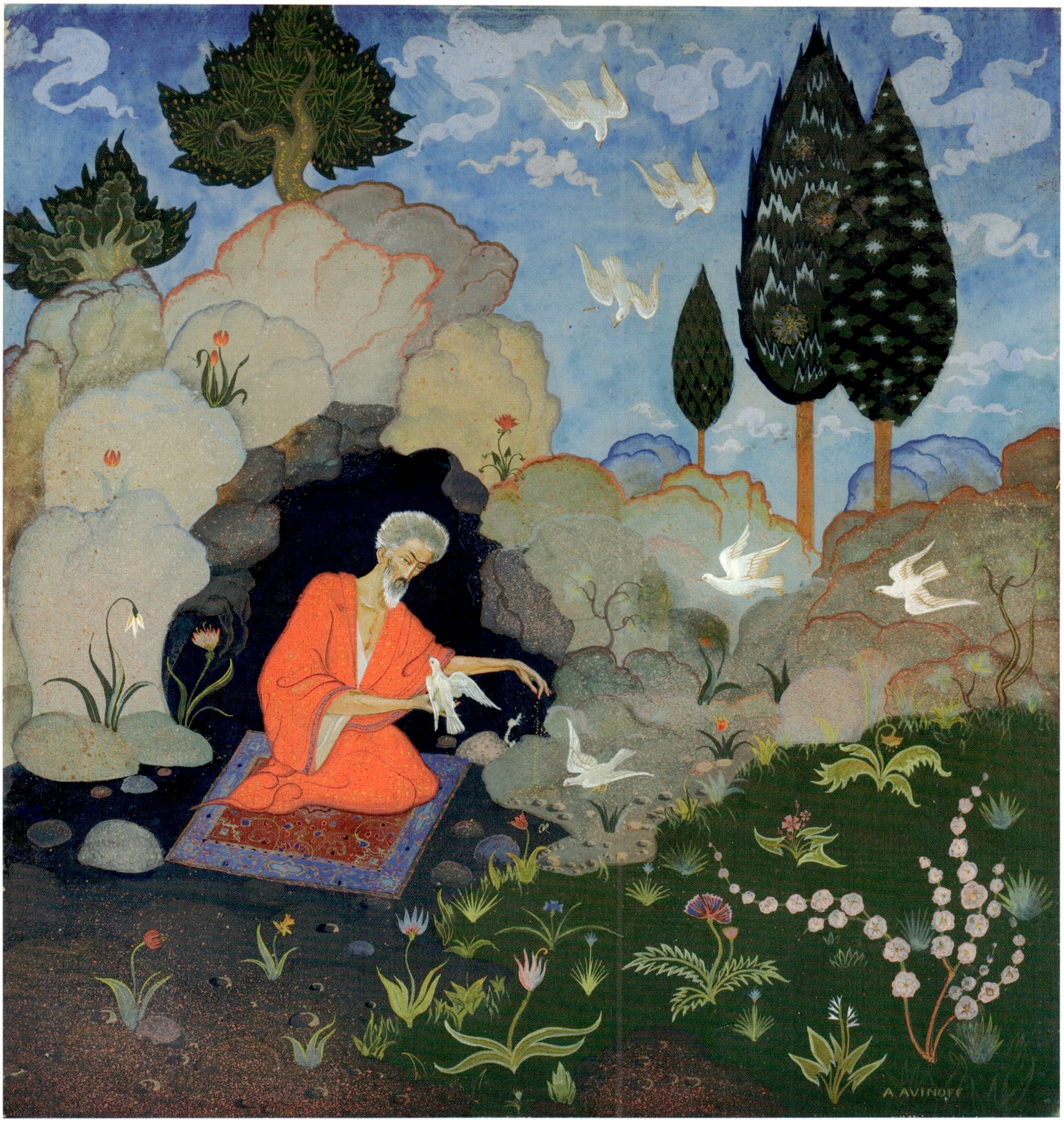

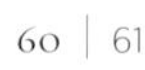

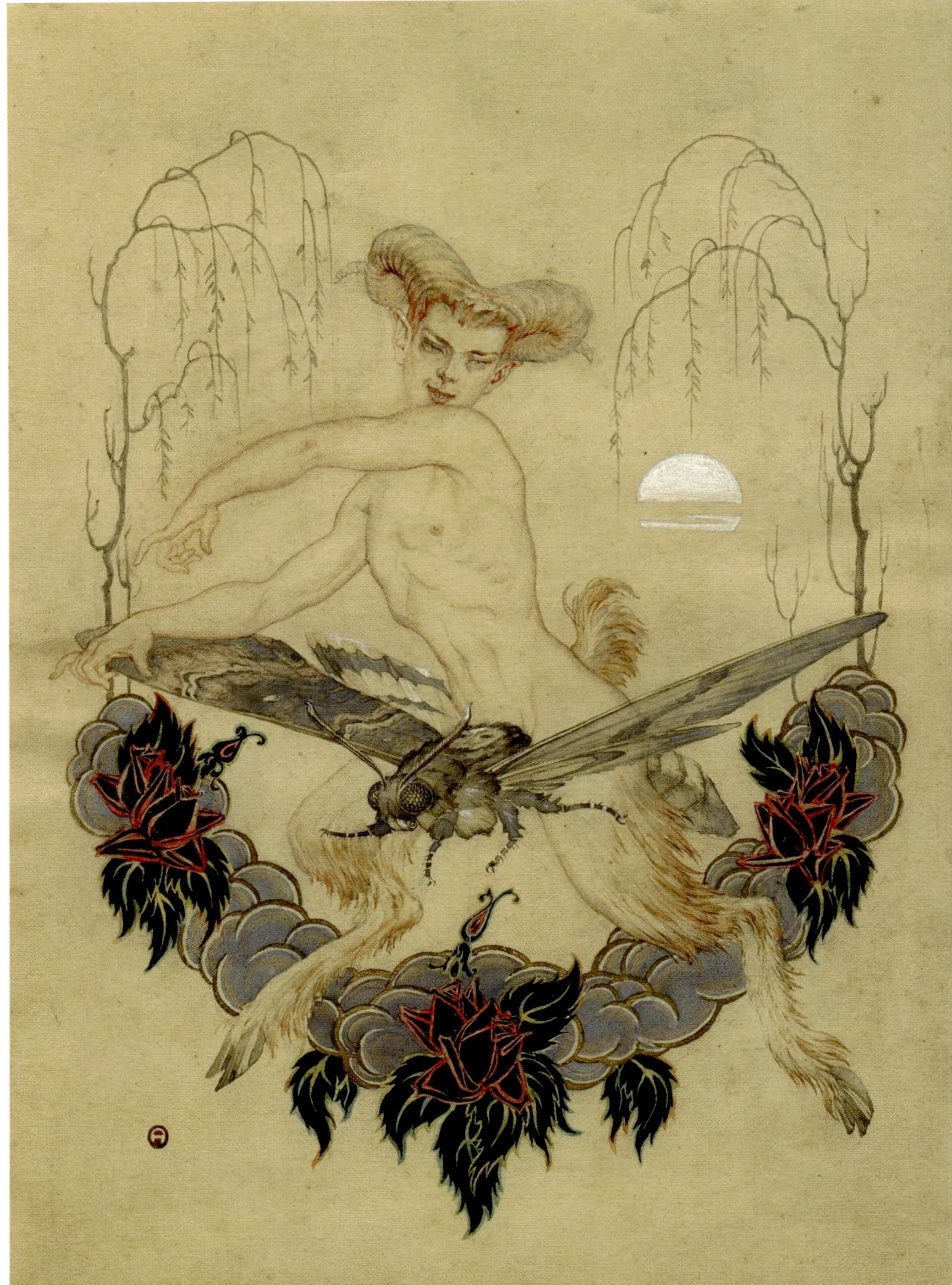

FIGURE 51
Nijinsky as Faun, 1918, ink and watercolor with gilding on paper, The Kinsey Institute for Research in Sex, Gender, and Reproduction, Indiana University, Bloomington, 290R Av9586.186. Cat. no. 11

exist in every species and every individual on a continuum, that homosexuality is the logical and acceptable orientation for an individual located near the midpoint of the continuum, and that an individual's place along that continuum is determined by the development of his or her protoplasm into increasingly specialized forms (idioplasm, etc.) that eventually produce a certain individual of a certain species.

It's not known when Andrey Avinoff grew his own set of wings. The family trip to Uzbekistan may have been important in his awareness of sexual identity. Quite likely, his collecting expeditions in 1908 and 1912 followed the model of the notorious all-male expeditions and camps led by Russian's most famous naturalist and explorer, Nikolai Przhevalsky, in the late nineteenth century. Avinoff was certainly a habitué of Russian bathhouses, which he described to Kinsey thus: "with private rooms, they used to have some young masseurs, 16 to 20 years old, who were always available—one or two at a time, to lend their willing services to the clients."[81] He idolized the ballet dancer Nijinsky; a

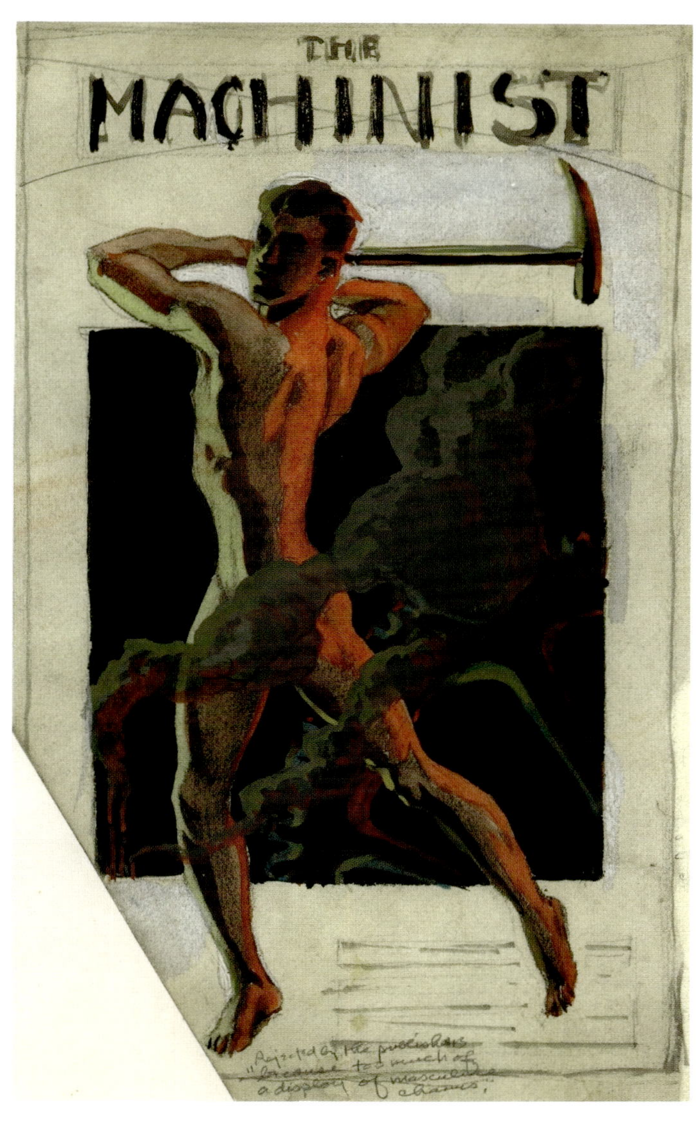

FIGURE 52
The Machinist, 1922, graphite, crayon, and gouache on paper, The Kinsey Institute for Research in Sex, Gender, and Reproduction, Indiana University, Bloomington, 290R Av 9586.215. Cat. no. 15

well-thumbed 1907 Nijinsky portrait with the stamp of a St. Petersburg photographer survives in the Avinoff collection of dance photographs at the Kinsey Institute, as does Avinoff's wonderfully perverse drawing of the dancer as a faun astride a hawkmoth (figure 51). The latter is perhaps a reference to Nijinsky's famously sexual performance in the lead role of the 1912 Ballets Russes production of *L' Après-midi d'un faune*—a performance that scandalized audiences with its final scene of simulated masturbation.

Once settled in the United States, Avinoff had to adjust to a different cultural climate from that of his native Russia. His design for a cover for *Machinist* magazine was "rejected by the publishers because [it was] too much of a display of masculine charms" (figure 52).[82] At Carnegie Museum, director W. J. Holland, the noted entomologist who tried to hire Avinoff for the entomology department, was notoriously homophobic. Holland's bitter relationship with his homosexual son must have been especially complicated for Avinoff, whom Holland seems to have regarded as a surrogate. Avinoff's other scientific supporter, the wealthy industrialist and hawkmoth collector B. Preston Clark, was also the father of a homosexual son, who committed suicide in 1930. Throughout the 1930s and 1940s, American homophobia and intolerance was on the rise, as reflected in legislation, law enforcement practices, and social conventions. Although Avinoff was a sexually active gay man throughout his life, he had to be exceedingly careful, as his peer group seems to have consisted of well-established (married, socially prominent) older men and a series of athletic, handsome college undergraduates, not all of them receptive to his advances. He was known and accepted as a perennial bachelor in the Pittsburgh establishment, but among his circle of close friends, "it [his homosexuality] was merely a small part of his charm, everybody knew about it, nobody was bothered by it."[83] In such an environment, liberal prewar St. Petersburg must have increasingly seemed like a lost paradise—a gay Atlantis.

The concept of St. Petersburg as a lost or dead city was a leitmotif in Russian émigré literature of the twentieth century.[84] With hindsight, its pre-Revolutionary Silver Age recalled Pompeii (destroyed by volcano in the first century CE), Imperial Rome, or, in the poetry of M. Vega and George V. Golokhvastoff, the drowned city of Atlantis. This was the theme of Golokhvastoff's lengthy poem *Gibel Atlantide*, published in Russian in the United States in 1938 with seventeen intricate illustrations by Avinoff.[85] The Avinoff designs reproduced in photogravures are symbolically elaborate, complex meditations on the rise and fall of civilizations, spirituality, ambition, and desire—populated by gorgeous winged male "spirits" modeled after Pittsburgh college athletes (figure 53). The most famous image from the set, *The Death of the High Priest,* depicts a withered hand reaching above the flood,

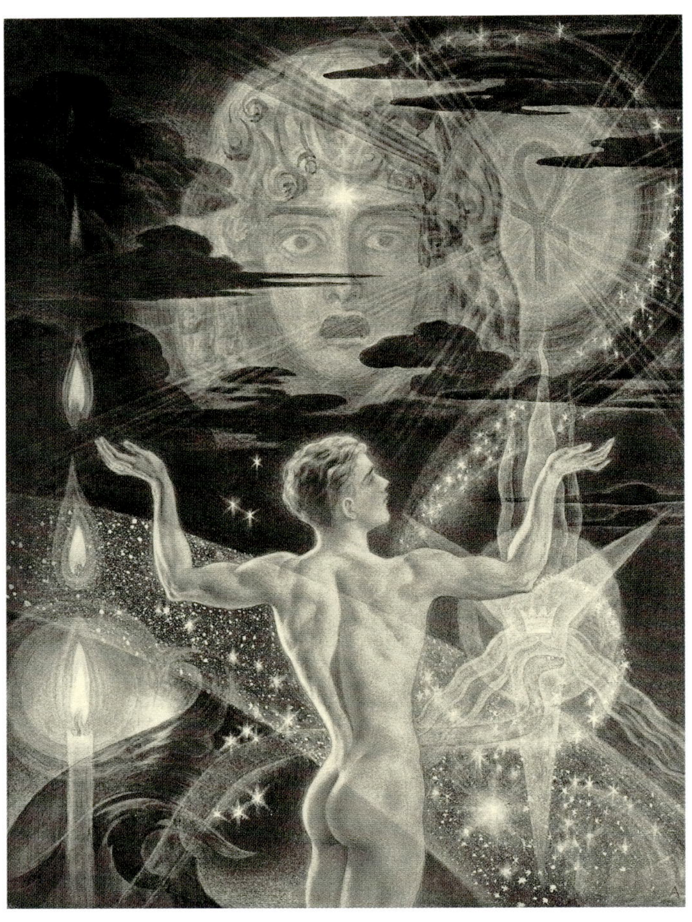

FIGURE 53
At the Gates of Immortality, plate 15 from *The Fall of Atlantis,* designed c. 1935–1938, folio edition published in 1944, gravure on paper, Carnegie Museum of Art, Gift of He Who Stands Firm (Nicholas Avinoff Shoumatoff), 2007. Cat. no. 26

FIGURE 54
The Death of the High Priest, plate 17 from *The Fall of Atlantis,* designed c. 1935–1938, folio edition published in 1944, gravure on paper, Carnegie Museum of Art, Gift of He Who Stands Firm (Nicholas Avinoff Shoumatoff), 2007. Cat. no. 27

as monuments of civilization break apart and burn, and a constellation of stars forms an ankh, a symbol of eternity (figure 54). A key element in the story is the survival of the androgynous spirit of Atlantis after the city descends to its final watery grave.

The 1938 Russian-language publication of *Gibel Atlantide* was produced only in a limited edition, now very rare. In 1944, with the support of George Hann, Avinoff published a folio-size version of the illustrations accompanied by his own commentary, describing his work as "a harmonic unfolding, a pictorial 'suite symphonique,' reflecting throughout in some way or other the central theme, the Spirit of Atlantis."[86] Several years later, in 1947 or 1948, he commissioned a set of photographic negatives of the plates and retouched them. This final version, preserved at the Kinsey Institute, endows the Spirits with impressive genitalia, absent (or veiled) in the 1944 edition.[87]

In his optimistic moments, as when he compared Old Russia to New York in his letter to Kinsey of December 14, 1947, Avinoff imagined that a rebirth of gay Atlantis in postwar America was possible. Settling on Long Island with his sister, and then moving to Fifth Avenue in spring 1948, he immersed himself in Kinsey's researches on male sexuality.[88] Their collaboration on a study of human sexuality through the medium of erotic art perfectly suited Avinoff's all-encompassing Silver Age ideology, in which scientific inquiry, artistic creativity, and sexuality are treated as inseparable elements of the human psyche. He introduced Kinsey to his friends, including prominent art museum professionals, painters, and dancers like Ted Shawn; Avinoff's letters to Kinsey discuss Salvador Dalí and the openly gay American artist Paul Cadmus, and his art from that period suggests their influence, as well as that of the Russian painter Pavel Tchelitchew (also homosexual), who had collaborated on Diaghilev's Ballets Russes productions in the 1920s, and who at the time was the darling of the New York avant-garde.

Avinoff bombarded Kinsey with examples of these artists' work in photographs and originals. He also spoke to Kinsey about his great project, "some Foundation or Fellowship which would bring together congenial people with similar emotional patterns and kindred esthetic philosophy."[89] Kinsey, ever cautious about creating public scandal, seems to have advised against anything so overt. Avinoff did describe some of his plans on paper, documents now preserved at the Kinsey Institute. He envisioned an elite men's club with dedicated rooms that would be decorated with frescoes depicting beautiful young men engaged in gravity-defying, anatomically impossible sexual combinations; his fresco designs survive at the Kinsey Institute.[90] The organization would

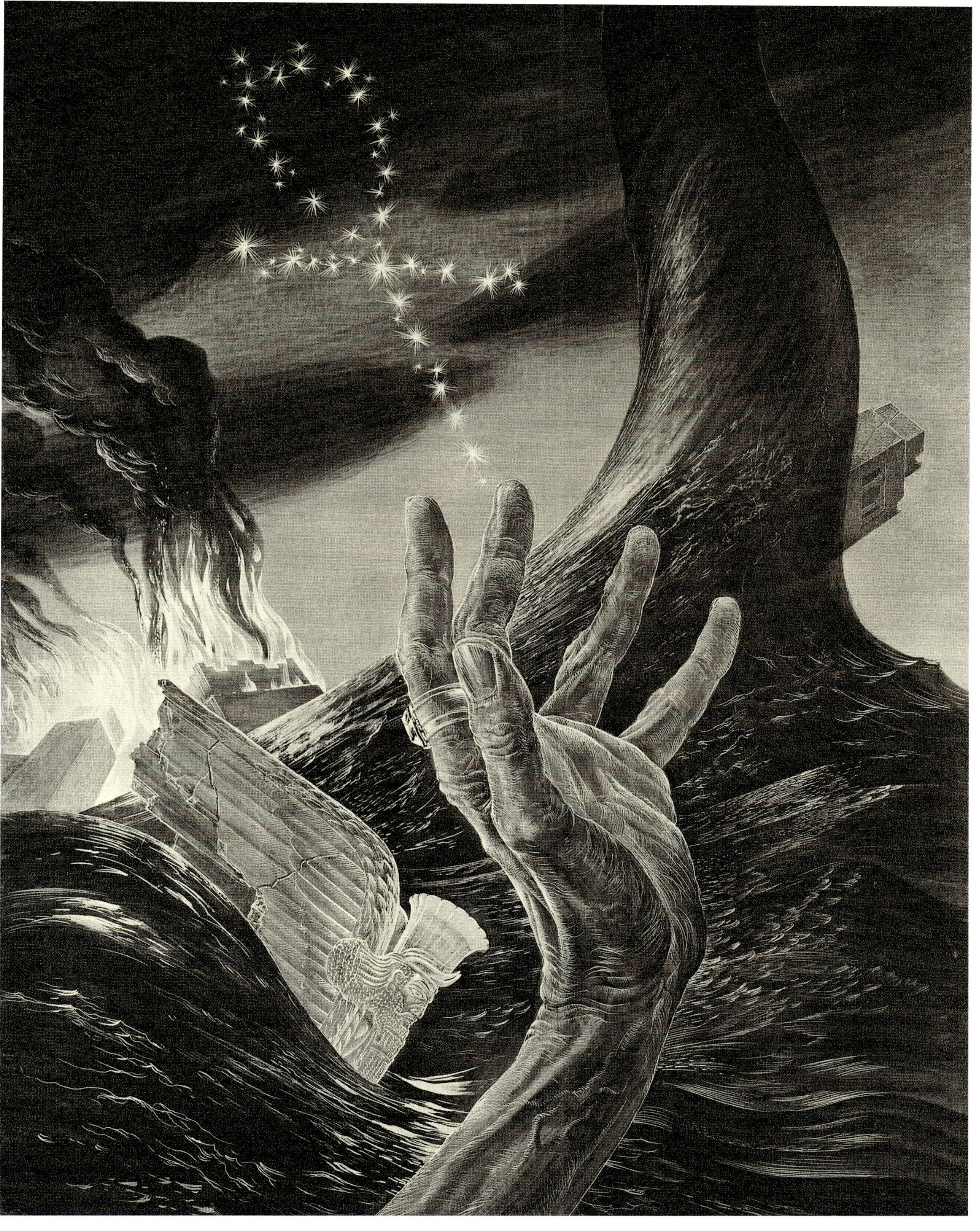

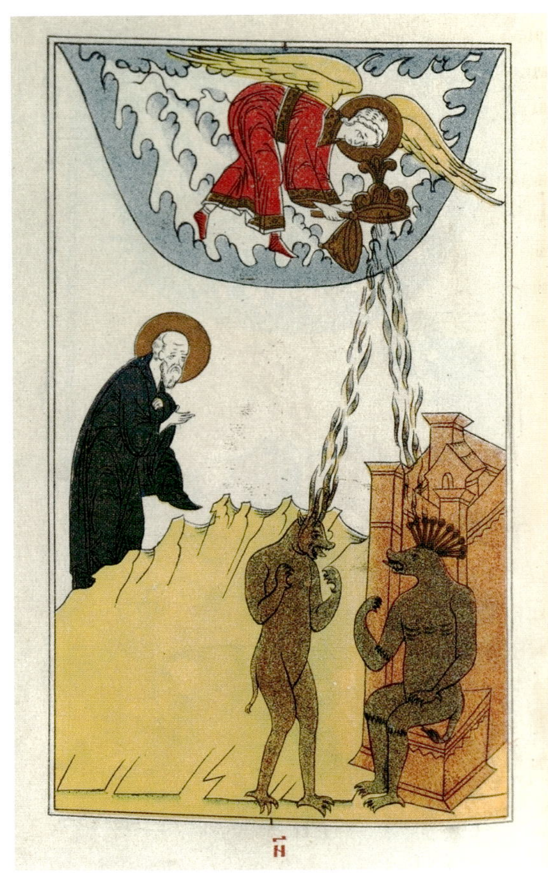

FIGURE 55
Bible, 1910, MS facsimile with leather binding, printed text, and illustrations, Hillwood Estate, Museum & Gardens Library, Washington, D.C., from the Avinoff-Shoumatoff Collection. Cat. no. 65

FIGURE 56
Icon, Anti-Communist Subject, c. 1940, graphite, watercolor, and gouache on pressed paperboard, Victoria Ward. Cat. no. 31

be composed of senior members, whose mission would be to recruit and indoctrinate likely young candidates, such as the handsome paratrooper featured in the composition *WINGS*. Avinoff named this organization "APOCATL"—the etymology of which is unknown. The Shoumatoffs think that it might have possibly inspired the Mattachine Society, one of the earliest U.S. organizations devoted to promoting the rights of homosexuals and educating the public about homosexuality.[91] The organization was founded shortly after Avinoff's death, in 1955.

From Atlantis to Apocalypse was a natural transition for Avinoff, as both entailed catastrophic destruction of decadent empires by winged spirits. Avinoff could apply these legends and symbols to the Bolsheviks' destruction of Silver Age Russia in the 1920s, to his dream of the fall of the Soviet regime in the 1930s, and/or to the defeat of Japan in World War II. Paralleling his development of the Atlantis illustrations, he created a series of apocalyptic compositions based on his rare 1910 facsimile of a thirteenth- or fourteenth-century illustrated manuscript written in Old Church Slavonic, one of the items that later ended up at Hillwood (figure 55).

The earliest such Avinoff interpretations date from the late 1930s or early 1940s, just as war was breaking out in Europe, and they allude to international politics; for example, Avinoff's treatment of Revelation 16:10, where an angel pours the wrath of god on the beast, includes a Soviet hammer and sickle on the throne of the beast (figure 56). Later, in response to the dropping of the atomic bomb, he painted a symbolic image of the four horsemen of the Apocalypse including death on his pale horse (private collection).[92] From there, it was another short step to imagining American military aviators as apocalyptic angels raining death and destruction upon the beast and his followers (figure 57). In May 1948, Avinoff sent some of these works to Kinsey: "You

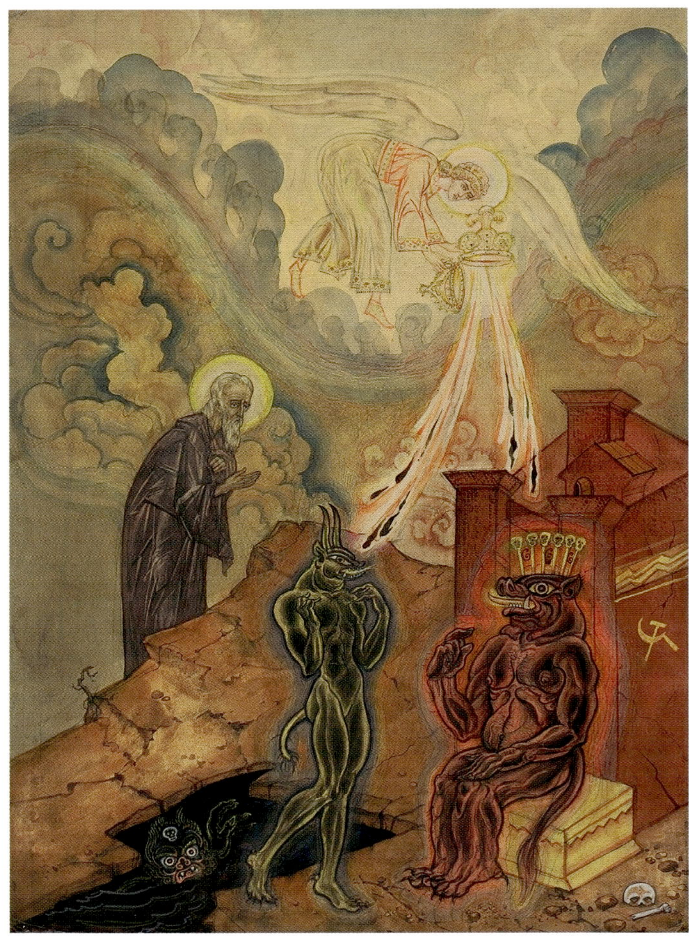

FIGURE 57
Apocalyptic Angel, c. 1945, pastel on paper, location unknown

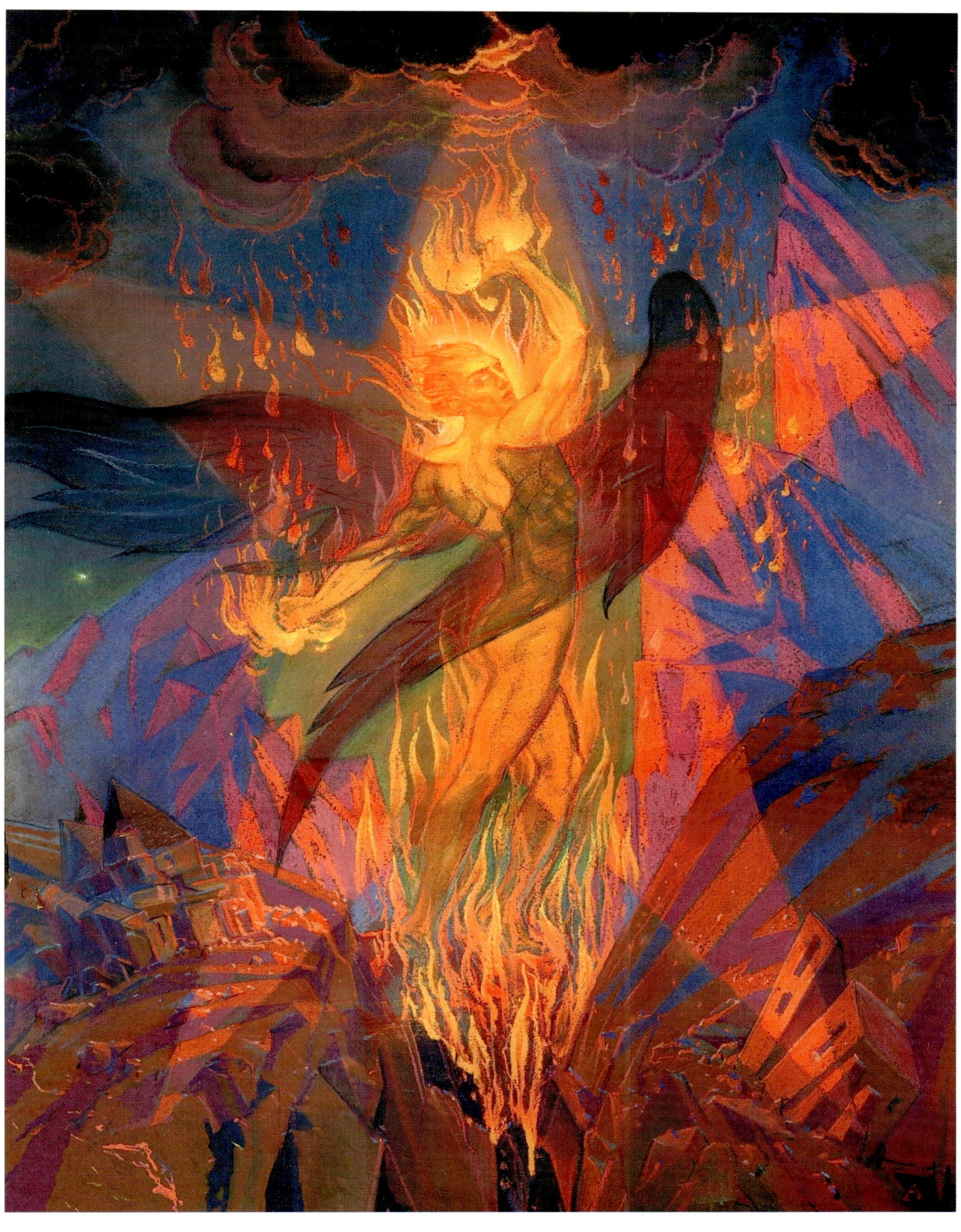

FIGURE 58
Male Nude as Apocalyptic Angel, c. 1940–1945, watercolor and crayon on paper, The Kinsey Institute for Research in Sex, Gender, and Reproduction, Indiana University, Bloomington, 290R Av9586.670. Cat. no. 32

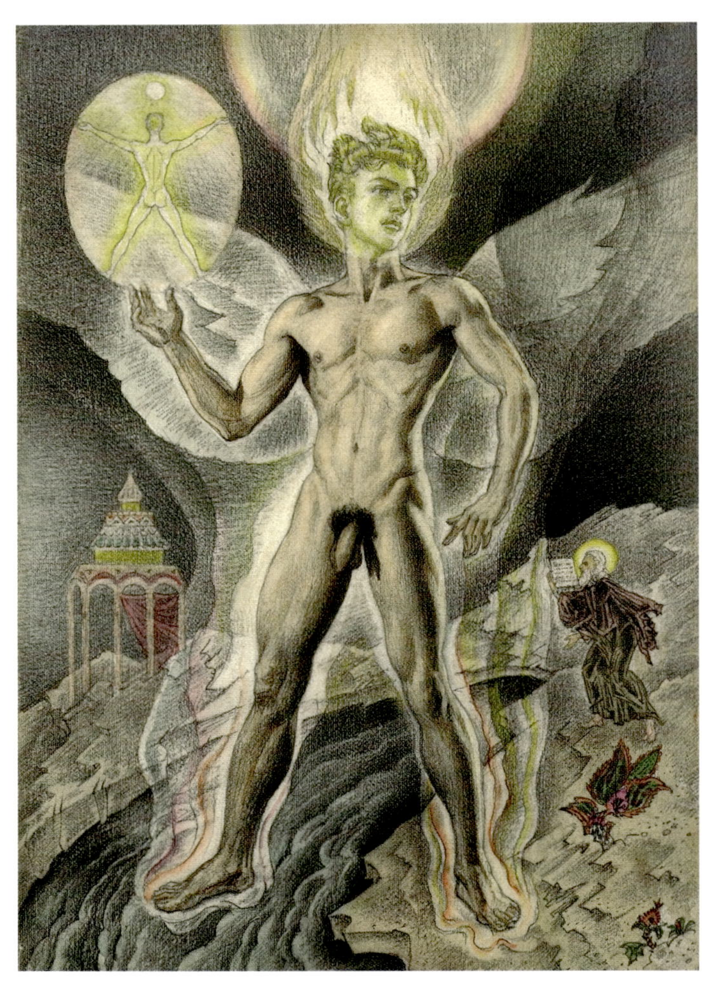

might be interested in an Apocalypse scene, inspired by an old Slavonic book [. . .] with portraits of young men I have known."[93] Avinoff sent Kinsey many of his destroying angels, and the identifications on the versos of several such drawings identify some models as members of the U.S. armed forces. Kinsey's associate Paul Gebhard later recalled, "The blonde young men who were Andre's [*sic*] ideal of spirituality and sexuality were like the bible's account of angels as being spiritual and beautiful" (figure 58).[94] In the Book of Revelation, of course, the apocalyptic angels' destruction of the corrupted world leads to the creation of a new paradise on earth—or a new Atlantis.

These images reveal Avinoff's last great project, a rebirth of the brilliant homosexual culture of Silver Age St. Petersburg in postwar New York, in which he seems to have imagined himself as the Atlantean High Priest. But his frail health, weakened further by his frenetic work with Kinsey, his move to Fifth Avenue, his production of dozens of flower paintings, and his involvement in numerous public exhibitions, seems to have exhausted him. The increasingly illegible handwriting of his letters to Rachel Hunt and Alfred Kinsey suggests that the last year of his life was a difficult one.

His homoerotic illustrations of the mid- to late 1940s are pervaded by an increasing sense of gloom. The outstretched, supplicating, drowning hand from *The Death of the High Priest* (see figure 54) appears in later works, notably the watercolor inscribed "Eddie," where it emerges, along with a despairing self-caricature, other significant body parts, and the beautiful Eddie, from the withered stump of a tree of life (figure 59). With rising frequency, the young male nudes appear in connection with the desiccated trees that seem to be symbolic self-portraits. Likewise, Avinoff's late floral compositions, with titles such as *Disintegration,* depict the collapse, death, and decay of beautiful

FIGURE 59
Eddie, c. 1941–1943, graphite, pen and ink, and watercolor on paper, The Kinsey Institute for Research in Sex, Gender, and Reproduction, Indiana University, Bloomington, 290R Av9586. Cat. no. 41

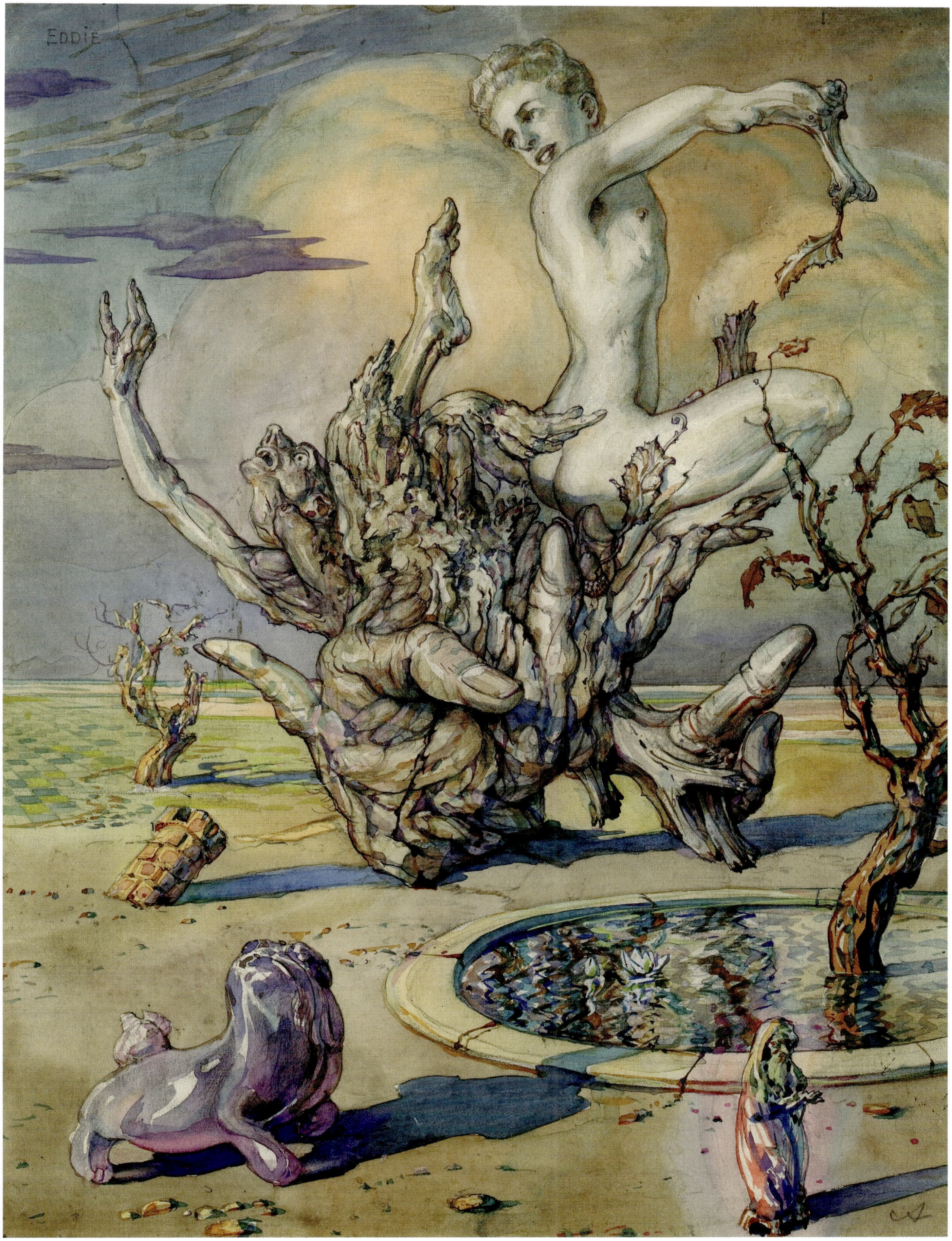

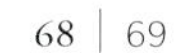

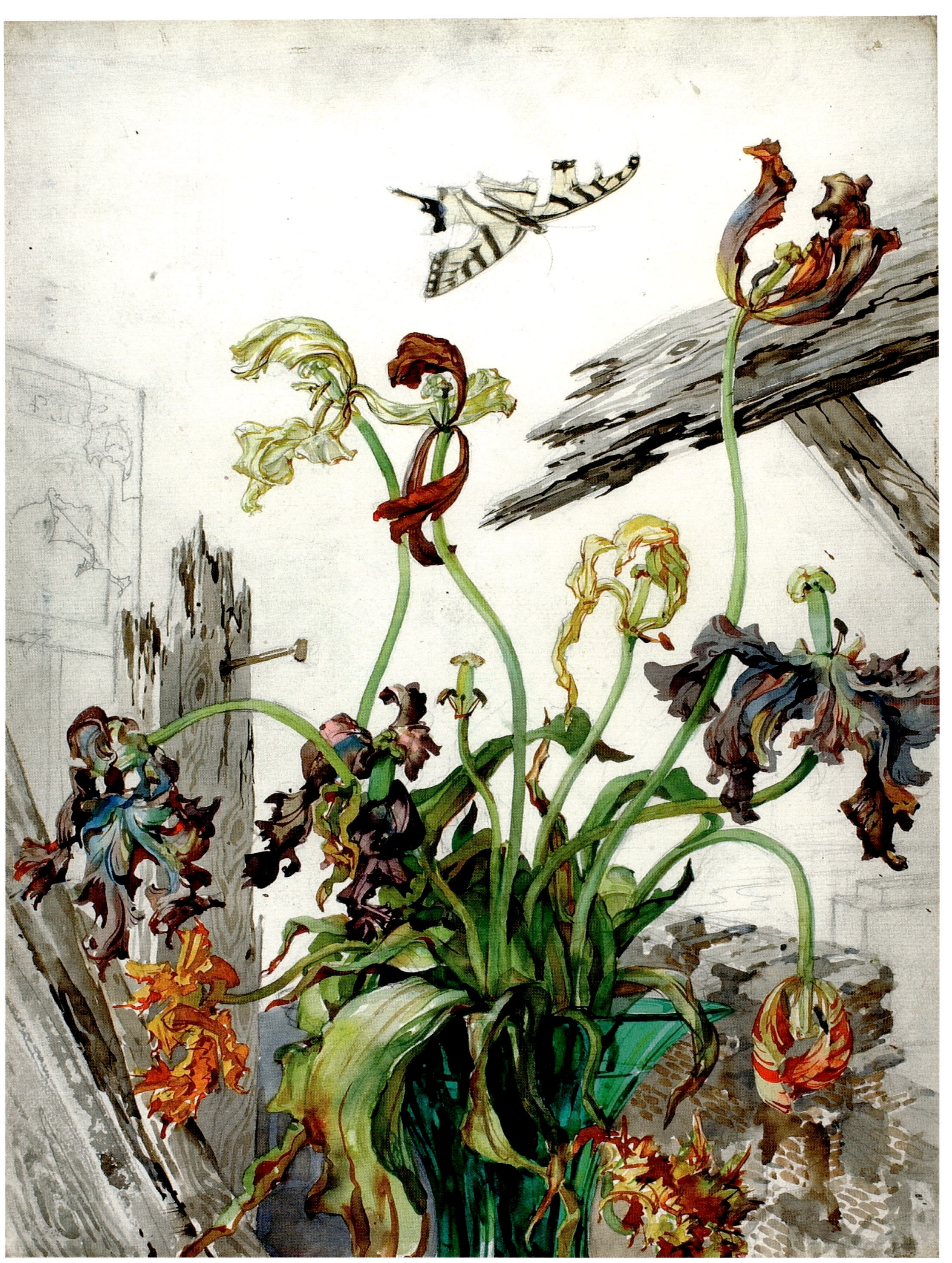

FIGURE 60
Tulips (Disintegration) (unfinished), c. 1949, graphite and watercolor on paperboard, Smithsonian American Art Museum, Gift of Elizabeth Shoumatoff, 1956.11.6. Cat. no. 60

flowers (figures 60, 63). Unlike in *Reminiscences of the House in Russia* or *Iridescence,* the dying flowers do not give rise to generative protoplasmic bubbles or new life. In 1947, he imagined his idol Nijinsky as a wrinkled old man clutching a wilted rose in bitter recollection of the role Avinoff had watched him dance when both were beautiful young men thirty years earlier (figure 61).

Such is the mood of Avinoff's last great visionary work, *Frustration* (figure 62), the pendant to his autobiographical composition *Morpho* (see figure 26). *Frustration's* compositional structure is the same as *Morpho's*, with flowers and lepidoptera in the foreground, stormy skies, and an urban landscape in the distance.[95] But *Frustration* seems to be looking westward—across Central Park from the vantage point of the new apartment at 952 Fifth Avenue—away from his inspirational origins in Russia and Tibet, and toward an American future. The river of life, a narrow, fast-moving stream in *Morpho,* has broadened out and slowed down, and the distant trees are brown and leafless. In this gloomy setting, two rainbows arc downward from heaven; where their prismatic colors meet, a brilliant bouquet of flowers and an image of the deity Guanyin materialize.

The figure of Guanyin appears four times in the painting, as a spectral head in the upper left, a dark silhouette balanced on a pillar, a ghostly head between the brown moth and the pink rose, and, finally, a white porcelain figure in the foreground, at the meeting point of the two rainbows. In the Buddhist religion, Guanyin is the bodhisattva of compassion, whose mission on earth is to relieve human suffering. Guanyin originated as a male, but in modern times appears most frequently as a female. The ability of this deity to encompass both male and female would have appealed to Avinoff, who idealized the androgyne; Guanyin might be seen as a spiritual embodiment of Otto Weininger's theory that every human being contains both male and female qualities.

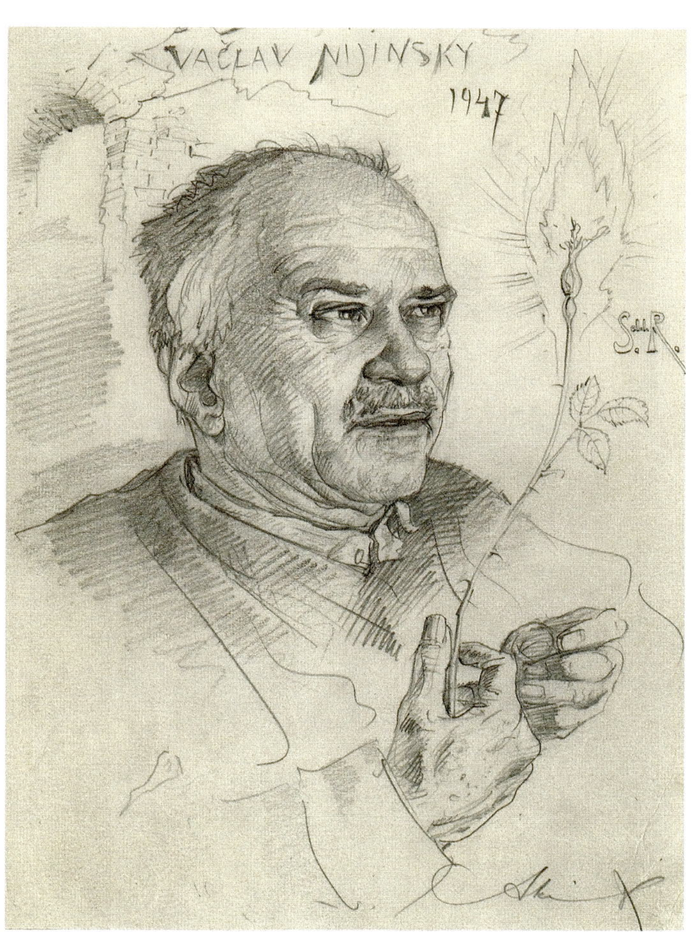

FIGURE 61
Vaslav Nijinsky "Spectre de la Rose," 1947, graphite on paper, The Kinsey Institute for Research in Sex, Gender, and Reproduction, Indiana University, Bloomington, 290R Av9586.565. Cat. no. 48

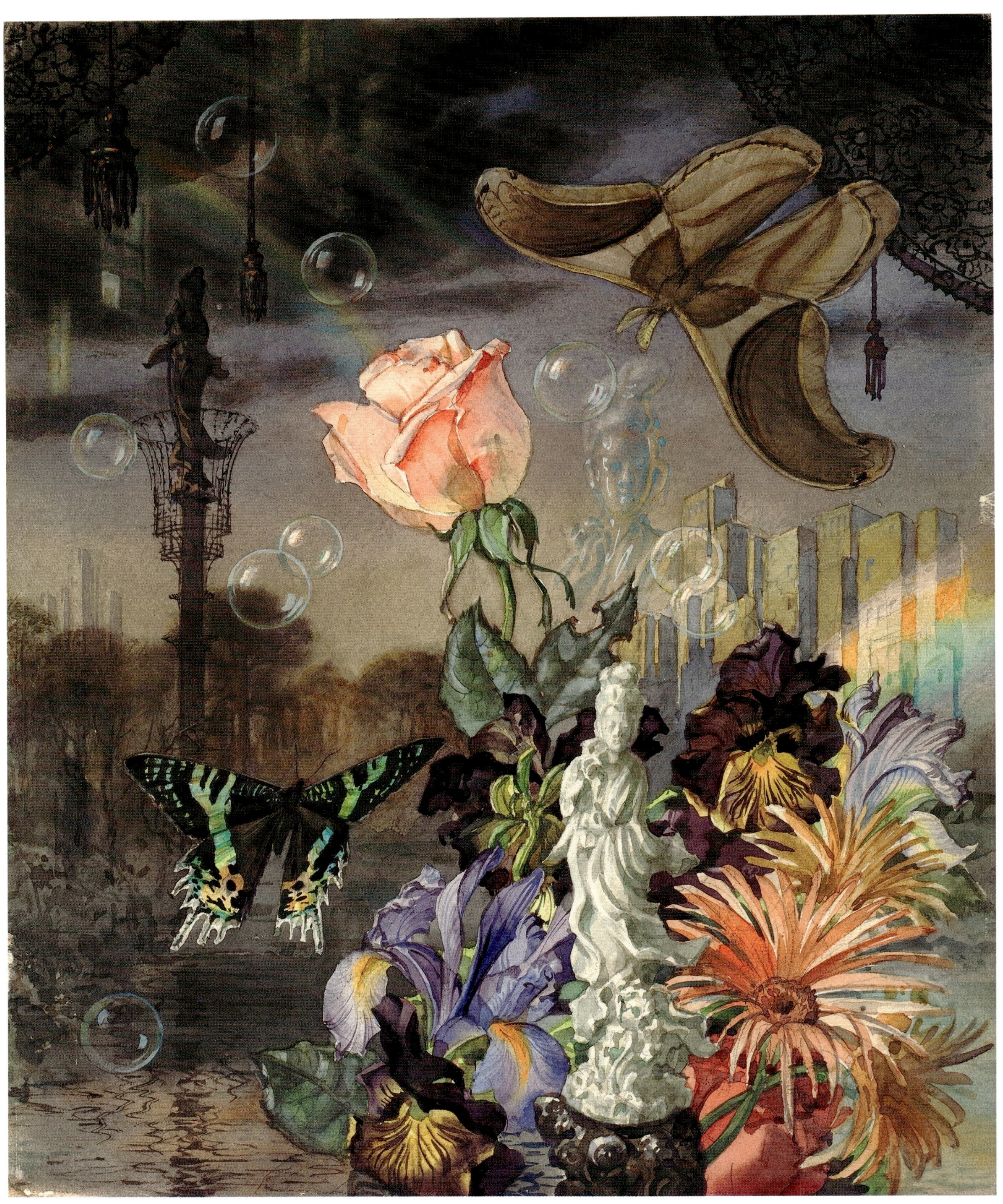

FIGURE 62
Frustration, 1948, graphite and watercolor on paper mounted on paperboard, Carnegie Museum of Art, Heinz Family Fund, 2007.46.3. Cat. no. 51

The meaning of the lepidoptera is more obscure. The brilliantly colored "butterfly" at lower left is actually a moth whose current scientific name is *Chrysiridia rhipheus.*[96] Like *Morpho aega* and *Apatura ilia, C. rhipheus* is another spectacularly iridescent animal highly prized by collectors. Unlike *M. aega*, it is not sexually dimorphic—males and females look and behave alike, giving it a certain Guanyin-like personality. The *M. aega* in *Remembrance of Things Past* (see figure 26) is a female, less iridescent than the male of the species, low-flying, and hard to observe. Eaters of rotten vegetation, carrion, and dung, *M. aega* of both genders are poisonous. As the embodiment of Avinoff's life, it is not a happy animal. Likewise, the yellow lilies it is frequenting usually symbolize greed or falsehood. Most apposite for Avinoff may have been *C. rhipheus*'s classification as member of the family *Uranidae*. In the human world in the nineteenth century, the term "Uranian" was applied to persons with "a female psyche in a male body" who were sexually attracted to men. Avinoff used the term in this sense in his description of the APOCATL fellowship, and it aligns the symbolism of the moth with that of the Guanyin figure. The large brown moth at upper right in *Frustration* is classified as *Rhescyntis pseudomartii* (formerly *R. hippodamia*); unlike *C. rhipheus*, it is nocturnal, secretive, and short-lived—perhaps it represents the antithesis of Avinoff's spectacularly colored, highly visible, Uranian self (as does the *M. aega*)—and the persistent reality of homosexual life in twentieth-century America.

In the 1930s and 1940s, Avinoff attended life-drawing classes at Carnegie Mellon University and Carnegie Institute. Among the others who took classes at those two institutions, and at around the same time, was none other than Andy Warhol. Born and raised in Pittsburgh as the child of Carpatho-Russian immigrants, Warhol began his career drawing butterflies, and went on to become one of the first openly homosexual major American artists—as well as one of the most renowned and controversial artists of all time.[97] It's intriguing to consider these and other parallels between the two artists, as well as what Avinoff would have made of Warhol's Factory, had he lived long enough to see it. With its foil-lined walls replete with icons of Jackie Kennedy, Elizabeth Taylor, and other notables, would Avinoff have recognized the birth of a new silver age?

TODAY, ANDREY AVINOFF stands in paradoxical relation to history. During his lifetime, he was one of the highest-profile Russian cultural figures active in the United States. As a museum director, natural scientist, botanical illustrator, collector, and balletomane, he moved in the most elite political, social, intellectual, and artistic circles in Pittsburgh and New York. However, his own works are small-scale and modest—lectures, watercolor paintings, and musical parodies, instead of novels, oil paintings, symphonies, or ballets—and as a result, his name has all but disappeared from present-day studies of émigré art and culture in twentieth-century America. He has almost been forgotten as a scientist, too, because his Silver Age, aesthetic approach to nature created the illusion of a lightweight intellectual in the macho world of American science. Paradoxical, too, is his growing prominence today as a homosexual artist and advocate, an aspect of his life that he never publicized.

When the known and unknown, remembered and forgotten aspects of his life are reconstituted, Avinoff should rightfully be considered one of the most important survivors of the Russian Silver Age to reach the United States. His influence extended into the familiar fields of art, music, and ballet, but also into less well-traveled territory such as museology, the natural sciences, and public education. Not only did he embody Silver Age ideals and practices in his life and work, he instilled them in the next generation of New York–based artists and intellectuals who would turn that city into the next great center of international modernist culture. Beauty will save the world.

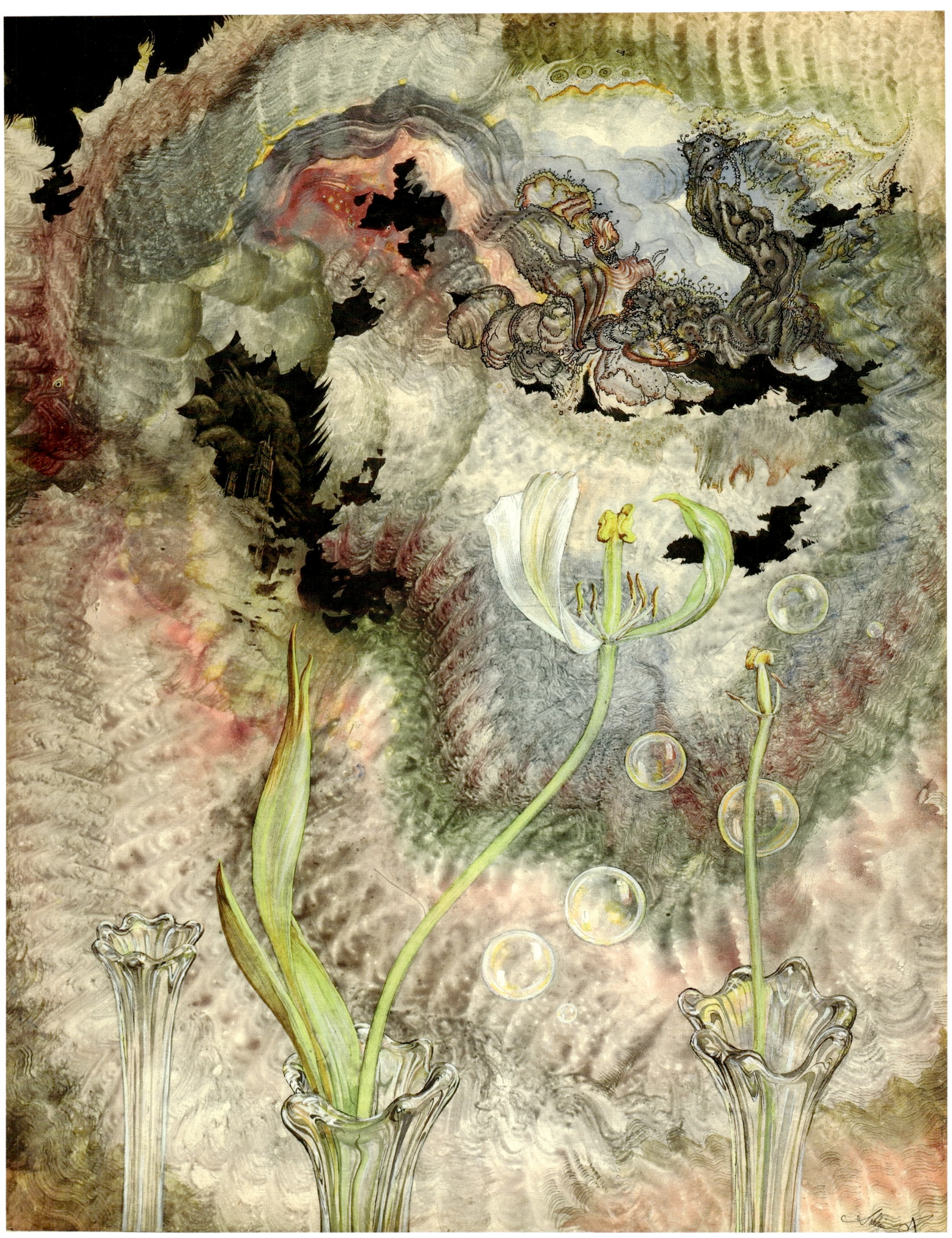

FIGURE 63
The Tulips Are Gone (Impermanence), c. 1945–1949, graphite, watercolor, and gouache with pen and brush and ink on paper, Antonia Shoumatoff Foster. Cat. no. 45

NOTES

1 Fyodor Dostoevsky, *The Idiot*, trans. Constance Garnett, rev. Elina Yuffa (New York: Barnes & Noble, 2004), 351.

2 Virginia E. Lewis and Walter Read Hovey, *An Exhibition of Andrey Avinoff: The Man of Science, Religion, Mysticism, Society, and Fantasy*, exh. cat. (Pittsburgh: Carnegie Institute and University of Pittsburgh, 1953). The exhibition was on view in Pittsburgh December 4, 1953–January 3, 1954.

3 The *Triptych* consists of three watercolors framed together. The central sheet is several inches taller than the flanking designs, suggesting an altarpiece with a central panel and subordinate wings. However, it is unlikely that Avinoff intended these three paintings to form a single work. First, the central panel can be securely dated to 1941, whereas the side panels were executed seven years later. Second, the central panel originated as a Christmas card, whereas the two side sheets are secular in origin and content. Third, the triptych was not included in any exhibition during Avinoff's lifetime. Its frame bears the label of the framer and is dated 1951. Fourth, while all three watercolors share the compositional scheme of flowers and lepidoptera placed in front of architectural landscapes, the stormy skies of the side panels do not match the radiant blues and yellows of the central sheet. Finally, when Avinoff sent Alfred Kinsey a set of annotated photographs of artworks with personally significant content in 1949, he sent only the two side panels. It seems likely that the current association of the three compositions is the work of Elizabeth Shoumatoff as she prepared her brother's paintings for the 1953 retrospective. Today, in order to fathom Avinoff's intentions, the side and central compositions must be understood independently.

4 Eugene F. Januzzi, "Ex-Head of Museum Here Excels in New Paintings," *Pittsburgh Post-Gazette*, April 16, 1949.

5 Geoffrey T. Hellman, "Black Tie and Cyanide Jar," *New Yorker*, August 21, 1948, 33.

6 Alex Shoumatoff, *Russian Blood: A Family Chronicle* (New York: Coward, McCann & Geoghegan, 1982). Portions of this book previously appeared in the *New Yorker*. I would like to acknowledge the wonderful generosity of the descendants of Elizabeth Shoumatoff for so willingly sharing with me their time, knowledge, and collections. Along with my debt to Alex Shoumatoff's published work and personal research, I must also acknowledge Antonia Shoumatoff Foster, whose management of the family archive and independent research on Avinoff has been a constant source of energy, inspiration, and primary material about the artist. Her research and collections are cited frequently hereafter. He Who Stands Firm (Nicholas Avinoff Shoumatoff) and Victoria Ward have kindly provided firsthand memories of "Uncle" and access to their personal art collections.

7 B. Preston Clark Papers, Carnegie Museum of Natural History (CMNH) Archives, 1999-1, Finding Aid, 4.

8 Andrey Avinoff (hereafter "AA") to J. Douglas Stewart, February 24, 1923, CMNH Archives. I am grateful to Kendal Shuber for sharing her copies of this material with me.

9 "Local Music Happenings," *New York Times*, March 9, 1930. Photograph of drawings for an insignia for Ballet Associates, 1942, Kinsey Institute Archives, 290R T2515.378.

10 Hellman, "Black Tie and Cyanide Jar," 32ff.

11 AA to Alfred Kinsey, December 14 [, 1947], Kinsey Institute Archives.

12 AA to Alfred Kinsey, undated [c. January 1948], Kinsey Institute Archives. In the letter, AA apologizes for not recalling Kinsey's visit to Carnegie Museum of Natural History of many years earlier; therefore, this correspondence must have followed soon after the first letter from AA to Kinsey of December 14 [, 1947].

13 AA to J. Douglas Stewart, February 24, 1923, CMNH Archives.

14 *Andrey Avinoff Watercolors: Flowers and Butterflies*, exh. cat. (New York: National Audubon Society, 1953), introduction by Alan Priest, quoted in Dorothy Adlow, "The Home Forum," *Christian Science Monitor*, June 4, 1954.

15 Andrey Avinoff and Walter R. Sweadner, "The Karanasa Butterflies: A Study in Evolution," *Annals of the Carnegie Museum* 32, part 1 (1951). My thanks to John Rawlins, Associate Curator of Invertebrate Zoology, Carnegie Museum of Natural History, for explaining the significance of the article in the context of Darwinian theories of evolution.

16 AA to Nicholas Petkovich, May or June 1948. Carbon copy of the original with Antonia Shoumatoff Foster, communicated to the author in an e-mail, June 30, 2009.

17 "Andrey Avinoff: His Artistic Credo," 2, undated typescript, c. 1945–1949. With Alex Shoumatoff.

18 Ibid., 7.

19 Black-and-white photograph of the painting in Kinsey Institute Archives, 290R T2515.367. The painting contains a pen-and-ink inscription in the lower left corner, in Avinoff's hand: *1925 finished 1947*.

20 John Rawlins kindly identified this insect.

21 *American Heritage Dictionary of the English Language*, 4th ed., s.v. "Protoplasm."

22 Austin Pardue, *He Lives* (1946; reprint, New York: Morehouse-Barlow Co., 1971). Pardue described Avinoff's role in developing the story in a letter to Elizabeth Shoumatoff, December 1, 1969. Original letter with Antonia Shoumatoff Foster. "You probably know that one night we sat up late after I had preached on Life after Death, and discussed, and created a story of a butterfly, growing from a caterpillar to full flight. I have written 11 books, but this story had more recognition than anything I have ever written."

23 Photostat of a letter from Nicholas Shoumatoff to Margherita Langer, June 30, 1976, referring to "a photograph of Heinz and yourself, the Hunts, Uncle Adja, & others in the butterfly costumes." Original with Antonia Shoumatoff Foster.

24 Hellman, "Black Tie and Cyanide Jar," last page.

25 Haniel Long, "Butterflies," *Poems* (1920), reproduced in "Haniel Long," PoemHunter.com, http://www.poemhunter.com/poem/butterflies-3 (accessed October 7, 2010).

26 Hellman, "Black Tie and Cyanide Jar," 32.

27 *New York Passenger Lists, 1820–1957,* Provo, Utah, Ancestry.com Operations, Inc., 2006, ancestry.com.

28 "This Week's Free Lectures," *New York Times*, April 4, 1915.

29 Fiske Kimball, preface to *Wild Flowers of Western Pennsylvania and the Upper Ohio Basin,* by O. E. Jennings, vol. 2 (Pittsburgh: University of Pittsburgh Press, 1953), ix.

30 *New York Passenger Lists, 1820–1957,* ancestry.com.

31 *Gaston & Co., Inc., v. All-Russian Zemsky Union*, Supreme Court of New York, Appellate Division, First Department, November 4, 1927. *Westlaw*. Thomson Reuters, 2009.

32 Paul Chavchavadze, *Marie Avinov: Pilgrimage through Hell* (Englewood Cliffs, N.J.: Prentice-Hall, 1968), 32.

33 *U.K. Incoming Passenger Lists, 1878–1960,* Provo, Utah, Ancestry.com Operations, Inc., 2008, ancestry.com.

34 *New York Passenger Lists, 1820–1957,* ancestry.com.

35 Chavchavadze, *Marie Avinov*, 114.

36 Kimball, preface to *Wild Flowers,* ix.

37 *Selected U.S. Naturalization Records—Original Documents, 1790–1974 (World Archives Project),* Provo, Utah, Ancestry.com Operations, Inc., 2009, ancestry.com.

38 "Stone House in Fox Chapel Sold," *Pittsburgh Sun-Telegraph,* December 22, 1935. Clipping in Pennsylvania Room, Carnegie Library, Pittsburgh, Avinoff clipping file.

39 I would like to acknowledge the assistance of John Rawlins and Mark Klingler, scientific illustrator at Carnegie Museum of Natural History, for the identification of the lepidoptera in this painting. Mary Murtland (Mernie) Berger identified the flowers and their symbolism in this painting as well as its pendant, described later in the essay.

40 Black-and-white photograph in the Kinsey Institute Archives, 290R T2515.369. Inscribed by Avinoff lower left: *1948*; lower center: *Morpho or a Remembrance of things past*. Inscribed by Kinsey lower left: *AA '49*.

41 For example, Salman Akhtar, "A Third Individuation: Immigration, Identity, and the Psychoanalytic Process," *Journal of the American Psychoanalytic Association* 43 (1995): 1051–1084. I am grateful for Dr. Joanne Selzer's insights on the impact of immigration on individual psychology, and on Avinoff in particular.

42 Avinoff note on a printed advertisement for Colgate Florient, 1923, Kinsey Institute Archives, 290R T2515.380.

43 In a 2008 conversation with the author, Mernie Berger recalled attending a debutante ball shortly after Pearl Harbor (December 7, 1941), at which Avinoff admired her Star of Bethlehem corsage and asked to borrow the flowers for a drawing. He sent her the drawing along with his Christmas card, a photogravure reproduction of the Star of Bethlehem painting. John Greenleaf Whittier, *The Star of Bethlehem* (1830), *The Complete Poetical Works of Whittier* (c. 1894; reprint, Boston and New York: Houghton Mifflin Company, 1947), 416.

44 The original drawings from this set are scattered among private collections. They are documented as having been published in *Country Life* in April 1924; however, they do not appear in that issue. The author has seen a printed version of the image with *Country Life Print* imprinted, so perhaps it was issued separately from the magazine.

45 This quote appeared on the printed version of the image offered on eBay, April 29, 2008 (http://wolverinelakechalet.com/ebay). The reference to Tarkington's new novel, *The Midlander* (1924), establishes the date of the image.

46 Chavchavadze, *Marie Avinov,* 33.

47 Inscription on Avinoff portrait drawing of a young boy, Kinsey Institute Archives, 290R Av9586.575.

48 B. Preston Clark Papers, CMNH Archives, 1999-1, Finding Aid, 4.

49 "A Group of Distinguished Rooms. Rose Cumming whose profession it is to create artistic rooms for other people has here used her imagination with delightful results in her own sitting room," *Arts & Decoration* (January 1927): 54. I am grateful to Alex Shoumatoff for a copy of this article.

50 AA to Peter Gray, Professor of Biology, University of Pittsburgh, November 11, 1948. I am grateful to Antonia Shoumatoff Foster for sharing the contents of this letter via e-mail, November 17, 2009.

51 John Thornton, *The Temple of Flora* (London, 1799).

52 AA, typed statement about the exhibition *Flower Paintings by Andrey Avinoff,* Department of Fine Arts, Carnegie Institute, Pittsburgh, 1948. Carbon copy in Carnegie Museum of Art, Avinoff artist file.

53 My thanks to Antonia Shoumatoff Foster for sharing her copy of the list of prices realized at Knoedler's in 1947–1948. Lenders of Avinoff paintings to exhibitions in 1947–1953 included Mrs. Richard King Mellon, Mrs. Alan M. Scaife, Mrs. E. F. Hutton, Halsted B. Vander Poel, Esq., Mrs. T. J. Oakley Rhinelander II, Mrs. Roy Arthur Hunt, Mr. and Mrs. Edwin Bechtel, Mrs. Thomas Hitchcock, Miss Helen C. Frick, Mrs. Ogden Phipps, and Mrs. Roland L. Redmond.

54 AA, [Introduction to an exhibition of Russian art], 2, typescript dated December 11, 1943. With Antonia Shoumatoff Foster.

55 Mikhail Lermontov, *The Demon* (1841), in *The Demon and Other Poems* (Yellow Springs, Ohio: Antioch Press, 1965), 159–197.

56 Penelope Redd, "Andre [*sic*] Avinoff's Works Put on Exhibition by College of Fine Arts," *Pittsburgh Sun-Telegraph,* March 2, 1930.

57 AA, "The Ever New Call," in John G. Bowman, Ruth Crawford Mitchell, and Andrey Avinoff, *Nationality Rooms of the University of Pittsburgh* (Pittsburgh: University of Pittsburgh Press, 1947), 7.

58 Bowman, Mitchell, and Avinoff, *Nationality Rooms,* 119.

59 Ibid.

60 AA, "The Ever New Call," in ibid., 7.

61 AA, "Cooperation in the Museum Field," address to the American Association of Museums meeting, New York, 1936; AA, "Introductory Remarks Made

at the Meeting of the American Association of Museums in Connection with a Project of a Universalium," c. 1944. Both typescripts with Antonia Shoumatoff Foster.

62 Reported in the *Bulletin Index*, February 1, 1940, Carnegie Library of Pittsburgh Pennslyvania Room, Andrey Avinoff clipping file: "The brutal, barbaric, unprovoked invasion of Finland perpetrated by the Soviet Union has justly aroused the condemnation of all decent, liberty-loving people throughout the world."

63 Anne Odom and Wendy R. Salmond, eds., *Treasures into Tractors: The Selling of Russia's Cultural Heritage, 1918–1938* (Seattle: University of Washington Press; Washington, D.C.: Hillwood Estate, Museum & Gardens, 2009).

64 Kristen Regina, "Hillwood Museum & Gardens: The Acquisition of the Avinoff-Shoumatoff Collection," *Slavic and East European Information Resources* 3, no. 1 (January 2002): 35–37. See also Kristen Regina, "Russian Art and Russian Studies in America, 1917–1945," symposium paper, Dartmouth College, October 2, 2008.

65 *Russian Icons and Objects of Ecclesiastical and Decorative Arts from the Collection of George R. Hann,* introduction and descriptive data by Andrey Avinoff (Pittsburgh: Carnegie Institute, 1944).

66 Michael Glenny, "Icons, Fakers, and Fools: The Rise and Fall of the Hann Collection of Russian Icons is a Chronicle of Cupidity, Greed, and Naivete," *Art & Antiques* (April 1984): 49–56.

67 Franklin Delano Roosevelt to AA, July 29, 1933. Original letter in the collection of Antonia Shoumatoff Foster.

68 Vladimir Teteriatnikov, *Icons & Fakes: Notes on the George R. Hann Collection* (New York: Teteriatnikov Art Expertise, Ltd., 1981), 30–31. Copy at the New York Public Library.

69 AA to Nicholas Shoumatoff, cited in Nicholas Shoumatoff, "Andrey Avinoff Remembered," *Carnegie Magazine* 62, no. 1 (January–February 1994): 24–28.

70 AA to Rachel Hunt, dated "Sunday" [August 1945], Hunt Family Archives. I am grateful to the family of Rachel Hunt for allowing access to her correspondence.

71 AA to Rachel Hunt, undated [February 1945], on University Club letterhead, Hunt Family Archives.

72 AA to Alfred Kinsey, January 10, 1948, on Hidden Hollow stationery, Kinsey Institute Archives.

73 AA to Alfred Kinsey, undated [late 1948–early 1949(?)], Kinsey Institute Archives.

74 AA to Alfred Kinsey, December 14 [, 1947], on Hidden Hollow stationery, Kinsey Institute Archives.

75 Dan Healey, *Homosexual Desire in Revolutionary Russia: The Regulation of Sexual and Gender Dissent* (Chicago and London: University of Chicago Press, 2001).

76 Mikhail Kuzmin, *Wings* (1906), trans. Hugh Aplin (London: Hesperus Press, Ltd., 2007), 20.

77 John E. Malmstad and Nikolay Bogomolov, *Mikhail Kuzmin: A Life in Art* (Cambridge and London: Harvard University Press, 1999), 111.

78 Uncatalogued watercolor with inscription on verso, Kinsey Institute Collection. Reproduced with date of 1946 in an uncatalogued photograph in Kinsey Institute Archives, Avinoff box 74.

79 Otto Weininger, *Sex and Character: An Investigation of Fundamental Principles* (1903), trans. Ladislas Löb, edited by Daniel Steuer and Laura Marcus, with an introduction by Daniel Steuer (Bloomington and Indianapolis: Indiana University Press, 2005).

80 Chavchavadze, *Marie Avinov,* 37.

81 AA inscription on a drawing of a Russian bathhouse attendant, Kinsey Institute Archives, 290R Av9586.673.

82 Inscribed on the lower left of the drawing by Kinsey, transcribing a conversation with AA of 1948.

83 Richard Hunt quoting Margherita Langer, letter to the author, May 30, 2010, Carnegie Museum of Art, Avinoff artist file.

84 Vladimir Khazan, "Petersburg in the Poetry of the Russian Emigration," in *Preserving Petersburg: History, Memory, Nostalgia*, ed. Helena Goscilo and Stephen M. Norris (Bloomington and Indianapolis: Indiana University Press, 2008), 124–125.

85 George V. Golokhvastoff, *Gibel Atlantide: Poema* (Privately published, 1938).

86 Andrey Avinoff and Percival Hunt, "Descriptive Brochure" [Fall of Atlantis] (Privately published, Pittsburgh, 1944).

87 In a letter to Kinsey of January 10, 1948, AA mentions, "I am forwarding you a set of photographs of my 'Atlantis' illustrations—not in the subdued state as they were published." Kinsey Institute Archives, Avinoff box 77.

88 The best description of the collaboration is to be found in the final chapters of John Gathorne-Hardy, *Kinsey: Sex the Measure of All Things* (Bloomington: Indiana University Press, 2000).

89 AA to Alfred Kinsey, undated [c. January 1948], Kinsey Institute Archives.

90 Kinsey Institute Archives. Inscriptions on two watercolors, *WINGS* (graphite and watercolor on artist board, 15 x 12 in.) and *The APOCATL Fellowship* (graphite and watercolor on artist board, 11⅛ x 8⅜ in.), uncatalogued.

91 Antonia Shoumatoff Foster interview with Paul Gebhard, Kinsey Institute. Typed transcript courtesy of Antonia Shoumatoff Foster in Carnegie Museum of Art, Avinoff artist file.

92 AA to Rachel Hunt, Sunday [August 1945], Hunt Family Archives.

93 AA to Alfred Kinsey, May 2 [, 1948], Kinsey Institute Archives.

94 Antonia Shoumatoff Foster interview with Paul Gebhard, Kinsey Institute.

95 Black-and-white photograph in Kinsey Institute Archives, Avinoff box 68B, 290R T2515.360. Inscribed by AA lower left: *1948*; lower center: *Frustration*. Inscribed by Kinsey lower left: *AA '49*.

96 Moth and butterfly identifications kindly provided by John Rawlins and Mark Klingler.

97 My thanks to Tom Sokolowski, director of The Andy Warhol Museum, Pittsburgh, for his brilliant suggestion about the possible connection between these two artists.

CHRONOLOGY

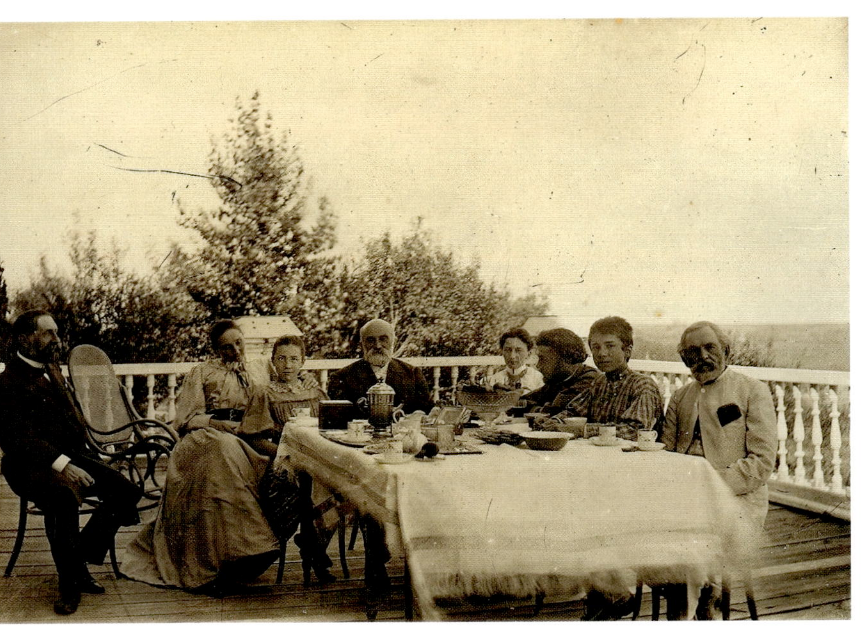

Family portrait at the family estate at Shideyevo, Avinoff second from right, 1898

1884. February 14. Born in Tulchin, Ukraine, the second son of Lieutenant General Nicholas Avinoff and his wife, Alexandra Lukianovitch.

1893–1894. The family accompanies Lieutenant General Avinoff on assignment to Tashkent, Uzbekistan.

1904–1905. Exhibits paintings in Moscow and St. Petersburg.

1905. Graduates from Imperial Law College, Moscow University; accepts government position in St. Petersburg.

1906. Avinoff's brother, Nicholas, marries; his wife's 1968 memoir, *Marie Avinov: Pilgrimage through Hell,* would become the best description of Avinoff family life in Russia.

1908. Inherits money from uncle, Serge Avinoff, which he uses to fund first butterfly-collecting expedition to Russian Turkestan and the Pamir region, Central Asia.

1911. Death of Avinoff's father; Avinoff joins the staff of Tsar Nicholas II as gentleman-in-waiting; transfers to position in protocol in 1913.

1912. Summer. Second butterfly-collecting excursion to Central Asia via India, from Kashmir through western Tibet (Ladakh), over Karakoram Pass to Kashgar and Chinese Turkestan (Tibet).

1914. Owns approximately 80,000 specimens of Palearctic butterflies, one of the largest collections in Europe. August. Russia enters World War I; Avinoff tends to wounded in Lodz, Poland, as part of war effort.

1915. April. Arrives in the United States as representative of All-Russian Zemsky Union to purchase war supplies for the Russian Army.

1916. April. Attends Ballets Russes performance of *Spectre de la Rose* in New York City, featuring Vaslav Nijinsky in the title role. Spring. Returns to Russia. Between 1916 and 1917, paints *Reminiscences of the House in Russia,* while serving as Marshal of the Nobility in province in Ukraine.

1917. February. Liberal Revolution in Russia. Avinoff's brother, Nicholas, joins newly installed Provisional Government. September. Avinoff departs for the U.S., arriving in San Francisco on October 11. Bolshevik Revolution takes place on November 7 (October 25 in the Julian calendar). Provisional Government is overturned, and its leadership subsequently sent into exile.

1918. Onset of Russian Civil War, with the Bolshevik Red Army fighting against the White Army for control of the country. Avinoff's sister, Elizabeth Shoumatoff, and her family arrive in the U.S., settling in New York. March 3. Signing of Treaty of Brest-Litovsk, marking Russia's exit from World War I. December. In Paris for Treaty of Versailles ending World War I, with party of Russian observers led by Prince George Lvoff.

1919. February. Returns to New York. Family estate of Shideyevo is destroyed amid popular unrest in Ukraine.

1920. Civil War in Russia ends with defeat of the Whites.

1921. One-man exhibition at Ainslie Galleries, New York; includes Russian and American subject matter.

1922. December. Soviet Union is established.

1923. Draws advertisements for Colgate-Palmolive. Active as a commercial illustrator and portrait painter until c. 1926. Begins to work intermittently at Carnegie Museum (now Carnegie Museum of Natural History) as curator and researcher in entomology department.

1924. Publishes "Ten Houses of Ten Authors" in *Country Life* magazine, in which he designs homes for best-selling American authors and/or their fictional characters.

1925. Begins work on *Iridescence,* autobiographical painting using butterfly imagery.

1926. Succeeds J. Douglas Stewart as director of Carnegie Museum.

1927. Attends Pittsburgh society gala with friends dressed as butterflies.

1928. September 10. Becomes U.S. citizen.

1930. Joins committee of League of Composers to support staging of avant-garde productions; League presents Igor Stravinsky's *Rite of Spring* and Sergei Prokofiev's *Age of Steel* ballets in 1931–1932.

1931. First butterfly-collecting expedition to Jamaica.

1932. Appointed chairman of the Committee on Museums of Science for the League of Nations; attends meeting in Geneva in July. Begins campaign to promote international cooperation among museums.

1933. February. Death of Avinoff's mother in Merrick, Long Island. U.S. recognizes the Soviet Union. Avinoff begins work on design of the Russian Nationality Room for University of Pittsburgh.

1935. Avinoff builds and briefly occupies a house in the Pittsburgh suburb of Fox Chapel. Asked to speak on "What the World Thinks of Pittsburgh"; famed explorer William Beebe responds, "I can truly say that I consider Dr. A. Avinoff… to be one of the most brilliant and versatile scientists alive today."

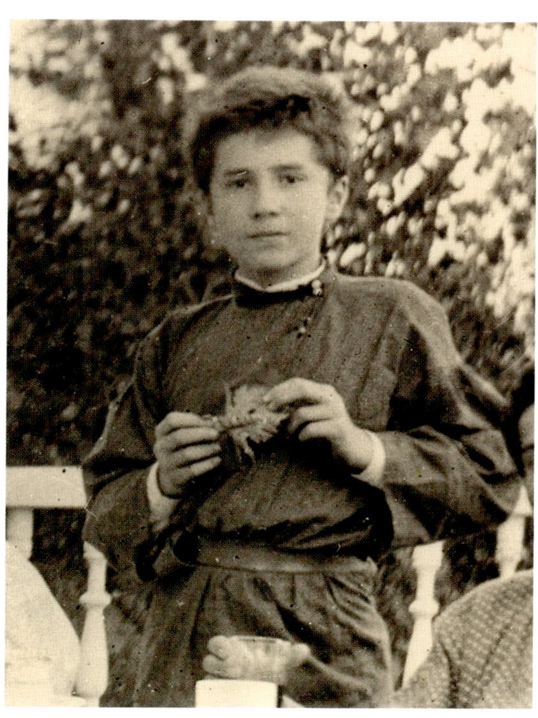

Avinoff with specimen, c. 1898

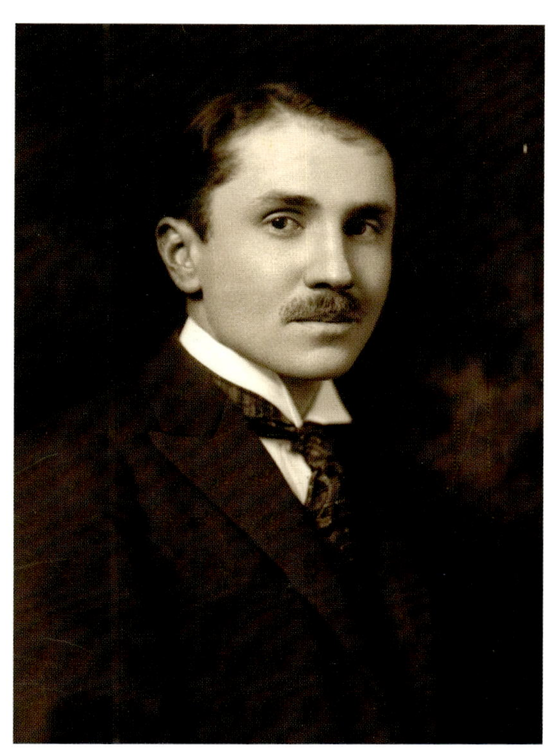

Avinoff as a young man, c. 1905–1915

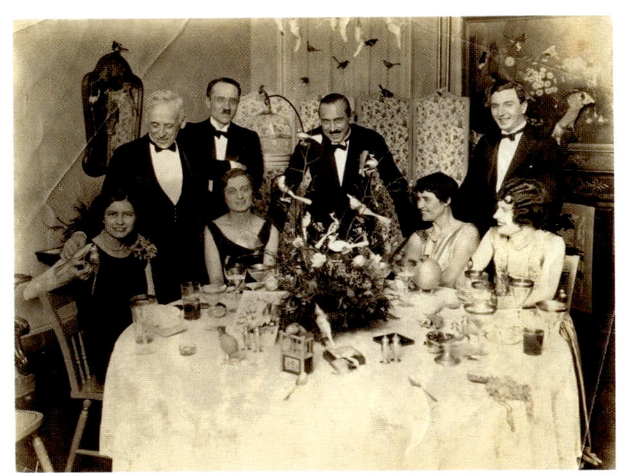

Dinner party with bird theme, Avinoff third from left, c. 1930s

1937. November. Seventh arrest of Nicholas Avinoff in Soviet Union. He is executed shortly afterward, but his death is unconfirmed for many years.

1938. George V. Golokhvastoff publishes poem *Gibel Atlantide* in Russian, with seventeen illustrations by Avinoff. July 8. Opening of Russian Nationality Room, designed by Avinoff.

1939. September. Onset of World War II. Avinoff joins other notables in signing letter of protest against Soviet invasion of Finland.

1941. June 22. Soviet Union enters World War II following German invasion of the country. Avinoff purchases *Tyrannosaurus rex* skeleton for Carnegie Museum from American Museum of Natural History. Opens new Hall of Botany at the museum with improved dioramas. Begins illustrations for *Wild Flowers of Western Pennsylvania and the Upper Ohio Basin;* intense work on publication until 1943. Fall. Attends Pittsburgh debutante ball; paints *Star of Bethlehem* using a guest's corsage as inspiration. December 7. Japanese attack Pearl Harbor; the next day, the U.S. officially enters the war.

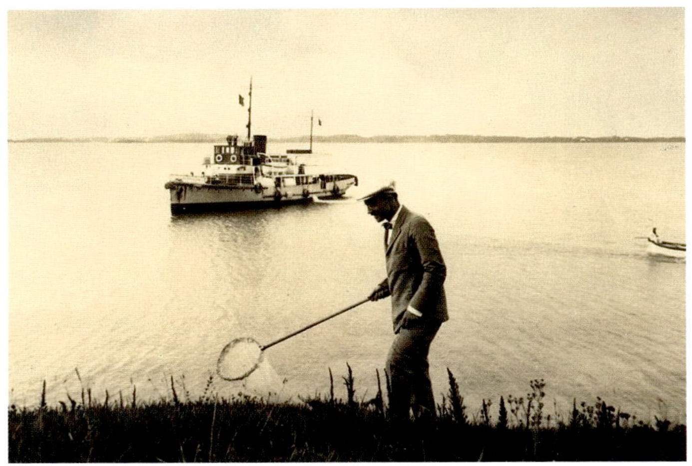

Pursuing butterflies in the Caribbean, c. 1930s

1943. Vladimir Nabokov borrows six female lepidoptera from Cuba (*Phoebis argante*) from "Avinov."

1944. January. The exhibition *Russian Icons and Objects of Ecclesiastical and Decorative Arts from the Collection of George R. Hann* opens at Carnegie Institute, with catalogue by Avinoff. Avinoff publishes *Gibel Atlantide* illustrations in larger format, and in 1948 retouches photographic negatives of the illustrations for limited distribution.

1945. February. Yalta Conference sets out future of liberated Europe. April. Avinoff suffers a serious heart attack. Following his recovery, he destroys most of his homoerotic art, resigns as director of Carnegie Museum (June), and moves to his sister's house on Long Island to continue his recuperation. May. Germany surrenders, ending World War II in Europe. August. U.S. drops atomic bomb on Hiroshima and Nagasaki; Japan surrenders in September.

1946. Episcopalian bishop Austin Pardue copyrights *He Lives,* a fable written with Avinoff's collaboration.

1947. Begins to show and sell flower paintings in New York and around the country. Draws imaginary portrait of aged dancer Nijinsky holding decaying rose, in reminiscence of Nijinsky's performance in *Spectre de la Rose* thirty years earlier. December. After reading preview of Alfred Kinsey's *Sexual Behavior in the Human Male,* writes letter introducing himself to Kinsey. Exhibition of Avinoff's flower paintings at Knoedler & Company, New York.

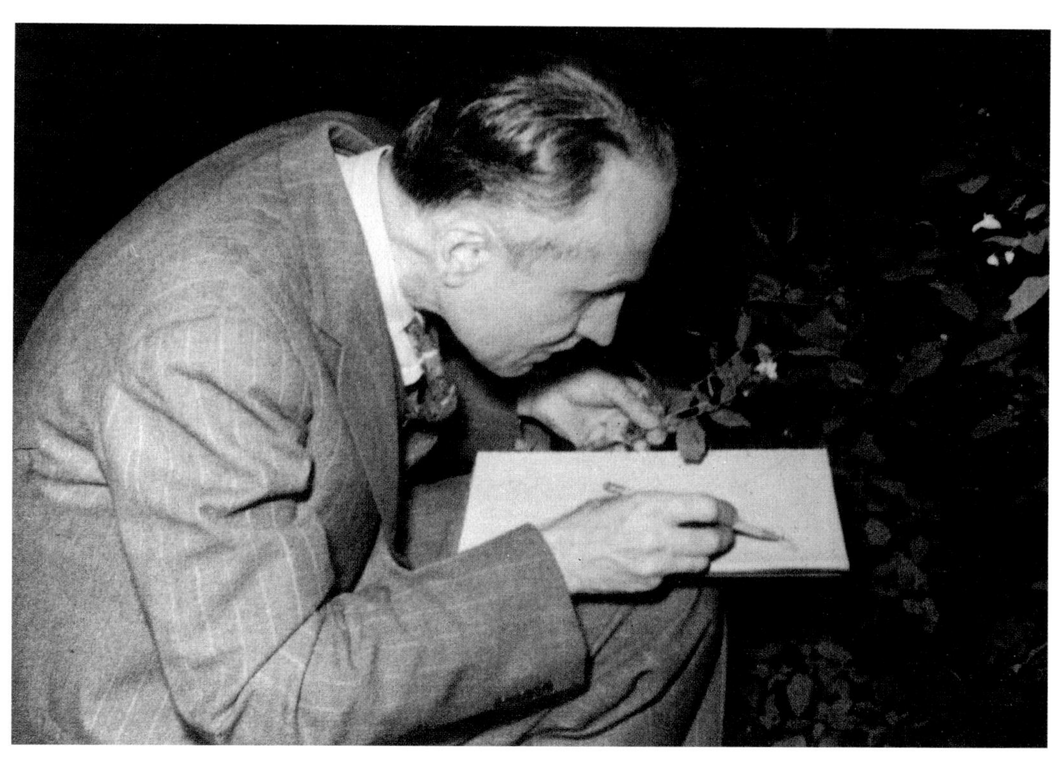

Drawing a specimen for *Wild Flowers of Western Pennsylvania and the Upper Ohio Basin*, c. 1941–1943

1948. January. Kinsey publishes *Sexual Behavior in the Human Male.* February. Avinoff and Elizabeth Shoumatoff move to 952 Fifth Avenue, New York. March. First meeting with Kinsey in New York. June. First trip to Kinsey Institute in Bloomington, Indiana. Paints *Morpho* and *Frustration,* autobiographical paintings. August. The *New Yorker* includes Geoffrey Hellman article on Avinoff. Avinoff develops plan for organization of artistically oriented male homosexuals to be called APOCATL Society. Begins to send artworks, books, and photographs to Kinsey.

1949. Early in the year, receives Afghan butterflies collected by the Third Danish Asiatic Expedition intended for Carnegie Museum; second trip to Kinsey Institute in June; *Life* magazine plans cover story on Avinoff for fall issue. July 16. He dies at Doctors' Hospital, New York, and is buried in Locust Valley Cemetery, Long Island. Kinsey collects materials from Avinoff's homes in New York City, Long Island, and Pittsburgh.

1951. Publication of "The Karanasa Butterflies: A Study in Evolution," co-authored with Walter Sweadner. Family members create *Triptych* by combining three separate paintings, *Star of Bethlehem, Morpho,* and *Frustration,* within one frame.

1953. Retrospective exhibition organized by Carnegie Institute and University of Pittsburgh. Walter Read Hovey and Virginia E. Lewis write catalogue. University of Pittsburgh Press publishes two-volume book *Wild Flowers of Western Pennsylvania and the Upper Ohio Basin,* featuring Avinoff's illustrations.

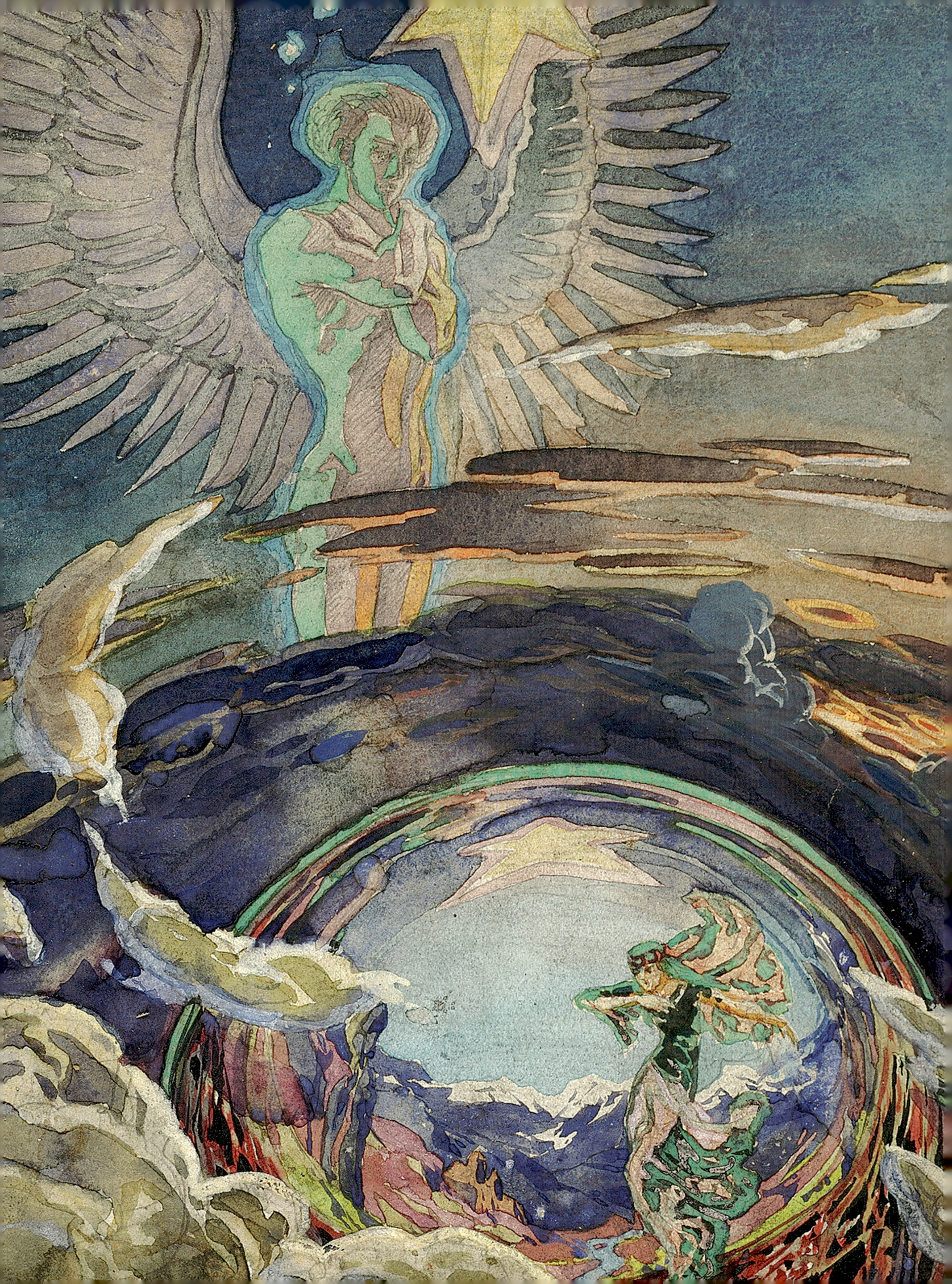

REMINISCENCES OF ANDREY AVINOFF

MY EARLIEST MEMORY OF MY GRANDUNCLE, Andrey Avinoff, whom I called "Djadja," is a fun one—sitting on his lap whirring up the flip-down electric seat lift to his studio-room over the kitchen, where he came to live after his heart attack. He was showing me his magic kingdom, fortified floor-to-ceiling with ancient books, some as high as I, opening mothball-scented wooden boxes of colorful butterflies and many paintings and icons. There was always work underway on the easel, usually one of his endless aquarelle bouquets on Whatman board, which he painted to carry his weight in supporting the family. There were always two large glasses of water, one for mixing and applying washes (what he called "controlled inundation") and the other for dipping and cleaning color off the many sable brushes sticking up in another jar near his little palette. From a small black box containing only cadmium red, cadmium yellow, ultramarine and cerulean blue, zinc white, yellow ocher, burnt umber, alizarin crimson, Prussian blue, and maybe burnt sienna, he mixed his treasury of colors and tones, mostly from three primaries. He showed me all with that authentic attentiveness that lets a child know he is being noticed and listened to. At visit's end, he gave me a smallish box with a huge golden-patterned rhinoceros beetle inside. Only years later did I realize that he had painted the gold decoration on the beetle for me.

Several years later, in the Fifth Avenue apartment where he and my grandmother, Elizabeth, moved in 1948, Uncle again brought me to his studio and asked me (then about seven) to help him as he carried a very wet and elaborate painting into the adjacent kitchen and placed it in the waiting oven: "Now, Nicky, bend way down to look and see that no edge of paper burns after we put it in." Decades later, I realized that this fast setting of thick washes of color in a very hot oven was how he achieved the iridescent effects in his fantastical paintings.

We are a family that has always been surrounded by and immersed in Uncle's creative legacy. Whether at the homes of my grandmother Elizabeth (Mopsy), one of America's premier portrait artists, or at my aunts' homes, or in the huge, museum-like setting of "The Barn" at my parents' house, or later in the dwellings of my siblings and cousins, we have lived among his books and paintings. Soon after his death, a tragedy that affected all of us and prevented the full recognition of his achievement, the

Detail of *Lermontov's Demon, part 1, stanza 9*, c. 1924 (figure 44)

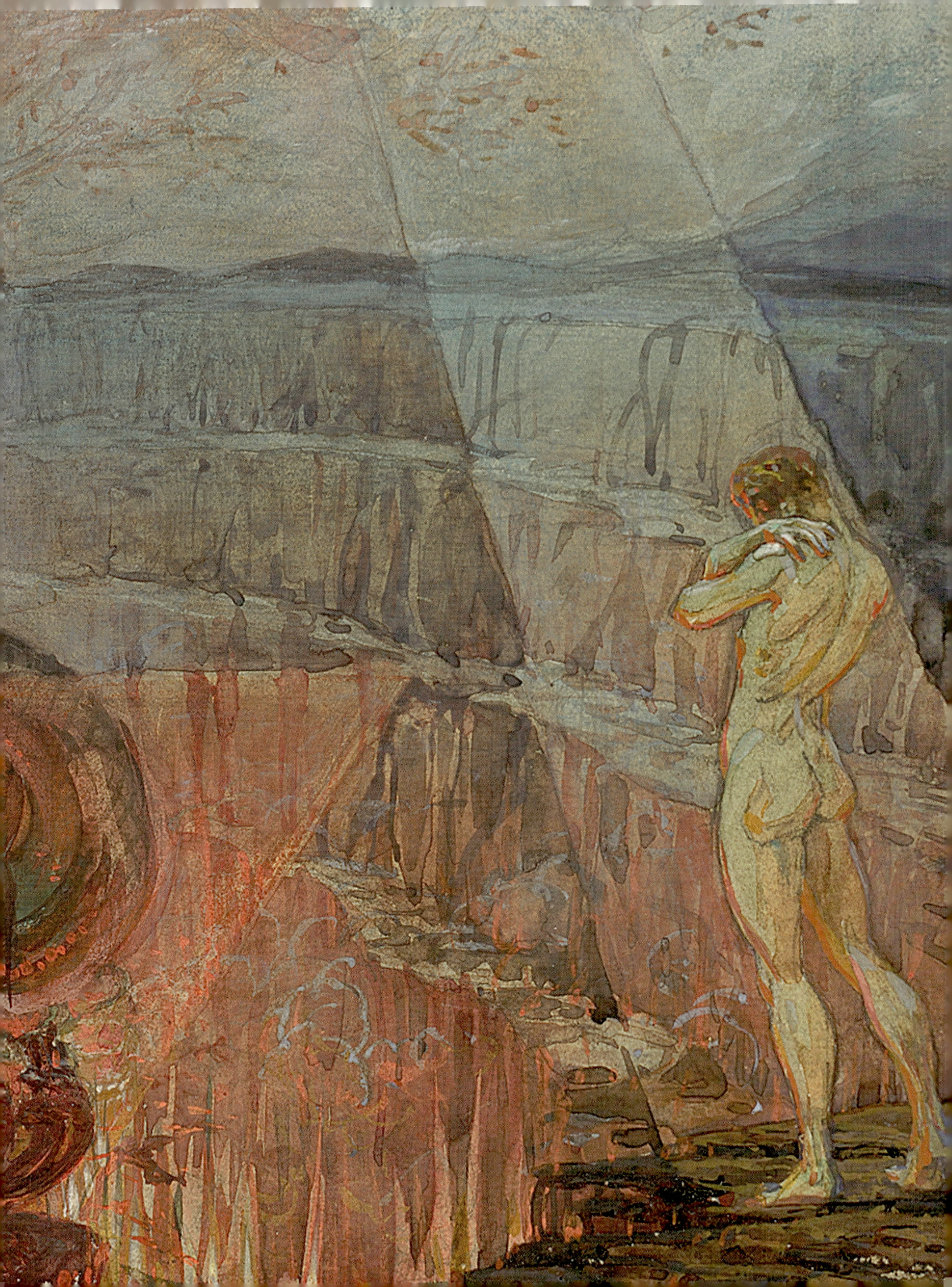

CHECKLIST OF THE EXHIBITION

NOTE TO THE READER

Andrey Avinoff signed his works for publication, exhibition, sale, or gift, but for the most part did not give them titles, and almost never dated them. Between the 1921 exhibition of selected works at Ainslie Galleries, New York, and the 1947 exhibition at Knoedler & Company, New York, he exhibited most of his work privately, if at all. Consequently, this checklist relies heavily on documentation from three sources to establish dates and titles: physical evidence from the works themselves including inscriptions, framing, and labels; the 1953 Carnegie Institute exhibition catalogue (the most extensive record to date of Avinoff's work, compiled by Virginia E. Lewis, Walter Read Hovey, and the artist's family); and the annotated drawings, photographs, and letters at the Kinsey Institute, Indiana University, Bloomington, compiled by Alfred Kinsey in conversation with Avinoff in 1948 and 1949. In all three instances, much of the data were compiled in the last years of Avinoff's life or shortly after his death.

Works are listed in chronological order. Titles are based on published titles where available, and on captions on photographs in the Kinsey or family collections; failing all else, the titles attempt to describe the subject matter. Avinoff's personal iconography combines a wide range of scientific and artistic sources and symbols. Many of these are still to be identified and deciphered, and the annotations are stunningly incomplete in this respect. Dates are based on publications of Avinoff's illustrations, annotations on drawings and photographs at the Kinsey Institute, known exhibitions, or dates in the artist's biography or personal correspondence (for example, the Bermuda drawings probably date from his trips to Bermuda, made in the 1920s and 1940s). As a last resort, the author has ascribed circa dates based on stylistic and technical similarities to other works with documented dates. Avinoff's tendency to work in series and sets over periods of two or three years at a time has provided the rationale behind most of the circa dates. In exhibition histories, dates, titles, or media are provided when they differ from the information given in the object description.

All dimensions are given in inches, height before width, followed by centimeters in parentheses.

Detail of *Sketch for the Last Judgment*, c. 1920–1925 (figure 47)

CAT. NO. 1

Cretan Motif, c. 1911–1915
Tempera on Bainbridge illustration board, 11 x 8 ½ in. (27.9 x 21.6 cm)
Antonia Shoumatoff Foster
Fig. 49

Signed lower right: *A AVINOFF*

Exhibited at Carnegie Institute, Pittsburgh, 1953, no. 216.

This painting has been assumed to be Avinoff's earliest surviving work, possibly dating from his years as an art student in Russia. However, the support is Bainbridge illustration board and the signature is in English, suggesting a date of 1911 (the year of his first trip to England) or later. The technique, using crosshatching to delineate anatomy, is consistent with his early work.

CAT. NO. 2

Ship Deck, 1912
Graphite and watercolor on paper, 9 ¾ x 6 in. (24.8 x 15.2 cm)
Carnegie Museum of Art, Gift of Antonia Shoumatoff Foster, 2009.39.2

CAT. NO. 3

Tibet: Camp Scene in the Karakoram at the Foot of the Mountain, 1912 (recto)
Tibet: Studies of Butterfly and Moth Wings, 1912 (verso)
Graphite and watercolor on paper, 9 ½ x 13 ¼ in. (24.1 x 33.7 cm)
Carnegie Museum of Art, Patrons Art Fund, 2008.12.1
Figs. 6, 7

Possibly exhibited at Ainslie Galleries, New York, 1921, nos. 18–20, 40; Carnegie Institute, Pittsburgh, 1953, no. 8.

CAT. NO. 4

Tibet: Camp Scene at Sonomarg in the Karakoram, 1912
Graphite and watercolor on paper, 9 x 12 ¾ in. (22.9 x 32.4 cm)
Carnegie Museum of Art, Gift of He Who Stands Firm (Nicholas Avinoff Shoumatoff), 2007.50.2

Possibly exhibited at Ainslie Galleries, New York, 1921, nos. 18–20, 40; Carnegie Institute, Pittsburgh, 1953, no. 7.

CAT. NO. 5

Tibet: Monastery in the Mountains, 1912
Graphite and watercolor on paper, 9 x 12 ¾ in. (22.9 x 32.4 cm)
Carnegie Museum of Art, Patrons Art Fund, 2008.12.3
Fig. 8

Possibly exhibited at Ainslie Galleries, New York, 1921, nos. 18–20, 40; Carnegie Institute, Pittsburgh, 1953, no. 12.

Reproduced in Nicholas and Nina Shoumatoff, eds., *Around the Roof of the World* (Ann Arbor: University of Michigan Press, 1996), chap. 2 (*A Buddhist Chorten at Gya, Karakorams*).

CAT. NO. 6

Tibet: Mountain with Camp Scene in the Karakoram, 1912
Graphite and watercolor on paper, 12 ¾ x 9 in. (32.4 x 22.9 cm)
Carnegie Museum of Art, Patrons Art Fund, 2008.12.2

Possibly exhibited at Ainslie Galleries, New York, 1921, nos. 18–20, 40; Carnegie Institute, Pittsburgh, 1953, no. 9.

CAT. NO. 7

Nightmare of Faces, 1915
Graphite and watercolor with ink and chalk on paper, 12 ½ x 8 ¾ in. (31.8 x 22.2 cm)
Carnegie Museum of Art, Gift of He Who Stands Firm (Nicholas Avinoff Shoumatoff), 2007.50.4
Fig. 25

Exhibited at Ainslie Galleries, New York, 1921, no. 2 (*Nightmare*); Carnegie Institute, Pittsburgh, 1953, no. 156.

According to the 1953 catalogue, this image was inspired by a nightmare following a séance, which Avinoff found "repulsive." It may also allude to the horrors of World War I. This is the earliest known example of Avinoff's use of "morphs" (one form flowing or "morphing" into something else) as a compositional device, anticipating by decades the Surrealism of Salvador Dalí and Pavel Tchelitchew.

CAT. NO. 8

Portrait of Nijinsky, 1916
Graphite on paper mounted on card, 10 x 8 in. (25.4 x 20.3 cm)
Victoria Ward

Inscribed center left by Avinoff: *W.NIJINSKY. / N.Y. 1916*; monogrammed lower right: *A* [in circle]

Exhibited at Ainslie Galleries, New York, 1921, no. 13 (*Portrait of V. Nijinsky, Cubist Suggestion*); Carnegie Institute, Pittsburgh, 1953, no. 154.

CAT. NO. 9

Reminiscences of the House in Russia, 1916–1917
Watercolor on paper mounted on card, 12 ½ x 9 in. (31.8 x 22.9 cm)
Victoria Ward
Figs. 21, 22

Monogrammed lower left in gold: *A* [in circle]

Exhibited at Ainslie Galleries, New York, 1921, no. 1 (*Reminiscences of My Country House*); Carnegie Institute, Pittsburgh, 1953, no. 157. Label on the back of the frame reads: *For exhibition at the Montclair Art Museum / Reminiscence of* [loss] *Shedéevo 1917.*

Most of the detail in this painting has been executed in stipple—minute dots of pigment from the tip of a very small brush. The technique, which Avinoff learned as a youth, is most commonly used for miniature paintings on ivory.

CAT. NO. 10

Tsar's Crown and Crown of Thorns in Stormy Landscape, c. 1917
Graphite, pen and ink, and ink wash heightened with white on paper, 7 ¼ x 11 in. (18.4 x 27.9 cm) (image); 9 ¾ x 14 in. (24.8 x 35.6 cm) (sheet)
Antonia Shoumatoff Foster
Fig. 24

CAT. NO. 11

Nijinsky as Faun, 1918
Ink and watercolor with gilding on paper, 9 x 6 ⅜ in. (22.9 x 16.2 cm) (sheet)
The Kinsey Institute for Research in Sex, Gender, and Reproduction, Indiana University, Bloomington, 290R Av9586.186
Fig. 51

Inscribed on mount by Kinsey: *1918*

Exhibited at Kinsey Institute, Indiana University, Bloomington, 2005, no cat. no.; Kinsey Institute, Indiana University, Bloomington, 2009, no cat. no.

The insect appears to be a hawkmoth, the collecting focus of B. Preston Clark, who befriended Avinoff in 1916 and promoted his entomological career in the United States.

CAT. NO. 12

Modern Music: Jazz Symphony, c. 1920–1925
Photogravure on paper, 12 x 8 in. (30.5 x 20.3 cm) (sheet)
Antonia Shoumatoff Foster
Fig. 4

Exhibited at Carnegie Institute, Pittsburgh, 1953, no. 160 (*Satire on Modern Music,* c. 1920).

Avinoff sent a black-and-white photograph of this composition to Kinsey with the following annotation on the back:

Modern music
Jazz symphony

This composition without any sexual connotations strives to reflect the confusion of a Jazz age in music. It was done at the time when Morris Guest [sic]*—with his typical racial features—was such a conspicuous figure among promotors* [sic] *of shows and "super colossal" attractions.*

Audience, admirers, gosts [sic], *cataracts of hands, huge ears, key boards on quicksands, fingers twirling passages and runs on pianos and violins, overcoats and programs . . . are spare parts of a continuum of inanities. The whole suggest an empty explosion* [sic].

Technically it might be interested [sic] *to note that the pen-and-ink manner is different in every part of the picture in the spirit of wasted precision and conflict of styles.*

Morris Gest's heyday as a Broadway producer spanned the years 1919–1924, suggesting likely execution dates for this drawing. Caricatures in the center foreground may represent Igor Stravinsky and Sergei Prokofiev. Antonia Shoumatoff Foster owns a copper-faced printing plate of the design, but the date and purpose of publication are unknown.

CAT. NO. 13

Sketch for the Last Judgment, c. 1920–1925
Graphite and watercolor heightened with white and gold on paper mounted on board, 21 ½ x 14 ½ in. (54.6 x 36.8 cm) (sheet)
Antonia Shoumatoff Foster
Fig. 47

Subject matter and technique suggest a date close to the Mikhail Lermontov *Demon* illustrations. The work might be identified with *Sketch for the Last Judgment,* watercolor and gouache, c. 1920, exhibited at Carnegie Institute, Pittsburgh, 1953, no. 56. The iconography combines elements of the Fall of Man (angel with flaming sword, Tree of Knowledge, serpentine Satan and repentant human figures) and the Apocalypse (opening scrolls in the heavens), along with Masonic symbols (golden triangle with eye of God in the heavens, burning triangle pointing downward in the realms of Hell). At the center of the lower edge, a tiny female figure, possibly the Whore of Babylon, seems to ride the Beast of the Apocalypse with multiple crowned heads. The five-pointed star on the serpent's forehead is Avinoff's symbol for the demonic. In another, more fully elaborated, version of the subject (location unknown, recorded in a black-and-white photograph in the collection of Antonia Shoumatoff Foster), the Tree of Knowledge has been eliminated and a castle added in the foreground.

CAT. NO. 14

The Bridge below Honk Falls at Naponoch, c. 1921
Pastel on illustrator's board, 14 ¾ x 18 ¾ in. (37.5 x 47.6 cm)
Carnegie Museum of Art, Second Century Acquisition Fund, 2007.47
Fig. 11

Probably exhibited at Ainslie Galleries, New York, 1921, no. 27 (*Under the Bridge*).

CAT. NO. 15

The Machinist, 1922
Graphite, crayon, and gouache on paper, 13 x 8 in. (33 x 20.3 cm) (sheet, irreg.)
The Kinsey Institute for Research in Sex, Gender, and Reproduction, Indiana University, Bloomington, 290R Av 9586.215
Fig. 52

Inscribed lower left by Kinsey: *Rejected by the publishers "because too much of a display of masculine charms."* Kinsey wrote the date *1922* and *AA 1948* (presumably the date they discussed the drawing) on the mount.

CAT. NO. 16

Tibet: A Caravan of Yaks on the Table-Land beyond Zoji-La, c. 1922
Pen and India ink on Bristol paper, 8 x 10 ⅜ in. (20.3 x 26.4 cm)
Carnegie Museum of Art, Gift of Antonia Shoumatoff Foster, 2008.26

Exhibited at Carnegie Institute, Pittsburgh, 1953, no. 10.

Reproduced in *Century Magazine* (January 1922), unpaginated; *Pittsburgh Record* (April 1931), unpaginated; Nicholas and Nina Shoumatoff, eds., *Around the Roof of the World* (Ann Arbor: University of Michigan Press, 1996), chap. 2.

The drawing, in a medium Avinoff used almost exclusively for work intended for publication, corresponds to no known studies from the 1908–1912 expeditions to the Pamir region and Tibet, which were mostly in watercolor. Possibly the original is lost, or this may be a later composite from on-the-spot drawings and/or memories and photographs.

CAT. NO. 17

Cave Interior, c. 1923
Pastel on black paper, 13 ½ x 10 ¼ in. (34.3 x 26 cm) (sheet)
Antonia Shoumatoff Foster
Fig. 15

Exhibited at Carnegie Institute, Pittsburgh, 1953, no. 28.

According to the 1953 catalogue, Avinoff made several such drawings during a Carnegie Museum expedition to Huntingdon County, Pennsylvania, possibly to collect materials and views for museum dioramas. Others from the set are in the collections of Antonia Shoumatoff Foster and Carnegie Museum of Art.

CAT. NOS. 18–19

Two illustrations for Mikhail Lermontov's *Demon,* c. 1924

Lermontov's Demon, part 1, stanzas 3–4
Graphite and watercolor on paper, 7 ⅜ x 7 ⅝ in. (18.7 x 19.4 cm)
Victoria Ward
Fig. 45

The exiled Demon in his flight
Beheld the Caucasus below:
Kazbék with peaks of diamond light
Aglow in their eternal snow
And, lower, like a trail of night,
Like a writhing serpent darkly coiling,
The chasm Daryàl; . . .
(*Demon,* part 1, stanza 3)

Before him then another scene
Spread far of beauty fair and tender:
The Gruzian vales lay robed in green
Like carpets rich in woven splendor.
(*Demon,* part 1, stanza 4)

Lermontov's Demon, part 1, stanza 9
Graphite and watercolor on paper, 13 x 10 ¼ in. (33 x 26 cm)
Antonia Shoumatoff Foster
Fig. 44

The Demon saw. . . . A strange elation
And pangs of wondrous adoration,
With music of some blissful rest
And harmonies of spheres above,
Then filled his lonely barren breast
With beauty, holiness, and love.
He watched the scene before him, feeling
His dreams of old and his unrest,
The dreams arising in his mind
Like star upon a star, revealing
The bliss of Heaven left behind.
(*Demon,* part 1, stanza 9)

Mikhail Lermontov, *The Demon and Other Poems,* trans. Eugene M. Kayden (Yellow Springs, Ohio: Antioch Press, 1965), pp. 159, 160–161, 164–165.

Exhibited at Carnegie Mellon University, 1930 (*Caucasian Saga*); one image from the set was included in Carnegie Institute, Pittsburgh, 1953, no. 59 (*Illustration for Lermontov's Demon*). Another illustration from the set at the Kinsey Institute is dated *1924* in Avinoff's handwriting on verso (A290R Av9586.455).

Judging from the many small, finished watercolors relating to Lermontov's *Demon* that survive today, Avinoff seems to have planned to illustrate the entire poem, stanza by stanza. The connection of Cat. no. 19 to Lermontov was lost by the 1970s, when it was called *Worlds*. The set is now scattered, so it has not been possible to determine whether Avinoff ever completed the project.

CAT. NO. 20
Iridescence, 1925/1947
Graphite, pen and ink, and watercolor on paper mounted on artist's board, 13 15/16 x 9 7/8 in. (35.2 x 25.1 cm)
Carnegie Museum of Art, Bequest of Howard Noble, by exchange, and the Margaret M. Vance Fund, 2008.81
Figs. 16, 17

Exhibited at Knoedler & Company, New York, 1947, no. 35; Carnegie Institute, Pittsburgh, 1948, no. 25; Cranbrook Institute of Science, Toledo, 1948, no. 13; Carnegie Institute, Pittsburgh, 1953, no. 65 (*The Chrysalis: Passage of the Flight of Time*). The title and dates are based on Kinsey's and Avinoff's inscriptions on a photograph of the painting at the Kinsey Institute (290R T2515.367).

CAT. NO. 21
"Persian" St. Francis, c. 1925
Gouache on card, 11 ¾ x 10 ¾ in. (29.9 x 27.3 cm) (sight)
He Who Stands Firm (Nicholas Avinoff Shoumatoff)
Fig. 50

Signed lower right: *A AVINOFF*

Exhibited at Carnegie Mellon University, March 1930, no cat. no.; Carnegie Institute, Pittsburgh, 1953, no. 222.

CAT. NO. 22
Bubbles and Rainbow, c. 1925–1930
Pastel on black card, 13 ½ x 9 ½ in. (34.3 x 24.1 cm)
Antonia Shoumatoff Foster
Fig. 12

CAT. NO. 23
Bermuda, c. 1927–1928
Watercolor on paper, 8 ¾ x 7 in. (22.2 x 17.8 cm)
The Kinsey Institute for Research in Sex, Gender, and Reproduction, Indiana University, Bloomington, 290R Av9586.303

CAT. NO. 24
Pterodactyls: Forerunners of the Airplane!, 1928
Pen and ink on paper, 11 ½ x 7 ¼ in. (29.2 x 18.4 cm)
Carnegie Museum of Art, Patrons Art Fund, 2009.36.4

Avinoff drew pterodactyls to illustrate his article "A Treasury from Many Lands," an overview of his plans for Carnegie Museum of Natural History, published in the *Pittsburgh Record* 3 (October 1928), p. 36.

CAT. NO. 25
Album, after 1931

Colgate's Cashmere Bouquet with the Tomb of Tamerlane, c. 1923
Photo offset lithograph on paper, 8 ½ x 6 in. (21.6 x 15.2 cm)

Colgate's Cashmere Bouquet with Paisley Shawl, c. 1923
Photo offset lithograph on paper, 10 ¼ x 8 ½ in. (26 x 21.6 cm)
Antonia Shoumatoff Foster
Fig. 27

The album was manufactured in 1931. It contains clippings of Avinoff's commercial illustrations from the 1920s, examples of his privately printed Christmas cards, and some later privately commissioned work, as well as a 1964 card from Elizabeth Shoumatoff.

CAT. NOS. 26–27
Two plates from *The Fall of Atlantis,* designed c. 1935–1938, folio edition published in 1944

At the Gates of Immortality, plate 15
Gravure on paper, 14 ⅛ x 10 ½ in. (35.9 x 26.7 cm) (image), 21 x 16 ½ in. (53.3 x 41.9 cm) (sheet)

The Death of the High Priest, plate 17
Gravure on paper, 13 ½ x 10 ½ in. (34.3 x 26.7 cm) (image), 21 x 16 ½ in. (53.3 x 41.9 cm) (sheet)
Carnegie Museum of Art, Gift of He Who Stands Firm (Nicholas Avinoff Shoumatoff), 2007
Figs. 53–54

Avinoff created his designs for *The Fall of Atlantis* in response to the lengthy poem *Gibel Atlantide*, by the Russian émigré poet George V. Golokhvastoff. The Avinoff illustrations and his explanatory text were published in the poem's quarto Russian-language edition in 1938 as an appendix (copy at New York Public Library). Avinoff published the designs privately in 1944 as an independent folio with text co-authored by Percival Hunt, and a few years later as a set of retouched photographic reproductions with homoerotic additions. The 1944 publication describes the subject matter of each plate:

15. At the Gates of Immortality. In contrast to the picture which to the High Priest embodied the apotheosis of his design, this composition reflects the design's frustration. The candlelight of the ritual is repeated in receding echoes of storm clouds, behind which emerges the tragical [sic] *mask embodying the verdict of the gods. As a 'terror antiquus,' the mask presages the cataclysm which will engulf Atlantis. The ancient wisdom embodied in the Kundalini serpent with a crown in the center of the dual triangles is defeated by the decree of the gods and the Ankh is emitting rays of darkness. The spirit of Atlantis is shown in a pose of farewell with the hands raised in the posture of prayer. The disturbance of symmetry of composition is significant of* [sic] *the impending cataclysm.*

17. The Death of the High Priest. A gigantic waterspout is carrying the burning ruins of Atlantis. These structures suggest the tomb of Darius and the palaces of Persepolis. The image of the High Priest, again an Assyrian winged bull, is sinking in the tidal wave of an ocean which has brought destruction to the island. From the hand of the High Priest, who is almost submerged, escapes the sign of the Ankh, which has been carried into the sky as a sparkling constellation beyond the veil of stormy clouds.

According to annotations on drawings, prints, and photographs at the Kinsey Institute, Avinoff based the Atlantis figures on life drawings made at Carnegie Mellon University art classes, or from models such as Johnny Bauer, an assistant in the entomology department at Carnegie Museum of Natural History, and athletes from the local universities. The hand of the high priest in plate 17 seems to have been modeled on Avinoff's own left hand; it is echoed in contemporaneous homoerotic works such as *Eddie* (Cat. no. 41).

CAT. NO. 28

The Russian Room, c. 1938–1944
Watercolor on paper, 11 7/8 x 8 7/8 in. (30.2 x 47.9 cm) (sheet)
University Art Gallery, University of Pittsburgh, 72.1.250.49
Fig. 46

Reproduced in John G. Bowman, Ruth Crawford Mitchell, and Andrey Avinoff, *Nationality Rooms of the University of Pittsburgh* (Pittsburgh: University of Pittsburgh Press, 1947), p. 118; probably one of seventeen Nationality Room watercolors exhibited at Carnegie Institute, Pittsburgh, 1953, no. 190.

The Russian Room, designed by Avinoff, opened on July 8, 1938. The tapestry on the back wall was also designed by Avinoff.

CAT. NO. 29

Jamaican Landscape: Blue Pool and Iris, 1930s
Gouache on card, 12 7/8 x 9 7/8 in. (32.7 x 50.5 cm)
Antonia Shoumatoff Foster
Fig. 9

Exhibited at Carnegie Institute, Pittsburgh, 1953, no. 23 (lent by Mrs. Russell Matthias).

The landscape was identified by Nicholas Shoumatoff as Rio Cobre, Jamaica, in his "Proposal for a Book on 'Rhapsody, Panorama, and Enlightenment in Avinoff's Art,'" undated typescript (1960s?) (original typescript with Alex Shoumatoff). Although close in size to other Jamaican landscapes in the collection of Alex Shoumatoff, it seems not to have been part of the set.

CAT. NO. 30

Crucifixion with Madonna, Child, and Angels, 1930s?
Graphite, crayon, pen and ink, and ink wash heightened with white on paper, 18 x 14 in. (45.7 x 35.6 cm)
Antonia Shoumatoff Foster

Possibly related to or the same as Carnegie Institute, Pittsburgh, 1953, no. 47 (*Madonna and Crucifixion*, crayon, collection of Margherita Chiari Langer).

CAT. NO. 31

Icon, Anti-Communist Subject, c. 1940
Graphite, watercolor, and gouache on pressed paperboard, 20 x 14 in. (50.8 x 35.6 cm)
Victoria Ward
Fig. 56

Possibly exhibited at Carnegie Institute, Pittsburgh, 1953, no. 50 or 51.

The inspiration and model for this composition was a plate from an extremely rare facsimile of an early illustrated Apocalypse written in Old Church Slavonic in Avinoff's collection (Cat. no. 65). The original motif illustrates Revelation 16:10: "And the fifth angel poured out his vial upon the seat of the beast; and his kingdom was full of darkness; and they gnawed their tongues for pain." Avinoff has followed the basic composition closely, but added his own details: a hammer and sickle, emblem of the Soviet Union, on the throne of the beast; a half-buried skull and bone; and an inky pool inhabited by a demonic creature. He endowed the beast with a porcine physique, symbolic of ugliness. The withered, tenuously rooted sapling tree next to St. John would become an increasingly important symbol in Avinoff's late work. The title is based on a label on the back of the frame.

CAT. NO. 32

Male Nude as Apocalyptic Angel, c. 1940–1945
Watercolor and crayon on paper, 18 x 12 in. (45.7 x 30.5 cm)
The Kinsey Institute for Research in Sex, Gender, and Reproduction, Indiana University, Bloomington, 290R Av9586.670
Fig. 58

Exhibited at Kinsey Institute, Indiana University, Bloomington, 2005, no cat. no.; Kinsey Institute, Indiana University, Bloomington, 2009, no cat. no.

A photograph of this work at the Kinsey Institute (290R T2515.562) records Avinoff's comments in Kinsey's handwriting: *Johnny Bauer. 22y [years old]. 'One of my best drw' Apocalypse angel. Holds (instd of bk) a luminous egg w a pentagon symbol of an ideal youth.* Johnny Bauer was an assistant in the entomology department at Carnegie Museum and a frequent model.

The supplicating pose of St. John mirrors the Avinoff self-portrait drawing as a nude with clasped hands (Cat. no. 43).

CAT. NO. 33

Star of Bethlehem, 1941
Graphite and watercolor on paper, 11 ½ x 8 5/8 in. (29.2 x 22 cm)
Carnegie Museum of Art, Gift of Mary Murtland Berger, 2007.67
Fig. 29

Inscribed in pencil lower right: *"Star of Bethlehem" / Eucaris grandiflora*

CAT. NO. 34

Star of Bethlehem, 1941
Graphite and watercolor on Whatman drawing board, 19 ½ x 13 in. (24.1 x 33 cm)
Carnegie Museum of Art, Heinz Family Fund, 2007.46.1
Figs. 2, 28

Monogrammed lower right: *A*

Probably related to Carnegie Institute, Pittsburgh, 1953, no. 58 (*Star of Bethlehem*, pastel, collection of Evangeline Zalstem Zalessky). Exhibited at Carnegie Institute, Pittsburgh, 1953, as central panel of no. 67 (*Triptych: The Old Dispensation and the New*); National Audubon Society, New York, 1953, no. 26 (*The Triptych*).

John Rawlins, Associate Curator of Invertebrate Zoology at Carnegie Museum of Natural History, has pointed out that the moths (*Eriogyna pyretorum*) are unfinished but recognizable; the shape and patterns of the wings are evident, even though final coloration is lacking. According to the donor of Cat. no. 33, Avinoff based the flowers in the painting on her Star of Bethlehem corsage (1941), and sent her the drawing and a black-and-white reproduction of this painting as his Christmas card that year (now in Carnegie Museum of Art curatorial files). The iconography corresponds to the content of John Greenleaf Whittier's 1830 poem *The Star of Bethlehem*. The ruined tower and brilliant turquoise bricks are reminiscent of the tomb of Tamerlane, depicted by Avinoff in the watercolor *Gur Emir, Tamerlane's Tomb in Samarkand* (1912?, location unknown), reproduced in Nicholas and Nina Shoumatoff, eds., *Around the Roof of the World* (Ann Arbor: University of Michigan Press, 1996), chap. 2. The column possibly refers to the Mausoleum of Halicarnassus in Rome; Avinoff may have drawn it from a plaster cast at Carnegie Institute (Hall of Architecture).

CAT. NOS. 35–40

Six plates from *Wild Flowers of Western Pennsylvania and the Upper Ohio Basin,* 1941–1943
Graphite and watercolor on paper, each 12 x 9 in. (30.5 x 22.9 cm) (sheet)

Green Dragon, plate 7
Wake Robin, plate 28
Coral Root & Lady's Tresses, plate 45
Juneberry and Ginger, plate 47
Pitcher Plant, plate 72
Cup Plant, plate 182

Carnegie Museum of Natural History, Section of Anthropology, Natural History Art Collection, 36,423
Figs. 31–36

Cup Plant is signed lower right in pencil: *A Avinoff*

Published in the second volume of *Wild Flowers of Western Pennsylvania and the Upper Ohio Basin,* text by O. E. Jennings and illustrations by Andrey Avinoff, 2 vols. (Pittsburgh: University of Pittsburgh Press, 1953).

Exhibited at Buhl Planetarium, Pittsburgh, 1946; selections from the set exhibited at Carnegie Institute, Pittsburgh, 1953, no. 41.

CAT. NO. 41

Eddie, c. 1941–1943
Graphite, pen and ink, and watercolor on paper, 13 ¼ x 10 in. (33.7 x 25.4 cm) (sheet)
The Kinsey Institute for Research in Sex, Gender, and Reproduction, Indiana University, Bloomington, 290R Av9586
Fig. 59

Exhibited at Kinsey Institute, Indiana University, Bloomington, 2005, no cat. no.; Kinsey Institute, Indiana University, Bloomington, 2009, no cat. no.

Eddie and his roommate, Robert, were Pittsburgh college students c. 1941–1943. Both modeled for Avinoff during those years, according to inscriptions on drawings and photographs in the Kinsey Institute. The withered male figure emerging from the tree stump can be interpreted metaphorically but not literally as an Avinoff self-portrait. The figure resembles another recorded in a photograph at Kinsey Institute of a lost painting depicting Robert, Eddie as a luminous shadow, and *Out right is a reprduct of me (AA) –x a portrait of me but simply an old + undesirbl creatur like a piece of drift wood...* [annotation by Kinsey; 200R T2515.569].

CAT. NO. 42

This Is the Army, c. 1942–1943
Graphite on paper, 12 x 7 ½ in. (30.5 x 19.1 cm)
The Kinsey Institute for Research in Sex, Gender, and Reproduction, Indiana University, Bloomington, Av9586.62

The mount for this drawing was inscribed by Kinsey apparently while in conversation with the artist in New York in 1948: *ex Army Show: The Soldiers. "The way the Show shld hv been" / "why dress ♂ as ♀ if they x shw ♂ qualities?"* [why dress men as women if they don't show male qualities?].

Irving Berlin's 1942 hit musical *This Is the Army* included a ballet performance in drag. The musical became a full-length motion picture in 1943; both were successful fundraisers for the war effort. Avinoff's drawing may have been inspired by either or both. Among the dance photographs Avinoff donated to Kinsey are three related to the musical (Kinsey reference nos. 69810, 69811, 69813), all annotated by Kinsey with the date of his conversation with Avinoff (October 1, 1948) and the title of the musical. One of the dancers is probably Nelson Barcroft impersonating Zorina, a well-known female classical dancer in New York in the early 1940s. The other may be A. Nelson (Kinsey Institute photograph 69813 and drawings Av9586.248, 249).

CAT. NO. 43

Self-Portrait, Half-Length Nude: Study for an Apocalypse, 1943
Graphite on paper, 7 ¾ x 6 in. (19.7 x 15.2 cm) (sheet)
The Kinsey Institute for Research in Sex, Gender, and Reproduction, Indiana University, Bloomington, A 290R Av9586.422

Exhibited at Kinsey Institute, Indiana University, Bloomington, 2005, no cat. no.; Kinsey Institute, Indiana University, Bloomington, 2009, no cat. no.

CAT. NO. 44

Interior at Hidden Hollow, c. 1945–1948
Graphite, gouache, and watercolor on Whatman drawing board, 12 x 9 in. (30.5 x 22.9 cm)
Carnegie Museum of Art, Gift of He Who Stands Firm (Nicholas Avinoff Shoumatoff), 2007.90

Hidden Hollow was Elizabeth Shoumatoff's Arts and Crafts–style home located in Locust Valley, Long Island. Avinoff lived there from summer 1945 until spring 1948, when he moved to an apartment at 952 Fifth Avenue, New York.

CAT. NO. 45

The Tulips Are Gone (Impermanence), c. 1945–1949
Graphite, watercolor, and gouache with pen and brush and ink on paper, 14 ½ x 11 ½ in. (36.8 x 29.2 cm) (sight)
Antonia Shoumatoff Foster
Fig. 63

Signed lower right: *Avinoff*

Probably exhibited at Knoedler & Company, New York, 1947, no. 34 (*The Tulips Are Gone*); Carnegie Institute, Pittsburgh, 1948, no. 40 *(The Tulips Are Gone*); Carnegie Institute, Pittsburgh, 1953, no. 73 (*The Tulips Are Gone,* watercolor, 1946). The 1953 catalogue text refers to the painting's "nacreous beauty" and mentions the Cathedral of Learning (the main building of the University of Pittsburgh's campus) floating in the clouds. A tiny image of the cathedral is visible in the black space above the leaf of the tulip.

CAT. NO. 46

Apatasaurus Luisae and the Victory, c. 1946
Graphite, pen, and india ink on board, 11 x 11 in. (27.9 x 27.9 cm)
Carnegie Museum of Art, Patrons Art Fund, 2009.36.6

According to annotations on its pendant, *Discobolus and Diplodocus,* at the Kinsey Institute (290R Av9586.208), this design was a proposal for the seal of the Society of Arts and Sciences, Carnegie Institute, in 1946. However, Avinoff had left Pittsburgh by that year, so an earlier date is possible.

CAT. NO. 47

Underwater Scene, c. 1946
Watercolor on paper, 11 ½ x 9 in. (29.2 x 22.9 cm) (sight)
Antonia Shoumatoff Foster
Fig. 14

One of a set of seven watercolors, two of which were exhibited at Carnegie Institute, Pittsburgh, 1953, nos. 99, 100 (this painting has both numbers on the back of the frame). A label from the 1970s bears the title *Underseascape.* According to the family, Avinoff painted the series in Bermuda in 1946.

CAT. NO. 48

Vaslav Nijinsky "Spectre de la Rose," 1947
Graphite on paper, 9 ⅛ x 6 ½ in. (23.2 x 16.5 cm)
The Kinsey Institute for Research in Sex, Gender, and Reproduction, Indiana University, Bloomington, 290R Av9586.565
Fig. 61

There is another version of this composition, with slight variations, in the collection of Antonia Shoumatoff Foster, which was most likely exhibited at Carnegie Institute, Pittsburgh, 1953, no. 151.

CAT. NO. 49

White Lilies and Caligo Butterfly, 1947
Watercolor on pressed paperboard, 14 ½ x 11 ½ in.
(36.8 x 29.2 cm) (sight)
Victoria Ward
Fig. 39

Monogrammed lower right: *A*

The title and date are based on Avinoff's annotations on a black-and-white photograph at the Kinsey Institute (290R T2515.328). It might be the same painting as *Lily and South American Butterfly,* exhibited at Carnegie Institute, Pittsburgh, 1953, no. 127.

CAT. NO. 50

Dutch Bouquet, 1948
Watercolor on paper mounted on Whatman board, 22 x 16 in.
(55.9 x 40.6 cm)
Victoria Ward
Fig. 38

There is a black-and-white photograph (290R T2515.338) of this composition at the Kinsey Institute with Kinsey's annotation on the back: *AA considers his best.*

CAT. NO. 51

Frustration, 1948
Graphite and watercolor on paper mounted on paperboard,
15 x 12 in. (38.1 x 30.5 cm)
Carnegie Museum of Art, Heinz Family Fund, 2007.46.3
Figs. 2, 62

Recorded as an independent work of art and titled *Frustration* by the artist and Alfred Kinsey on a black-and-white photograph in the Kinsey Institute (290R T2515.360).

Exhibited at Carnegie Institute, Pittsburgh, 1953, as the left-hand panel of no. 67 (*Triptych: The Old Dispensation and the New*); National Audubon Society, New York, 1953, no. 26 (*The Triptych*).

CAT. NO. 52

Morpho: Remembrance of Things Past, 1948
Graphite and watercolor on paper mounted on paperboard,
15 x 12 in. (38.1 x 30.5 cm)
Carnegie Museum of Art, Heinz Family Fund, 2007.46.2
Figs. 2, 26

Monogrammed lower right: *A*

Recorded as an independent work of art and titled *Morpho: Remembrance of Things Past* by the artist and Alfred Kinsey on a black-and-white photograph in the Kinsey Institute (290R T2515.369). It seems likely that after the artist's death, *Morpho* and its pendant, *Frustration* (Cat. no. 51), were associated with the *Star of Bethlehem* watercolor (Cat. no. 34) in one frame. The framer's label on the verso of the resulting triptych is dated May 1951, two years after the artist's death. *Morpho* was exhibited at Carnegie Institute, Pittsburgh, 1953, as the right-hand panel of no. 67 (*Triptych: The Old Dispensation and the New*); National Audubon Society, New York, 1953, no. 26 (*The Triptych*). Nicholas Shoumatoff reproduced *Morpho* alone with the title *Manhattan Discontinuity* in his "Proposal for a Book on 'Rhapsody, Panorama, and Enlightenment in Avinoff's Art,'" undated typescript (1960s?) (original typescript with Alex Shoumatoff).

CAT. NO. 53

Talisman Roses, 1948
Graphite and watercolor on pressed paperboard, 16 x 12 in.
(40.6 x 30.5 cm)
Victoria Ward
Fig. 10

Dated *1948* by Avinoff on a photograph at Kinsey Institute (290R T2515.333).

CAT. NO. 54

Orchid with Butterfly, 1948–1949
Graphite and watercolor on Whatman board, 19 x 15 in.
(48.3 x 38.1 cm)
Victoria Ward
Fig. 41

CAT. NO. 55

White Orchid, 1948–1949
Graphite and watercolor on paper mounted on pressed paperboard,
17 x 14 in. (43.2 x 35.6 cm)
Victoria Ward
Fig. 43

Inscribed lower left: *12*; inscribed in pencil on verso by Avinoff: *B.C. Albion*; inscribed in pencil on verso in another hand: *BC. ALBION / BC THORNTONI X C.TRIANAEI, VAR. ALBA / STUART LOW CO. 1921*

CAT. NO. 56

Yellow Orchid, 1948–1949
Graphite and watercolor on paper,
17 x 14 in. (43.2 x 35.6 cm)
Victoria Ward
Fig. 42

Signed lower left: *Avinoff*

The *Orchids* (Cat. nos. 54–56) were published in 1960 in *Andrey Avinoff's Portraits of Orchids, Faithfully Reproduced from Original Water-Colors, with Bibliographical Notes by Helen H. Adams* (New York: C. Harrison Conroy, 1960). Sixty orchid paintings were exhibited in 1949 at the American Museum of Natural History, no cat. no.

CAT. NO. 57

Spring Flowers, Manner of Vincent van Gogh, 1948–1949
Pastel on card, 14 x 11 in.
(35.6 x 27.9 cm)
Victoria Ward
Fig. 40

Monogrammed lower left: *A*

Exhibited at Knoedler & Company, New York, 1947, no. 25; Carnegie Institute, Pittsburgh, 1948, no. 44; Cranbrook Institute of Science, Toledo, 1948, no. 10.

CAT. NO. 58

Memories (unfinished), 1949
Graphite and watercolor on Whatman drawing board,
29 x 21 ½ in. (73.7 x 54.6 cm)
Antonia Shoumatoff Foster
Fig. 23

Exhibited at Carnegie Institute, Pittsburgh, 1953, no. 210.

The composition incorporates family portraits of Avinoff ancestors including the Panayev children. Avinoff's maternal grandmother, Alexandra, is one of the little girls, who reappears as a mature woman in the miniature at the center of the composition. According to Alex Shoumatoff, *Russian Blood: A Family Chronicle* (New York: Coward, McCann & Geoghegan, 1982), pp. 62–65, both portraits were the work of the renowned Russian painter Aleksei Venetsianov (1780–1847), and the children's portrait was a 1928 gift from Nicholas Avinoff to the Tretyakov Gallery, Moscow.

CAT. NO. 59

Study for *Tulips (Disintegration),* c. 1949
Pastel on card, 6 ¾ x 13 ¾ in.
(17.2 x 34.9 cm)
Carnegie Museum of Art, Leisser Art Fund, 2008.11

CAT. NO. 60

Tulips (Disintegration) (unfinished), c. 1949
Graphite and watercolor on paperboard, 20 ⅝ x 15 ⅛ in.
(52.4 x 38.4 cm)
Smithsonian American Art Museum, Gift of Elizabeth Shoumatoff, 1956.11.6
Fig. 60

CAT. NO. 61

Self-Portrait with Butterfly Eye, 1940s
Graphite on fragment of envelope, with typescript and stamps,
5 ¾ x 5 ¼ in. (14.6 x 13.3 cm)
Antonia Shoumatoff Foster
Fig. 5

Signed lower right: *Avinoff*

CAT. NO. 62

Brooch, 1940s
Elbaite, opal, pearl, and diamond set in gold and platinum, approx. 4 x 3 x 1 in. (10.2 x 7.6 x 2.5 cm)
Carnegie Museum of Natural History
Fig. 13

According to Victoria Ward, who owns Avinoff's drawing for the jewel, he designed it and had it made as a Christmas gift for Elizabeth Shoumatoff after she requested "No more pocket-books" (correspondence in curatorial files).

WORKS BY OTHER ARTISTS

CAT. NO. 63

John Abbot, British, 1751–c. 1840
Album of 106 drawings and notes, including some illustrations of American insects, 1767–1773
Carnegie Museum of Natural History

This volume was perhaps used as studies for James Edward Smith's *Natural History of the Rarer Lepidopterous Insects of Georgia* (London, 1797). Avinoff took the album with him when he left Russia in 1917.

CAT. NO. 64

Russian, 19th century
The Mother of God Vladimirskaya, 19th century in the style of 16th century
Tempera and gilding on gesso on panel, 34 x 24 ¾ in. (86.4 x 62.9 cm)
Carnegie Museum of Art, Gift of O. John Anderson in memory of Mr. and Mrs. George Hann, 80.63.1
Fig. 48

Exhibited in *Russian Icons and Objects of Ecclesiastical and Decorative Arts from the Collection of George R. Hann,* Carnegie Institute, Pittsburgh, 1944, no. 30 (traveled to Metropolitan Museum of Art, New York; Syracuse Museum of Fine Arts; Columbus Gallery of Fine Arts; John Herron Art Museum, Indianapolis; Allen Memorial Art Museum, Oberlin; St. Louis Art Museum, 1944–1945).

In the catalogue for the exhibition, Avinoff attributed this icon to the Novgorod School, late 15th century. At the 1980 Christie's sale of Hann's collection (New York, April 17, lot 56), it was called "possibly central Russia, 16th century" and also cited as possibly a later work in the sixteenth-century style. After viewing the icon at Carnegie Museum of Art in 1989, the Soviet émigré art expert Vladimir Teteriatnikov redated it to "19th century in imitation of 16th century."

CAT. NO. 65

Bible, 1910
MS facsimile with leather binding, printed text, and illustrations, closed dimensions approx. 18 x 12 in. (45.7 x 30.5 cm)
Hillwood Estate, Museum & Gardens Library, Washington, D.C., from the Avinoff-Shoumatoff Collection
Fig. 55

CAT. NO. 66

Elizabeth Shoumatoff
American, 1888–1980
Portrait of Andrey Avinoff, 1943
Watercolor on paper, 38 x 30 in. (96.5 x 76.2 cm)
Carnegie Museum of Art, Transfer from Museum Department of Carnegie Institute, 48.21
Fig. 1

BIBLIOGRAPHY AND EXHIBITION HISTORY

Entries are organized chronologically within each section.

PUBLISHED WRITINGS OF ANDREY AVINOFF

"Contributions à la faune des Rhopalocera du Pamir oriental" [Russian]. *Horae societatis entomologicae Rossicae* 39 (1910): 225–246, pl. 14.

"Formes nouvelles de Rhopalocères de la Fergana" [Russian]. *Horae societatis entomologicae Rossicae* 39 (1910): 247–250, pl. 14.

"Quelques formes nouvelles du genre Parnassius Latr." [Russian]. *Horae societatis entomologicae Rossicae* 40, no. 5 (1912): 1–21, pl. II.

"Butterflies of the Genus Parnassius in the Collection of the Indian Museum." *Records of the Indian Museum* (1913): 327–331.

"Contribution toward a Problem of a More Precise Zoogeographical Subdivision of the Palearctic Regions of British India on the Ground of the Distribution and Grouping of Rhopalocera." *Bulletin of the Imperial Russian Geographical Society* 49 (1913): 523–563.

"Zoogeographical Subdivision of Palearctic Regions of British India Based on Distribution and Grouping of Rhopalocera." *Bulletin of the Imperial Russian Geographical Society* 49 (1913): 1–41.

"Some New Forms of Parnassius (Lepidoptera Rhopolecera)." *Transactions of the Entomological Society of London 1915* 3–4 (1916): 351–360, pls. 52–54.

"Notice sur la collection de Lepidoptères formée par A. Avinoff." *Etudes de Lépidoptérologie comparée* 17 (March 1920): 71–84.

"Tibetan Drawings by Andrew [*sic*] Avinoff." *Century Magazine,* 103, n.s. 81, January 1922, unpaginated.

"Considérations sur les Parnassiens d'Asie Centrale." *Etudes de Lépidoptérologie comparée* 19 (1922): 41–70.

"Descriptions of Some New Species of Rhopalocera in the Carnegie Museum." *Annals of the Carnegie Museum* 16 (1926): 355–374, pls. 30–33.

"Flyers: From Pterodactyls to Lindbergh." *Bulletin of the Carnegie Institute* (February 1928).

"Educational Work in the Museum." *Carnegie Magazine* 2, no. 1 (April 1928): 71–74.

"The Natural History Museum: A Treasury from Many Lands; An Address Given Over the University of Pittsburgh Radio." *Carnegie Magazine* 2, no. 1 (April 1928): 6.

"The Carnegie Museum Looks Ahead." *Pittsburgh Record* 2, no. 4 (June 1928): 247–254.

"International Congress of Entomology." *Carnegie Magazine* 2, no. 3 (August 1928): 146–148.

"The Clark Collection." *Carnegie Magazine* 2, no. 4 (September 1928): 120.

"The Ortmann Library." *Carnegie Magazine* 2, no. 4 (September 1928): 122.

"A Treasury from Many Lands: The Natural History Museum." *Pittsburgh Record* 3 (October 1928): 35–40.

"Museums and the People." *American Magazine of Art* 19 (1928): 596–601.

"Competitive Drawings by High-School Pupils." *Carnegie Magazine* 2, no. 8 (January 1929): 252.

"The Museum's Lecture Course." *Carnegie Magazine* 2, no. 9 (February 1929): 279.

"Testimonial to Dr. Holland on His Eightieth Birthday [1928]." *Annals of the Carnegie Museum* 19 (1929): 11–13, pl. 1.

"On the Art of Knowing." *Pittsburgh Record* 4 (April 1930): 13–19.

"Old World Museums." *Carnegie Magazine* 4, no. 7 (December 1930): 215–219.

"Two New Subspecies of Melitaea Harrisi with Remarks upon Related Forms." *Annals of the Carnegie Museum* 19 (1930): 161–166, pl. 6.

"More Old World Museums." *Carnegie Magazine* 4, no. 8 (January 1931): 233–236.

"The Roof of the World." *Pittsburgh Record* 5 (April 1931): 39–47.

"A Trip to Western Tibet." *Pittsburgh Record* 5 (April 1931): 38, 42, 46.

"Animals That Were Not." *Carnegie Magazine* 6, no. 1 (April 1932): 3–7.

"The Art of Paleolithic and Neolithic Man." *Sigma Xi Quarterly* (Easton, Pa.) 20, no. 2 (June 1932): 78–81.

"International Cooperation among Museums of Science." *Carnegie Magazine* 6, no. 4 (September 1932): 113–114.

"Obituary." *Science* (February 24, 1933): 204–205.

"The Clark Entomological Library." *Carnegie Magazine* 6, no. 10 (March 1933): 301.

"The Giant Sable Antelope." *Carnegie Magazine* 7, no. 3 (June 1933): 82–83.

"The Coptic Textile Collection: Fabrics from the Tombs of the Christianized Egyptians from the Fourth to the Twelfth Centuries." *Carnegie Magazine* 7, no. 9 (February 1934): 266–268.

"International Trends in Science Museums." *Carnegie Magazine* 8, no. 4 (September 1934): 104–106.

"A Persian Garden." *Carnegie Magazine* 9, no. 1 (April 1935): 10–11.

"The Giant Ground Sloth: An Important Pleistocene Specimen Acquired for the Hall of Fossils." *Carnegie Magazine* 9, no. 2 (May 1935): 54–55.

"St. George and the Dragon: The Traditions of Old Russia to Be Preserved in an Artistic Hanging." *Carnegie Magazine* 9, no. 3 (June 1935): 82–84.

Holland, W. J., and Andrey Avinoff. "The Lepidoptera Collected by G. M. Sutton on Southampton Island: Rhopalocera, Heterocera." *Memoirs of the Carnegie Museum* 12, pt. 2, sec. 5 (December 1935): 34 pp., 3pls.

"In Honor of A. Semenov Tian-Shansky." *Annals of the Entomological Society of America* 29 (December 1936): 557–560.

"An Elusive Butterfly [*Parnassius Przewalskii* Alph.]." *Carnegie Magazine* 11, no. 4 (September 1937): 103–107.

"The Heinz Gift: The Entire Collection on Exhibition now Belongs to Carnegie Institute." *Carnegie Magazine* 12, no. 1 (April 1938): 267.

"The Preston B. Clark Bequest: An Important Collection Comes to the Carnegie Institute." *Carnegie Magazine* 12, no. 1 (April 1938): 300–302.

"A Variable Palearctic Satyrid." *Fourth International Congress of Entomology* (Ithaca) 2 (1938): 290–293.

"Go to the Ant: New Glass Insects in the Museum." *Carnegie Magazine* 13, no. 5 (October 1939): 143–147.

"The Douglas Stewart Memorial: New Habitat Groups Portraying Pittsburgh in the Coal Age Dedicated in the Carnegie Museum." *Carnegie Magazine* 14, no. 3 (June 1940): 67–71.

"Jamaican Summer." *Carnegie Magazine* 14, no. 6 (November 1940): 171–182.

"Memorial Library of Dr. Hugo Kahl Presented to the Museum." *Carnegie Magazine* 15, no. 3 (June 1941): 69–70.

"The New Botanical Hall: A Revolutionary Change in the Museum's System of Display." *Carnegie Magazine* 15, no. 9 (February 1942): 273–277.

"Life in the Museum." *Carnegie Magazine* 15, no. 10 (March 1942): 310–311.

"A Memorial Exhibition: Miniature Models of Specimens Mounted by Remi H. Santens on Display in the Carnegie Museum." *Carnegie Magazine* 17, no. 1 (April 1943): 12–13.

"Russian Icons: An Exhibition of the Hann Collection in the Fine Arts Galleries." *Carnegie Magazine* 17, no. 8 (January 1944): 227–235.

"A Loan Exhibition of Russian Icons." *Metropolitan Museum of Art Bulletin*, n.s. 2, no. 8 (April 1944): 227–232.

"The Story of Russian Icons." *Russian Orthodox Journal* 18, no. 3 (July 1944).

"The Pacific Show: New Exhibit Staged by the Museum in the Gallery of Ornithology." *Carnegie Magazine*, 18, no. 6 (November 1944): 163–166.

Avinoff, Andrey, and Percival Hunt. "Descriptive Brochure [Fall of Atlantis]." Privately published, Pittsburgh, 1944.

Russian Icons and Objects of Ecclesiastical and Decorative Arts from the Collection of George R. Hann. Introduction and descriptive data by Andrey Avinoff. Pittsburgh: Carnegie Institute, 1944.

"Postwar Plan for Science Museums." *Carnegie Magazine* 19, no. 1 (April 1945): 10–11.

"A Library of Entomology Is Given." *Carnegie Magazine* 19, no. 10 (April 1946): 296–299.

Avinoff, Andrey, and Nicholas Shoumatoff. "An Annotated List of the Butterflies of Jamaica." *Annals of the Carnegie Museum* 30 (December 1946): 263–295.

"Asiatic Butterflies in Manhattan." *Carnegie Magazine* 20, no. 10 (May 1947): 301–302.

"The Ever New Call." In *Nationality Rooms of the University of Pittsburgh,* by John G. Bowman, Ruth Crawford Mitchell, and Andrey Avinoff. Pittsburgh: University of Pittsburgh Press, 1947.

Avinoff, Andrey, et al. "After All, What Is Art?" *Carnegie Magazine* 22, no. 5 (December 1948): 158.

"An Analysis of the Color and Pattern in Butterflies of the Asiatic Genus Karanasa." *Annals of the Carnegie Museum* 31 (1950): 321–332, 2 pls.

Avinoff, Andrey, and Walter R. Sweadner. "The Karanasa Butterflies: A Study in Evolution." *Annals of the Carnegie Museum* 32, part 1 (1951).

UNPUBLISHED WRITINGS OF ANDREY AVINOFF

"Soul and Matter." Typescript dated June 8, 1928, with Antonia Shoumatoff Foster.

"Carnegie Museum: Our Position and Aim in the Study of Natural History." Address to the WCAE, June 6, 1932. Typescript with Antonia Shoumatoff Foster.

"Cooperation in the Museum Field." Address to the American Association of Museums meeting, New York, 1936. Typescript with Antonia Shoumatoff Foster.

[Introduction to an exhibition of Russian art]. Typescript dated December 12, 1943, with Antonia Shoumatoff Foster.

"Introductory Remarks Made at the Meeting of the American Association of Museums in Connection with a Project of a Universalium." Undated typescript, c. 1944, with Antonia Shoumatoff Foster.

Russian Ecclesiastical and Decorative Objects in the Collection of George R. Hann: Watercolor Illustrations by A. Avinoff. Typescript with water-color illustrations, 2 albums, 1944 (formerly Westmoreland Museum of American Art, Greensburg, Pa.; James R. Cummins, New York; private collection).

"Andrey Avinoff: His Artistic Credo." Undated typescript, c. 1945–1949, with Alex Shoumatoff.

"Painting in Watercolor." Undated holograph manuscript, c. 1949, and typescript with Antonia Shoumatoff Foster.

"The Nature of Evil." Undated typescript, final pages missing, with undated editorial notes by Nicholas Shoumatoff, original with Antonia Shoumatoff Foster.

PUBLICATIONS ILLUSTRATED BY ANDREY AVINOFF

Powell, E. Alexander. "A Modern Magic Carpet." *Century Magazine* 104 (June 1922): 203–214.

Masson, Thomas L. "Ten Houses of Ten Authors." *Country Life,* April 1924, 34–41.

The St. Nicholas Magazine 57, no. 10 (August 1930): cover.

White, Jane Ava. "Christmas in Many Lands." *Carnegie Magazine* 4, no. 8 (January 1931): 238.

Noel, Sibylle. *The Magic Bird of Chomo-Lung-Ma: Tales of Mount Everest; The Turquoise Peak.* New York: Doubleday, Doran & Co., 1931.

S. H. C. "The Magic Bird of ChoMo-Lung-Ma." *Carnegie Magazine* 5, no. 8 (January 1932): 246.

White, Jane Ava. "Mother Nature's Helpers." *Carnegie Magazine* 6, no. 2 (May 1932): cover.

Langer, Dr. Heinz. "Diseases which Present Signs of Over-Irritation of the Sympathetic Nerves and Their Treatment by X-Rays." *Illinois Medical Journal* (March 1936).

Memoirs of the Carnegie Museum 11 (1936).

Golokhvastoff, George V. *Gibel Atlantide: Poema* [Russian]. New York, 1938.

[Avinoff drawings of Apatasaurus and T. Rex reconstructed]. *Carnegie Magazine* 16, no. 7 (December 1942): 201–202.

The Commons Room at the University of Pittsburgh: Ten Pencil Drawings. Pittsburgh: University of Pittsburgh Press, 1942.

Gilmore, Charles W. *The Great Dinosaurs of the Carnegie Museum.* Pittsburgh: Carnegie Museum of Natural History Pamphlet 2, undated [1942?].

"Cover Picture." *Carnegie Magazine* 18, no. 7 (December 1944): 193, 213.

Golokhivastoff, George V. *The Fall of Atlantis: A Series of Graphic Impressions of the Poem by George V. Golokhivastoff Drawn by Andrey Avinoff.* Pittsburgh: Eddy Press Corporation, 1944.

Osborn, Fairfield. *The Pacific World: Its Vast Distances, Its Lands and the Life upon Them, and Its Peoples . . . with Illustrations by . . . Andrey Avinoff . . . .* New York: W. W. Norton & Company, 1944.

Bidwell, Marshall. "Rachmaninoff, Threefold Musician." *Carnegie Magazine* 19, no. 10 (March 1945): 304.

Bowman, John G., Ruth Crawford Mitchell, and Andrey Avinoff. *Nationality Rooms of the University of Pittsburgh.* Pittsburgh: University of Pittsburgh Press, 1947.

Jennings, O. E. *Wild Flowers of Western Pennsylvania and the Upper Ohio Basin,* 2 vols. Preface by Fiske Kimball. Pittsburgh: University of Pittsburgh Press, 1953.

Andrey Avinoff's Portraits of Orchids, Faithfully Reproduced from Original Water-Colors, with Bibliographical Notes by Helen H. Adams. New York: C. Harrison Conroy, 1960.

Evans, Burtt. *Rooms with a View: Achievements of the Nationality Committees and the Office of Cultural and Educational Exchange*. Pittsburgh: University of Pittsburgh [1960?].

WRITINGS ON ANDREY AVINOFF

[Untitled review of Ainslie Galleries exhibition]. *New York American* (February 13, 1921). Typescript with Alex Shoumatoff.

[Untitled review of Ainslie Galleries exhibition]. *American Art News* (February 19, 1921). Typescript with Alex Shoumatoff.

Cortissoz, Royal. "Good Landscapes Made In the East and the West." *New York Tribune,* February 20, 1921, B7.

[Untitled review of Ainslie Galleries exhibition]. *Brooklyn Daily Eagle,* February 20, 1921. Typescript with Alex Shoumatoff.

[Untitled review of Ainslie Galleries exhibition]. *New York Herald,* February 20, 1921. Typescript with Alex Shoumatoff.

[Untitled review of Ainslie Galleries exhibition]. *New York Sun,* February 20, 1921. Typescript with Alex Shoumatoff.

"Our Neighboring Communities: Sunday Afternoon Lectures Scheduled at Carnegie Museum." *Jewish Criterion* 64, no. 24 (October 24, 1924).

Matthias, Blanche C. "The Art of the Spectrum and the Butterfly: A Russian Painter in the Catskills." *Chicago Evening Post Magazine of the Art World,* September 8, 1925.

Suydam, Emma B. "[Twentieth Century] Club Hears Unusual Lecture on Tendencies of Art: A. Avinoff Describes General Trend of Modern Painting; Calls Futurists and Cubists Imitators of Primitive Art." *Post,* November 29, 1925.

"Avinoff Is Named Museum Director: Native of Russia Succeeds Douglas Stewart at Carnegie Institute." *Pittsburgh Chronicle-Telegraph,* July 24, 1926.

"Avinoff Succeeds Stewart as Carnegie Museum Head." *Pittsburgh Gazette-Times,* July 24, 1926.

"Ex-Member of Czar's Staff Is Elected as Director of Museum." *Pittsburgh Sun,* July 24, 1926.

"The New Museum Director." *Pittsburgh Sun,* July 26, 1926.

Gillette, Berenice. "Avinoff, Carnegie Museum Director: After the Russian Revolution This Master of Many Professions Came to Pittsburgh to Begin Life Anew." Unattributed clipping, c. 1926.

"A Group of Distinguished Rooms; Rose Cumming Whose Profession It Is to Create Artistic Rooms for Other People Has Here Used Her Imagination with Delightful Results in Her Own Sitting Room." *Arts & Decoration,* January 1927, 54.

"Award of the John Scott Medals." *Science* 65 (June 17, 1927): 591–592.

"Scientific Notes and News." *Science* 65 (June 17, 1927): 592–594.

"Talented." *Pittsburgh Sun-Telegraph,* September 30, 1928, 1, 3.

"Avinoff, Russ Nobleman, Becomes Citizen Here." *Pittsburgh Sun-Telegraph,* January 6, 1929.

"Expedition for the Study of Gorillas." *Science* 69 (May 24, 1929): 538–539.

"Research Reserves in the National Forests." *Science* 69 (May 24, 1929): 538.

Gaul, Harvey. "Andrey Avinoff, Entomologist, Exhibits His Pictures at Carnegie Tech." *Pittsburgh Post-Gazette,* February 27, 1930.

Redd, Penelope. "Andre [*sic*] Avinoff's Works Put on Exhibition by College of Fine Arts." *Pittsburgh Sun-Telegraph,* March 2, 1930.

"Dr. Avinoff's Visit Anticipated." *News/Record of the Baltimore Museum of Art* 3 (January 1931): 4.

"Andrey Avinoff... His Butterflies Were famed." *Bulletin Index*, March 5, 1931.

"Bachelors: Reasons Unknown." *Bulletin Index,* May 19, 1932.

Silverman, Alexander. "Luba Rubin Goldsmith: An Appreciation." *Jewish Criterion* 80, no. 7 (June 24, 1932).

"Minute Biographies: Andrey Avinoff." *Pittsburgh Post-Gazette,* November 11, 1932.

"International Cooperation of Science Museums." *Science* 76 (December 9, 1932): 534.

"The North India Expedition of Yale University." *Science* 76 (December 9, 1932): 534–535.

"Dr. Avinoff's Tour." *Carnegie Magazine* 6, no. 3 (June 1932): 94.

Nationality Rooms in the Cathedral of Learning. Pittsburgh: University of Pittsburgh, 1933.

"Spanish Honors for Director Avinoff." *Carnegie Magazine* 7, no. 9 (February 1934): 265.

"Stone House in Fox Chapel Sold." *Pittsburgh Sun-Telegraph,* December 22, 1935.

"Scientific Notes and News." *Science* 83 (March 13, 1936): 255–259.

George, James R. "Avinoff: The Expert 'Amateur'; A Master of Many Arts." *Pittsburgh Post-Gazette,* December 12, 1936.

"Jamaica Lecture." *Carnegie Magazine* 10, no. 10 (March 1937): 311.

"Andrey Avinoff: Director, Carnegie Museum." *Town & Country Review* (London), June 1937, 43–44.

Starrett, Agnes Lynch. *Through One Hundred and Fifty Years: The University of Pittsburgh*. Pittsburgh: University of Pittsburgh Press, 1937.

"Museum Official Owns Valuable Library." *Pittsburgh Sun-Telegraph,* February 7, 1939.

[Profile]. *American Slav* 2 (February 1939): 5.

"Russian Letter." *Bulletin Index,* February 1, 1940.

"Pan-American Union: Member of the Advisory Committee of the American Scientific Congress." *Carnegie Magazine* 14, no. 1 (April 1940): 7.

"Red Admirals Found on Jamaica Island." *Pittsburgh Post-Gazette,* September 6, 1940.

Jena, Jeanette. "Avinoff Fascinates at Fine Art Galleries: Excellence of Individual Pieces Emphasizes Wide Range of Sensitive Mind." *Pittsburgh Post-Gazette,* November 13, 1941.

"Avinoff Drawings Published: Portfolio of Sketches Shows Commons Room; Intricate Details of Mellon Gift to Cathedral of Learning Shown in Work." *Pittsburgh Post-Gazette,* April 1, 1942.

"Russian Icons and Dr. Avinoff." *Baltimore Museum News* 4 (May 1942): 37–38.

Sweadner, Walter R. "Three Miles Up: The Avinoff Collection of Butterflies from Central Asia." *Carnegie Magazine* 16, no. 6 (November 1942): 163–167.

Danver, Charles F. "Pittsburghesque," *Pittsburgh...,* December 1, 1942.

Classrooms in the Cathedral of Learning. Pittsburgh: University of Pittsburgh, 1944.

"Dr. Avinoff Resigns as Director of Carnegie Museum." *Carnegie Magazine* 19, no. 3 (June 1945): 71.

"Dr. Avinoff to Resume Writing on Retirement." *Pittsburgh Sun-Telegraph,* June 24, 1945.

"Avinoff Resigns." *Museum News* 23 (September 1, 1945): 3.

"Portrait of Andrey Avinoff Acquired." *Carnegie Magazine* 19, no. 5 (November 1945): 157.

"Scientific Work of Art? Or Art Worthy of Science? They Don't Know What to Call Watercolor Show of Dr. Avinoff at Planetarium." *Pittsburgh Press,* January 17, 1946.

"Avinoff Library Given to Carnegie Museum." *Museum News* 24 (May 15, 1946): 3.

Pardue, Austin. *He Lives.* 1946. Reprint. New York: Morehouse-Barlow Co., 1971.

Burrows, Carlyle. "Art of the Week: Group Shows Opening the Summer Season." *New York Herald-Tribune,* June 8, 1947.

J[ewell], E. A. "Some One-Man Shows." *New York Times,* June 8, 1947.

"Exhibition, Knoedler." *Art News* 46 (June 1947): 43.

J. K. R. "Paintings by A. Avinoff at Knoedler Galleries." *Art Digest* 21 (June 1947): 31.

Jennings, O. E. "A Gift of Flower Paintings." *Carnegie Magazine* 21, no. 2 (July 1947): 41–42.

Carlson, Helen. "Current Exhibitions: A Primitive and an Expressionist Have Their First Showing; Other Displays." Unattributed clipping [summer 1947].

Stow, Charles Messer. "The Quester: Russian Icons as a Heritage of the Golden Age of Greece." *New York Sun,* December 12, 1947.

Hovey, Walter R. "Flower Paintings by Andrey Avinoff." *Carnegie Magazine* 21, no. 10 (May 1948): 291–293.

Hellman, Geoffrey T. "Black Tie and Cyanide Jar." *New Yorker,* August 21, 1948, 32ff.

Januzzi, Eugene F. J. "Ex-Head of Museum Here Excels in New Paintings: 71 Flower Works of Andrey Avinoff Point Up Technique and Imagination." *Pittsburgh Post-Gazette,* April 16, 1949.

"Andrey Avinoff: An Entomologist." *New York Times,* July 18, 1949.

"Death Ends Avinoff's Career as Unusual Scientist-Artist." *Pittsburgh Press,* July 18, 1949.

"Museum Officials Eye Plans for Publishing 300 Color Prints." *Pittsburgh Sun-Telegraph*, July 18, 1949.

"News and Notes." *Science* 110 (August 26, 1949): 221–224.

"Obituary." *Museum News* 27 (September 1, 1949): 3.

"Buhl Foundation Grant Subsidy to Guarantee Publication of Wildflowers of Western Pennsylvania." *Carnegie Magazine* 23, no. 3 (October 1949): 99.

Jennings, Otto E. "In Memoriam." *Carnegie Magazine* 23, no. 3 (October 1949): 98–99.

Shoumatoff, Nicholas. "Andrey Avinoff (1884–1949)." *Lepidopterists' News* 4, nos. 1–2 (1950): 7–9.

Kantner, Dorothy. "Two Volumes Tell Story of Wild Flowers." *Pittsburgh Sun-Telegraph,* July 12, 1953.

"Memorial Exhibition of Art by Avinoff Opens Tomorrow: Elizabeth Shoumatoff, Artist's Sister, Arrives here to Attend Grand Show." *Pittsburgh Press,* December 3, 1953.

Jena, Jeanette. "Exhibit Proves Avinoff Man of Many Talents: Collection of 234 Items Shows Diversity of Work of Late Head of Carnegie Museum." *Pittsburgh Post-Gazette,* December 4, 1953.

"In Calm of Carnegie Institute: Collection of Wildflower Paintings on Display; Book Tells Story Behind Works." *Pittsburgh Press,* December 27, 1953.

Hovey, Walter R. "Andrey Avinoff, 1889–1949." *Carnegie Magazine* 27, no. 10 (December 1953): 332–334.

Adlow, Dorothy. "The Home Forum." *Christian Science Monitor,* June 4, 1954.

Miller, Donald. *Nationality Classrooms, University of Pittsburgh.* Pittsburgh: University of Pittsburgh Press, 1955.

Moorhead, Elizabeth. "Andrey Avinoff the Entomologist." In *Pittsburgh Portraits,* 69–85. Pittsburgh: The Boxwood Press, 1955.

"Watercolor: Orchid Art on Display at Pitt." *Pittsburgh Post-Gazette,* January 10, 1961.

"Andrey Avinoff Chair." *Carnegie Magazine* 38, no. 10 (December 1964): 339.

Bruhns, E. Maxine. "The Avinoff Family Ikon." *Carnegie Magazine* 42, no. 1 (January 1968): 27.

Chavchavadze, Paul. *Marie Avinov: Pilgrimage through Hell.* Englewood Cliffs, N.J.: Prentice-Hall, 1968.

Fox, Lyndra Pate. *Andrey Avinoff.* Griggsville, Ill.: Nature House, 1975.

Teteriatnikov, Vladimir. *Icons & Fakes: Notes on the George R. Hann Collection.* New York: Teteriatnikov Art Expertise, Ltd., 1981. Copy of type-script at New York Public Library.

Shoumatoff, Alex. *Russian Blood: A Family Chronicle.* New York: Coward, McCann, & Geoghegan, 1982. Portions previously published in the *New Yorker.*

Glenny, Michael. "Icons, Fakers, and Fools: The Rise and Fall of the Hann Collection of Russian Icons Is a Chronicle of Cupidity, Greed, and Naivete." *Art & Antiques* (April 1984): 49–56.

Alberts, R. C. *Pitt: The Story of the University of Pittsburgh, 1787–1987.* Pittsburgh: University of Pittsburgh Press, 1986.

Chew, Paul A., ed. *Southwestern Pennsylvania Painters: Collection of Westmoreland Museum of Art.* Greensburg, Pa.: Westmoreland Museum of American Art, 1989.

Nabokov, Vladimir. *Selected Letters, 1940–1977.* Edited by Dmitri Nabokov and Matthew J. Bruccoli. San Diego, New York, and London: Harcourt, Brace, Jovanovich, 1989.

Shoumatoff, Elizabeth. *FDR's Unfinished Portrait: A Memoir.* Pittsburgh: University of Pittsburgh Press, 1990.

Shoumatoff, Nicholas. "Andrey Avinoff Remembered." *Carnegie Magazine* 62, no. 1 (January–February 1994): 24–28.

Berenbaum, May R. *Bugs in the System: Insects and Their Impact on Human Affairs,* 333. Cambridge, Mass.: Perseus Books, 1995.

Shoumatoff, Nicholas, and Nina Shoumatoff, eds. *Around the Roof of the World.* Ann Arbor: University of Michigan Press, 1996.

Collins, Michael M. "Walter Sweadner and the Wild Silk Moths of the Bitteroot Mountains." *Carnegie Magazine* 63, no. 7 (January–February 1997): 20–25.

Bown, Matthew Cullerne. *A Dictionary of Twentieth-Century Russian and Soviet Painters, 1900–1980s.* London: Izomar, Ltd., 1998.

Falk, Peter, ed. *Who Was Who in American Art, 1564–1975,* vol. 1. Madison, Conn.: Sound View Press, 1999.

Johnson, Kurt, and Steve Coates. *Nabokov's Blues: The Scientific Odyssey of a Literary Genius.* Cambridge, Mass.: Zoland Books, Inc., 1999.

Gathorne-Hardy, Jonathan. *Sex, the Measure of All Things: A Life of Alfred C. Kinsey.* Bloomington: Indiana University Press, 2000.

Manos-Jones, Maraleen. *The Spirit of Butterflies.* New York: Abrams, 2000.

Regina, Kristen. "Hillwood Museum & Gardens: The Acquisition of the Avinoff-Shoumatoff Collection." *Slavic and East European Information Resources* 3, no. 1 (January 2002): 35–37.

Callery, Bernadette. "Andrey Avinoff: The Carnegie Connection; Books and Blooms." Unpublished PowerPoint lecture, October 2002.

Starodubtseva, Zinaida. "Andrei Avinov's Atlantis" [Russian]. *Novyi mir iskusstva* (June 14, 2004). Translation by Susan Johnson-Roehr in type-script at Kinsey Institute.

Waugh, Thomas, et al. *Lust Unearthed.* San Francisco: The Gay, Lesbian, Bisexual, and Transgender Historical Society, 2004.

"A Piece of History: The Story of the Winged S." *Sikorsky Archives News* (January 2005): 5.

Osterrieder, Markus. "From Synarchy to Shambala: The Role of Political Occultism and Social Messianism in the Activities of Nicholas Roerich." Paper presented at "The Occult in 20th Century Russia: Metaphysical Roots of Soviet Civilization," European Academy, Berlin, March 11–13, 2007. The Harriman Institute, Columbia University. http://www.harrimaninstitute.org/MEDIA/00741.pdf (accessed October 7, 2010).

Kroek, L. John, Heather H. Semple, and Harton S. Semple, Jr. "The Russians Landed: Avinoff and Shoumatoff in Sewickley." *Sewickley Valley Historical Society Signals* 35, no. 3 (November 2007).

Heinrichs, Allison M. "Fangs Sharpened for T. Rex's Long-Awaited Revival," *Pittsburgh Tribune-Review,* February 23, 2008.

Regina, Kristen. "From the Imperial Court to the Iron City: Andrei Avinov, the Soviet Sales, and Russian Books." Conference paper, Dartmouth University, October 2008.

Sanger, Martha Frick Symington. *Helen Clay Frick: Bittersweet Heiress.* Pittsburgh: University of Pittsburgh Press, 2008.

Lippincott, Louise. "Recollecting Andrey Avinoff." *Carnegie Magazine* 73, no. 1 (Spring 2009): 26–29.

Rawlins, John. "Andrey Avinoff: Master of Arts and Sciences." *Carnegie Magazine* 73, no. 1 (Spring 2009): 30–31.

Salmond, Wendy R. "Russian Icons and American Money, 1928–1938." In *Treasures into Tractors: The Selling of Russia's Cultural Heritage, 1918–1938,* edited by Anne Odom and Wendy R. Salmond, 237–263. Seattle: University of Washington Press; Washington, D.C.: Hillwood Estate, Museum & Gardens, 2009.

Gangewere, Robert. *Palace of Culture: Andrew Carnegie's Institute and Library in Pittsburgh.* Pittsburgh: University of Pittsburgh Press, forthcoming 2010.

EXHIBITION HISTORY

GROUP EXHIBITIONS

Moscow Artists Society, Moscow, 1904–.

Imperial Academy of Art, St. Petersburg, 1910.

American Museum of Natural History, New York, October 1928.

Roses. The Hunt Institute for Botanical Decoration, Carnegie Mellon University, Pittsburgh (traveling exhibition, date unknown), nos. 6, 7.

Out of Russia: *The Art of Chagall, Tchelitchew, and Avinoff.* Kinsey Institute, Indiana University, Bloomington, 2005.

Pre-Revolutionary Queer: Gay Art and Culture before Stonewall. Kinsey Institute, Indiana University, Bloomington, 2009.

Revealed: The Tradition of Male Homoerotic Art. Central Connecticut State University, New Britain, April 2010; The Leslie Lohman Gay Art Foundation, New York, May 12–29, 2010.

SOLO EXHIBITIONS

Paintings by A. Avinoff. Ainslie Galleries, New York, 1921. Reviewed in *New York American,* February 13, 1921; *American Art News* 19 (February 19, 1921); *New York Tribune,* February 20, 1921; *New York Sun*, February 21, 1921.

[Retrospective]. College of Fine Arts, Carnegie Institute of Technology, Pittsburgh, March 1930.

Exhibition of Paintings and Drawings by Andrey Avinoff. Fine Arts Galleries, University of Pittsburgh, November 1941. Typescript list at Frick Art Reference Library, New York.

Flowers by Andrey Avinoff. Cranbrook Institute of Science, Toledo, Ohio, 1945.

Wildflowers of Western Pennsylvania. The Buhl Planetarium and Institute of Popular Science, Pittsburgh, January 17–February 11, 1946.

Flower Paintings by A. Avinoff. Knoedler & Company, Inc., New York, June 2–20, 1947. Reviewed in Edward Alden Jewell, *New York Times,* June 8, 1947; Carlyle Burrows, *Herald Tribune;* Laura Marden, *New York Sun;* Emily Genauer, *New York World-Telegram.*

Flower Paintings by Andrey Avinoff. Carnegie Institute, Department of Fine Arts, Pittsburgh, 1948.

[Flower paintings]. National Academy of Design, New York, 1948.

[Flower paintings]. New York Botanical Garden, January 1949.

[Orchid paintings]. American Museum of Natural History, 1949.

Andrey Avinoff Watercolors: Flowers and Butterflies. Introduction by Alan Priest. National Audubon Society, New York, October 7–November 26, 1953.

An Exhibition of Andrey Avinoff: The Man of Science, Religion, Mysticism, Society, and Fantasy. Catalogue by Virginia E. Lewis and Walter Read Hovey. Department of Fine Arts, Carnegie Institute, Pittsburgh, and University of Pittsburgh, December 4, 1953–January 3, 1954.

Watercolors of Orchids by Andrey Avinoff. Henry Clay Frick Fine Arts Gallery, Cathedral of Learning, University of Pittsburgh, January 10–February 6, 1961.

Andrey Avinoff: Botanical Paintings. Catalogue by George H. M. Lawrence. Hunt Botanical Library, Carnegie Institute of Technology, Pittsburgh, May 2–October 15, 1965.

Wonderful Wildflowers: Botanical Watercolors by Andrey Avinoff. Carnegie Museum of Natural History, Pittsburgh, April 28–December 1986.

Visions Through the Apocalypse. The Heritage Gallery of the Edgar Cayce A.R.E., Virginia Beach, November 2005.

CARNEGIE MUSEUMS OF PITTSBURGH TRUSTEES

CARNEGIE MUSEUM OF ART BOARD

PHOTOGRAPHY CREDITS

Unless otherwise noted, all works of art appear courtesy of the lender.

Unless otherwise noted, all photographs of works of art are by Carnegie Museum of Art.

The following credits apply to all images for which separate acknowledgment is due.

Page 25, figure 13; page 47: Photos by Tom Little

Page 29, figure 18: Photo by Jane C. Hyland

Page 30: Courtesy Carnegie Library of Pittsburgh Archives

Page 32, figure 20; page 67: Photos courtesy Antonia Shoumatoff Foster

Page 55: The University of Pittsburgh Art Gallery owns the painting titled "The Russian Room" by Andrey Avinoff, which is protected by copyright and is reproduced with permission from the University of Pittsburgh.

Pages 62–63, 68–69, 71: Photos courtesy The Kinsey Institute for Research in Sex, Gender, and Reproduction

Page 70: Photo courtesy Smithsonian American Art Museum

Pages 78–81: Photos courtesy the Andrey Avinoff Foundation